高等学校规划教材·语言学

英汉互译实用教程

（第 2 版）

雷晓峰　编著
［美］Michael Wherrity　审校

西北工业大学出版社

西　安

【内容提要】 本书分理论篇(第一章至第五章)和实践篇(第六章至第九章)两部分,共九章。本书先讲述基础理论,后以篇章为单位讲解英汉互译实践,由易及难,环环相扣。

第一章介绍翻译的基本知识(翻译分类、翻译标准和翻译过程等);第二章罗列了英语和汉语在9个方面的差异;第三章介绍翻译措辞;第四章介绍句子翻译,涉及句子翻译常用的方法以及从句和长句翻译的方法和技巧;第五章介绍篇章翻译,讲解篇章翻译的过程和方法。第六章至第九章分别涉及新闻、旅游、科技和工作留学语篇翻译等话题,介绍了这些语篇的语言特点和翻译过程,是对理论知识的应用。本书末尾还附有自主翻译实践材料,可供读者进行翻译练习。

本书可作为高等学校英汉互译课程的教材,也可供广大英汉互译爱好者自学使用。

图书在版编目(CIP)数据

英汉互译实用教程 / 雷晓峰编著. — 2版. — 西安：西北工业大学出版社，2020.12
高等学校规划教材. 语言学
ISBN 978-7-5612-7485-9

Ⅰ. ①英⋯ Ⅱ. ①雷⋯ Ⅲ. ①英语-翻译-高等学校-教材 Ⅳ. ①H315.9

中国版本图书馆 CIP 数据核字(2020)第 249705 号

YING-HAN HUYI SHIYONG JIAOCHENG
英 汉 互 译 实 用 教 程

责任编辑：隋秀娟 李 欣	策划编辑：何格夫
责任校对：万灵芝 陈松涛	装帧设计：李 飞

出版发行：西北工业大学出版社
通信地址：西安市友谊西路127号　　邮编：710072
电　　话：(029)88491757，88493844
网　　址：www.nwpup.com
印 刷 者：兴平市博闻印务有限公司
开　　本：787 mm×1 092 mm　　1/16
印　　张：12.375
字　　数：325千字
版　　次：2017年9月第1版　2020年12月第2版　2020年12月第1次印刷
定　　价：50.00元

如有印装问题请与出版社联系调换

第 2 版前言

一、培养翻译能力的重要性

翻译是最重要、最古老的跨语言和跨文化交流活动,是推动人类社会进步最重要的手段和途径之一。长久以来,翻译为我国各领域对内和对外发展都做出了巨大贡献。

翻译是外语学习和使用的一个重要手段,外语应用的五项基本技能(即听、说、读、写和译)在实践过程中或多或少都应用到了"翻译"能力。比如,我们能听懂、读懂外语,是因为语言、文本交际经历了从接受信息到转换(涉及翻译能力)信息这个信息"解码"和"编码"的过程。同样,我们会说、会写和会译,主要是因为我们将源语信息"解码"后重新进行"编码"(涉及翻译能力),为另一方所接受和理解,实现了交际目的。事实证明,翻译能力最能体现一个人的双语驾驭能力。故此,我国现行的外语类考试(如全国大学生英语四级和六级考试、英语专业四级和八级考试、硕士和博士研究生入学考试英语试题等)一般都有翻译类测试题。

二、本教材的修订背景

2017 年 9 月,《英汉互译实用教程》第 1 版出版发行,距今已过去 3 年多了。3 年多来,每年约有 1 200 名学生使用本教材,学习名为"英汉互译"的英语拓展课程,通过使用本教材内外的新鲜材料,学生的英语应用(尤其是英汉互译)能力有了较大程度的提高,对外交流能力也提高了。

3 年多来,结合本课程收到的反馈意见,课程组教师不断探索翻译教学技巧和方法,顺应学生译者翻译能力发展规律,与时俱进,更新教学内容和方法,经过访谈、问卷、测试等方法,确定了本教材的更新内容,以加快教材和课程建设,力争出精品教材,建设高水平课程。

三、本教材的修订内容

与第 1 版教材相比,本版教材在内容上主要做了以下修订。

1.进一步丰富了教材内容

比如,在教材修订过程中,编者增加了一些典型例句/例段,以增强翻译讲解的说服力,方便读者提升翻译能力;在"附录"中增加了更多的自主翻译练习材料,并附有参考译文;还增加了"附录 4",罗列了一些常见的翻译术语,供读者了解、学习;等等。

2.调整了教材的部分结构

比如,本版教材中删除了第 1 版教材中的"第七章 广告语篇的翻译",是因为汉语和英语广告有明显的风格差异。不同语言风格的转换对翻译初学者而言有一些困难。

此外,对原先译文中存在的错讹及不妥之处进行了修正和完善。

在编写本书的过程中,笔者参考了国内外专家学者所编写的教材、论文等资料,得到了所在单位的大力支持,在此一并表示衷心的感谢!

由于笔者水平有限,书中难免有不妥之处,诚请广大读者多多包涵,批评指正。

雷晓峰
2020 年 11 月

第1版前言

翻译是人类最重要、最古老的语言和思维活动之一。古往今来,翻译在人际沟通、商务往来、经济发展、科技振兴、文化传播、学术交流、国际关系、全球治理等方面都起着不可代替的重要作用。

传统意义上讲,翻译是用目的语忠实、通顺地再现原文信息和风格的一项重要技能,应用面很广,实用性强。要掌握翻译这个技能,不但需要双语语言和文化知识,而且需要翻译专业知识、翻译决策能力,甚至需要具备很强的心理和生理要素(如情绪控制力、毅力、判断力等),非下苦功夫不可。

一、本书的编写思想

翻译能力的发展需经历一个循序渐进的过程。一个人需要掌握一定量的词汇及其用法、完备的语法知识、篇章处理(如阅读)能力以及较强的双语转换能力才能开启初步的翻译工作,而较完美的翻译工作还需要译者掌握翻译专业知识(如翻译理论、翻译方法等)和大量的翻译实践活动。

二、本书的框架结构

本书分两部分:理论篇和实践篇。

第一部分:理论篇,共5章。第一章介绍了我国历史上的翻译高峰期、翻译分类、翻译标准和翻译过程等基础知识;第二章介绍了英语和汉语在9个方面的差异,旨在增强学习者在英汉互译过程中的差异意识,从而可从容地做出恰当的差异转换;第三章关注措辞,这是保证翻译准确性的关键;第四章讲解句子翻译,涉及句子翻译常用方法、从句翻译和长句翻译,这是翻译能力迈向成熟的关键所在,因为大多数翻译工作是在句子层面操作;第五章关于篇章翻译,通过例子讲解篇章翻译的过程和方法。

理论篇从翻译基本知识到英汉差异,从措辞到句子搭建,再到布局谋篇,贯彻了"理论导向、学习过程'自下而上'"的编写思想,符合翻译能力发展的一般规律。

第二部分:实践篇,共5章。从第六章到第十章,编者分别精心选择了新闻稿、广告、旅游、科技和留学语篇等与我们生活、工作和学习相关的话题,介绍各种语篇语言、文体风格上的特点和翻译过程,这是对本书第一部分相关理论知识的应用讲解。

三、本书的编写特色

1. 翻译理论与翻译实践相结合

时至今日,翻译研究已形成了语言学派、阐释学派、功能学派、文化学派、解构学派、女性主义、后殖民主义、苏东学派等理论学派。尽管如此,笔者仅选择了翻译的标准、过程和方法等相关理论,以及词、句和篇章翻译操作规范等翻译操作框架作为一般难度笔译的基础理论知识,让读者学有所用,用了即会。本教材中有大量典型实用的翻译实例,课文中的实例部分有讲解,课后练习题和"附录"中的翻译材料均附有参考译文。只有在理论指导下的翻译实践才有助于译者翻译能力的快速培养;只有大量的翻译实践才能检验、发展翻译理论,从而进一步指导翻译实践。

2.关注翻译能力发展过程

事物的发展总是循序渐进的,翻译能力发展也不例外。翻译界普遍认为,翻译操作应该"自上而下"(即按照篇章—段落—句子—小句—词汇—语音顺序),高瞻远瞩,这样可以尽最大可能避免翻译错误。然而,翻译能力是由量变到质变,"自下而上"的发展过程(即按照语音—词汇—小句—句子—段落—篇章顺序进行),需要不断积累。因此,在本书第一部分,笔者在讲解了翻译的基本概念和英汉常见差异后,逐章讲了词、句子和篇章翻译,辅以大量例句,以提高译者的翻译操作层次意识,关注翻译过程,逐渐培养译者的翻译能力。

3.强调翻译实践的重要性

真正的翻译能力是通过大量的翻译实践培养出来的。本书每章最后都有翻译练习。此外,本书"附录"部分有大量的翻译练习,供读者练笔用。笔者认同"自上而下"的翻译操作模式,翻译者需处理篇章及篇章以下层面信息(即段落、句子、小句、词汇等)。读者可以尝试做这些翻译练习,然后与笔者给出的参考译文对比,体会翻译过程,总结翻译得失,再进行更多的翻译练习,假以时日定收获多多。

在编写本书的过程中,笔者参考了国内外专家学者所编写的教材、论文等资料,得到了所在单位的大力支持,在此一并表示衷心的感谢。

由于编写水平有限,书中难免有不妥之处,诚请广大读者批评指正,以便进一步修订。

雷晓峰

2017年6月

目　录

第一部分　理　论　篇

第一章　翻译概论 ·· 3
　一、翻译的重要性 ··· 3
　二、翻译分类 ··· 4
　三、我国历史上的翻译高峰期 ··································· 6
　四、翻译原则/标准 ·· 8
　五、翻译过程 ·· 10
　练习题 ·· 15

第二章　英汉比较 ·· 17
　一、词义不对等 ·· 17
　二、搭配不对等 ·· 20
　三、形合与意合 ·· 20
　四、主语显著与话题显著 ······································ 22
　五、被动与主动 ·· 23
　六、物称与人称 ·· 24
　七、静态与动态 ·· 25
　八、"化整为零"与"化零为整" ·································· 26
　九、思维方式的转变 ·· 27
　练习题 ·· 28

第三章　遣词用字 ·· 30
　一、词语搭配 ·· 30
　二、选词用字 ·· 31
　练习题 ·· 39

第四章　句子翻译 ·· 41
　一、翻译常用方法 ·· 41
　二、从句的翻译 ·· 49
　三、长句的翻译 ·· 51
　练习题 ·· 53

— 1 —

第五章　篇章翻译·····57
一、篇章的定义、特点及布局模式·····57
二、篇章翻译的过程·····59
三、篇章翻译译文的评判标准·····62
练习题·····62

第二部分　实　践　篇

第六章　新闻语篇的翻译·····67
一、新闻语篇的语言特点·····67
二、新闻语篇翻译实例·····71
练习题·····78

第七章　旅游语篇的翻译·····80
一、旅游语篇的特点·····80
二、旅游语篇翻译实例·····81
练习题·····90

第八章　科技语篇的翻译·····92
一、科技语篇的特点·····92
二、科技语篇翻译实例·····94
练习题·····102

第九章　工作留学语篇的翻译·····104
一、书信的翻译·····104
二、个人简历的翻译·····109
三、个人陈述的翻译·····114
练习题·····119

附录·····122
附录1　练习题参考译文·····122
附录2　翻译补充练习·····134
附录3　翻译补充练习参考译文·····161
附录4　部分翻译术语·····187

参考文献·····190

第一部分 理 论 篇

第一章 翻译概论

一、翻译的重要性

统计表明,世界上有 7 000 多种语言。随着全球化进程的发展,世界正变成一个"村落"。国家、机构、人之间的联系越来越紧密,翻译也变得越来越重要。无论是近代还是现代,在重大时刻,都有翻译工作者(见图 1.1)的身影。

玄奘　　　　　　林纾　　　　　　严复　　　　　　傅雷

图 1.1　中国著名的翻译家代表人物

优秀的翻译能促进来自不同社会文化背景的人交流、合作、分享,发展友好关系,推动国家和社会的发展。改革开放 40 多年来,我国取得了举世瞩目的辉煌成就,尤其是我国科技的飞速发展,正改变着我们生活各方面的面貌。

我国日新月异的变化离不开翻译工作者的贡献,是他们架起了语言与文化的桥梁,方便了人文、科技等很多领域信息的流通,加速了人类共同进步的步伐。我国已故国学大师季羡林先生曾说过,在四大文明中,只有中华文明延续了下来,其中翻译起了很大作用。翻译给中华文明不断注入异域文化的新鲜血液,中华文明得以永葆青春和活力。

然而,错误的翻译会带来危害,轻则造成人与人、机构与机构、国家与国家之间的误解,重则造成人民的生命和财产损失,所以要尽全力避免误译。

E. g. They have not much of an opinion of him.
　　误译:他们对他没有多大意见。
　　正译:他们对他印象不怎么好。

E. g. I have an opinion of you, sir, to which it is not easy to give mouth.
　　先生,我对你有意见,不过很难说出口。

[分析]　have an opinion of sb. 意思是"对某人有意见"。但是,have no opinion of sb. 意思是"对某人反感""对某人印象不好"等。

E. g. I have no opinion of that sort of man.
　　我对这类人很反感。

E. g. This is a smoke-free area.

误译:这是个自由吸烟区。

正译:这是个无烟区。

E. g. Tom, Dick and Harry

阿猫阿狗

[分析] 旧时人们常用小名,引申为任何轻贱的、不值得重视的人。西方人和我们一样,提到人名,不总是指其字面意思,有时会有特殊含义。"名从主人,文从读者。"一般情况下,采用音译法将外国人名译成汉语,如将"Tom, Dick and Harry"译为"汤姆、迪克和哈里",但是在特殊情况下(如某个文学作品情景中)若有其他含义,译为"阿猫阿狗"会更好,切合我国文化,更接地气。

E. g. Last night I heard him driving his pig to market.

昨夜我听到他鼾声如雷。

[分析] 这里,如果将"driving his pig to market"字对字翻译则会让人贻笑大方。当译文违背常识(如把前文短语译为"把猪赶到市场去")时,译者一定要查阅资料,确保译文正确,千万不可望文生义。

E. g. 你想灌醉他? 他可是海量,从来没有醉过。

Want to drink him under the table? Well... you can never do it. He's got a hollow leg, you know.

[分析] 汉语"海量"的言外之意是"喝不醉",指"能喝很多"。在谈及某人的酒量大时,常有人说"He can drink many bottles of wine."。虽不能说此句完全有错,但听来总感觉不地道。汉语的"海量"与英语的"have a hollow leg"十分接近,字面意思为"有一条中空的腿",而真实意思是"无论喝多少都不会醉"。

二、翻译分类

1959 年,苏联杰出的语言学家、诗学家罗曼·雅各布森(Roman Jakobson,1896—1982 年)从符号学的观点出发,把翻译分为以下几种。

1. 语际翻译 (interlingual translation)

语际翻译是将一种语言的文本翻译成另一种语言文本。这是传统意义上的翻译。

E. g. 给力

brilliant/cool

E. g. 时间都去哪了?

Where did the time go?

E. g. 我读书少,你别骗我。

I don't have much education. Please don't try to fool me.

E. g. 《非诚勿扰》

If You Are the One

E. g. 这样的好机会,你应该抓住。怎能眼睁睁地看着它跑掉呢?

You should have jumped at such a good chance. How could you let it slip through your fingers?

E. g. 我的工作有一定的危险性。

Danger is part of my job.

E. g. 今天什么风把你给吹来了?
What brings you here today?

E. g. 他都 80 岁了,身子骨还那么硬朗。
He is already eighty but still going strong.

E. g. 在大江大海中游泳,既可以锻炼身体,又可以锻炼意志。
Swimming in big rivers and seas helps to build up both physical strength and willpower.

2. 语内翻译(intralingual translation)

语内翻译是用同一种语言将较难理解的信息以较简单的方式表达出来。如将粤语译为标准汉语;将英语字母 A 译为 the first letter in the English alphabet;将古汉语译为白话文。

3. 符际翻译(intersemiotic translation)

符际翻译是用非语言符号系统解释语言符号,或用语言符号解释非语言符号。

E. g. (摇头)译为 No(不)

E. g. 译为 No Smoking!(禁止吸烟!)

E. g. 译为 Wheelchair Accessible(无障碍通行)

E. g. (红灯)译为 STOP(停车)

E. g. 译为 Construction Ahead(前方施工)

E. g. Parking 译为

E. g. Somebody pulls a long face. 译为 Probably she/he is not happy now.(可能她/他不高兴。)

另外,如果按照方向、模式、材料和处理方式划分,翻译具体类别也不同(见表 1.1)。

表 1.1 翻译分类

划分方式	项目
方向	本族语—外语、外语—本族语
模式	口译、笔译、机器翻译
材料	文学翻译、科技翻译等
处理方式	全译、摘译、编译等

三、我国历史上的翻译高峰期

1. 第一次翻译高峰期：佛经翻译（东汉至唐宋时期）

三国时期，支谦的《法句经序》中提出了"因循本旨，不加文饰"（即按照原文的意思翻译，不添加额外的说辞）的译经原则。这是"直译"概念的雏形。

北朝末年及隋初，彦琮著《辩证论》。这本书可以说是我国第一篇翻译专论。彦琮主张译经"宁贵朴而近理，不用巧而背源"。由此可见，彦琮倾向于直译。

玄奘是享誉世界的著名翻译家。在古今佛经翻译者中，他的翻译水平最高，翻译的佛经数量最突出。二十年间，玄奘及其翻译团队（译场）共翻译佛经74部、1 335卷，每卷万字左右，占整个唐代译经总数的一半以上，相当于中国历史上另外三大"译经翻译家"（即鸠摩罗什、真谛和不空）译经总数的一倍多，而且玄奘的翻译作品质量大大超越前人，成为翻译史上的杰出典范。

人类古代的翻译活动大都与宗教的发展密切相关（见图1.2）。我国的翻译始于佛经的翻译，西方的翻译则是从翻译《圣经》开始的。

图1.2　翻译与宗教

2. 第二次翻译高峰期：科技翻译（明末清初）

图1.3是坤舆万国图（局部），由16世纪意大利传教士利玛窦（Matteo Ricci，1552—1610年）参与绘制翻译。

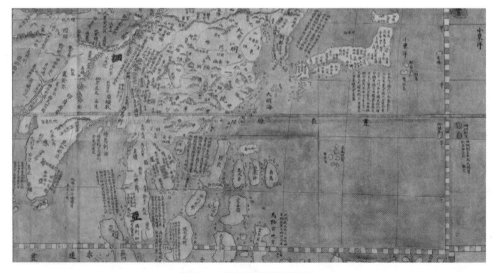

图1.3　坤舆万国图（局部）

马祖毅和范祥涛的相关研究指出：数学方面，比如李之藻、利玛窦编译的《同文算指》，傅兰雅译、华蘅芳述的《代数术》，傅兰雅译、江衡述的《算式集要》，傅兰雅评、华蘅芳述的《三角数理》等；物理学方面，比如傅兰雅译、徐建寅述的《电学》，傅兰雅译、王季烈述的《通物电光》，金楷理译、赵元益述的《光学》等；化学方面，比如傅兰雅译、徐寿述的《化学鉴原》《化学考质》《化学求数》，傅兰雅译、徐建寅述的《化学分原》等。天文学家高鲁编译了《空中航行术》，秋瑾译有《看护学教程》，孙中山译有《红十字会救伤第一法》等。

3. 第三次翻译高峰期：西学翻译（鸦片战争至五四运动后）

比如，林纾（1852—1924年），翻译外国文学著作达170余种，如《巴黎茶花女遗事》（见图1.4）、《黑奴吁天录》（后译为《汤姆叔叔的小屋》）、《王子复仇记》等。

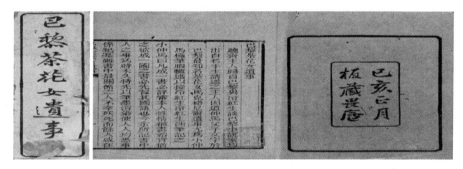

图1.4 《巴黎茶花女遗事》中文版

严复（1853—1921年）的译著主要有赫胥黎的《天演论》（图1.5是严复为《天演论》所写的序言的一部分）、亚当·斯密的《原富》、斯宾塞的《群学肄言》、约翰·穆勒的《群己权界论》和《名学》、甄克斯的《社会通诠》、孟德斯鸠的《法意》和耶芳斯的《名学浅说》，后人称它们为"严译八大名著"。

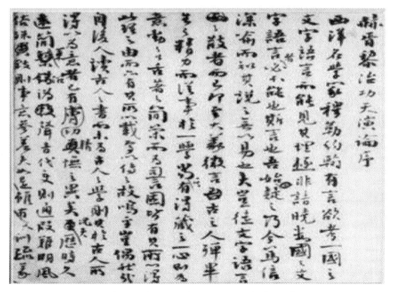

图1.5 严复为《天演论》所写的序言（局部）

此外，还有郭沫若、泰东、钱钟书、傅雷、鲁迅等一大批翻译家。

4. 第四次翻译高峰期：各个领域全面开花期（中华人民共和国成立至今）

中华人民共和国成立后，我国翻译事业的成就超过了历史上任何一个时期，在范围、规模、质量、从业人数、译著数量方面的发展都是空前的。翻译活动在文学、社科、科技、军事、外交、贸易、法律、文教、卫生等领域"全面开花"。比如，我国有组织、有计划、有系统地翻译了《马克思恩格斯全集》和《毛泽东选集》等。

四、翻译原则/标准

不同的人/组织对翻译的原则/标准有不同的看法（见表1.2）。

表1.2　不同人/组织的翻译原则/标准

提出者	观　点
马建忠	善译
严复	信、达、雅
鲁迅	宁信而不顺
赵景深	宁错而务顺
许渊冲	诗歌翻译的三原则："三美"（意美、音美、形美）以及"三化"（浅化、等化、深化）
林语堂	音美、意美、神美、气美、形美
郭沫若	好的翻译等于创作
朱光潜	译者"须设身处地在作者的地位，透入作者的心窍，和他同样感，同样想，同样地努力使所感所想凝定于语文"
傅雷	以效果而论，翻译应当像临画一样，所求的不在形似而在神似
钱钟书	文学翻译的最高理想可以说是"化"，把作品从一国文字转变成另一国文字，既能不因语文习惯的差异而露出生硬牵强的痕迹，又能完全保存原作的风味，那就算得入于"化境"
[美]奈达	动态对等：译文读者或译语听众对于译文或译语的反应，要和原文读者或原文讲话听众对于原文或原讲话的反应进行比较，如果大体一致，就是质量上乘的译文
[英]泰勒	翻译三原则：① 要将原作的意思全部转移到译文上来；② 译文应当具备原作的风格和文体；③ 译文和原作要同样地流畅
国际译联的《翻译工作者章程》	译文应忠实于原文，准确表现原作的思想与形式

可见，不同的人/组织对翻译原则/标准的看法各异。一般认为，一般文本的翻译原则/标准是"忠实"和"通顺"，即译文"忠实"于原文的信息内容和风格，译文读来"通顺"即可。

E.g.《死魂灵》（[俄]果戈理著，鲁迅译）译文摘选

省会NN市的一家旅馆的大门口，跑进了一辆讲究的，软垫子的小小的篷车，这是独身的人们，例如退伍陆军中佐、步兵二等大尉、有着百来个农奴的贵族之类——一句话，就是大家叫

作中流的绅士这一类人所爱坐的车子。车里面坐着一位先生,不很漂亮,却也不难看;不太肥,可也不太瘦,说他老是不行的,然而他又并不怎么年轻了。他的到来,旅馆里并没有什么惊奇,也毫不能惹起一点怎样的事故;只有站在旅馆对面的酒店门口的两个乡下人,彼此讲了几句话,但也不是说坐客,倒是大抵关于马车的。

[评价]　这段译文读来拗口,用词不够简练,时有啰唆之嫌。鲁迅先生的翻译原则是"宁信而不顺",即翻译时力保译文忠实于原文,哪怕读来不通顺。在信息爆炸时代,这个翻译原则已落后了,因为几乎没有几个人有很大耐心去阅读不通顺的文字了。

E.g.《约翰·克利斯朵夫》([法]罗曼·罗兰著,傅雷译)译文摘选

江声浩荡,自屋后上升。雨水整天的打在窗上。一层水雾沿着玻璃的裂痕蜿蜒流下。昏黄的天色黑下来了。室内有股闷热之气。

初生的婴儿在摇篮里扭动。老人进来虽然把木靴脱在门外,走路的时候地板还是格格地响,孩子哼啊嗐的哭了。母亲从床上探出身子抚慰他;祖父摸索着点起灯来,免得孩子在黑夜里害怕。灯光照出老约翰·米希尔红红的脸,粗硬的白须,忧郁易怒的表情,炯炯有神的眼睛。他走近摇篮,外套发出股潮气,脚下拖着双大蓝布鞋。鲁意莎做着手势叫他不要走近。她的淡黄头发差不多像白的;绵羊般和善的脸都打皱了,颇有些雀斑;没有血色的厚嘴唇不大容易合拢,笑起来非常胆怯;眼睛很蓝,迷迷惘惘的,眼珠只有极小的一点,可是挺温柔;她不胜怜爱地瞅着孩子。

[评价]　通过大量的翻译实践,傅雷总结出的翻译原则是"以效果而论,翻译应当像临画一样,所求的不在形似而在神似"。这与美国翻译理论家尤金·奈达的"等效论"(equivalent effect)有几分相像。"等效论",简单地说,即译文读者阅读译文的效果应该等同于原文读者阅读原文的效果。正是傅雷以效果而论译文,力求译文"神似",所以他的译文通常措辞讲究,读来朗朗上口,译文如同汉语原作。

综上所述,忠实准确、通顺流畅和风格得体可以说是所有标准的共核,三者的次序不可颠倒。"忠实准确"指译文必须忠实于原文的内容,把原文内容完整准确地转达出来,译者不能随意歪曲、增删、遗漏、篡改原文的内容;"通顺流畅"指译文要充分发挥译入语的语言优势,译文语言必须标准规范、通俗易懂、符合译入语的表达习惯,不存在死译、硬译、生搬硬套、文理不通的现象;"风格得体"指译文应尽量忠实转达原文的文体特征和写作风格。

请试译:
1. I've heard so much about you, sir.
2. a user-friendly camera
3. lunar New Year's Day
4. a logo bag
5. a commercial break
6. 搀扶
7. 炒货
8. 陈醋

9. 出诊

10. 窗花

【参考译文】

1. 久仰先生大名。
2. 傻瓜相机
3. 大年初一
4. 有某机构/部门标识的专用袋
5. （节目中）商业广告插播时间
6. support sb. by the arm
7. roasted seeds and nuts
8. mature vinegar
9. visit a patient at home
10. paper cut for window decoration

五、翻译过程

翻译有严格的操作流程。

翻译过程可分为理解、转换、表达及校对等四个阶段。其中，理解是所有翻译操作的总前提，否则任何翻译操作将变得毫无意义；转换是关键，涉及词、词组、小句、句子、段落和篇章各语言层，是生成正确译文的重要保证；表达是译文产出阶段，需将已理解并转换成恰当的信息从连词成句到连句成段，再到连段成篇生成第一稿译文，对译者的双语转换能力要求高；校对同样很重要，可以说，高质量的译文都是校对出来的。

1. 理解阶段：主要通过原文的上下文进行

(1) 理解语言现象

比如：

1) balance

E. g. For the **balance** of the section, let's speak in straightforward and elementary terms to describe the function and form of the electronic computer.

在本节的**剩余部分**，我们将用简单明了的术语来描述这种电子计算机的功能和形式。

E. g. I'd like to check the **balance** in my account please.

我想查一下我账户的**余额**。

E. g. The monarchy has to create a **balance** between its public and private lives.

王室不得不在公众生活和私生活之间建立一种**平衡**。

2) 复原

E. g. 他身体已经**复原**了。

He has already **recovered.**

E. g. **复原**后的金缕玉衣充分显示出中国古代劳动人民的精湛工艺。

The **restored** jade burial suit fully reveals the consummate skill of the laboring people of ancient China.

E. g. 这座在战争中惨遭破坏的城市已经**复原**了。

The city, which was destroyed in the war, has been **restored**.

3) 个别

E. g. **个别**辅导

individual coaching

E. g. **个别**照顾

special consideration for **individual cases**

E. g. 只有**个别**人请假。

Only one or two people asked for leave.

E. g. 这是极其**个别**的事例。

Such instances are very **rare**.

E. g. 这是**个别**情况。

These are **isolated** cases.

(2) 理解逻辑关系

有时，原文里的一个词、一个词组或一个句子可能有几种不同的意思，就得仔细推敲，分析来龙去脉，估计实际情况，根据逻辑推理来决定哪一种是确切的译法。

E. g. Nothing really prepared the world for the 1997 announcement that a group of Scottish scientists had created a cloned sheep named Dolly.

1997年，苏格兰一群科学家克隆出"多莉"羊。整个世界为之哗然。

要正确翻译这句话，必须正确翻译"Nothing really prepared the world"，不可按照字面翻译。透过本句字面意思，"the world"可理解为"全世界的人"，可将"Nothing really prepared the world"理解为"the 1997 announcement"的反应，根据深层逻辑关系，可译为"整个世界为之哗然"。另外，还要妥当翻译多义词"create"，最好不译为"创造"或"创建"，因为与其作用词"sheep"搭配不当。所谓"create a cloned sheep"，实际上是说"克隆了一只羊"。

E. g. 那时，曾子住在乡下，一边种地，一边读书，日子过得很清贫。

Zencius lived a poor life in the countryside, farming and studying at that time.

这里"住"和"过"都可用 live 表达，所以翻译时合并了"同类项"，一并翻译，使英语译文表达更精练。

E. g. 他饮他的花酒，我喝我的清茶。人生需要一种境界：自我安定。

Human life, it seems to me, needs a placidity of mind. While others may be wining and dining, I'm content with plain tea.

由于英文写作中逻辑模式常为先总述、后分说，所以译者将先分说、后总述的原文汉语信息翻译成英语时做了调整。

(3) 理解原文所涉及的事物

E. g. 鱼和熊掌不可兼得。

这句话的本意不是说二者必然不可兼得，而是强调如果不能兼得的时候，我们应当做出取舍。

误译：You can not have fish and bear's paws at the same time.

正译：You cannot have your cake and eat it.（英文中的对应说法）

如果直译，英语读者会"丈二和尚摸不着头脑"。

E.g. 惊蛰

the Waking of insects——the 3rd of the 24 solar terms in China (when creation stirs after the winter sleep)

E.g. 农历

lunar calendar

E.g. 天方夜谭

Arabian Nights（图书《天方夜谭》，又名《一千零一夜》）；quite unreal；virtually impossible；a miracle（具体选取哪种译法要看上下文）

2. 转换阶段

"转换"可对应英语中"transfer"一词，是译者在很强的英汉差异意识下，按照译入语的行文习惯向着译入语方向做出的文本调整。转换往往按照词汇—小句—句子—段落—篇章这个顺序进行，信息层级越高，语言单位越大。具体而言，各层级信息转换的常规做法是：

第一，在词汇层，译者要做到措辞准确：对（尤其是外来语中的）专有名词翻译而言，一般采用音译法，措辞符合音译规范（一般采用中性词汇，译法不可令人费解甚至误解）；术语翻译须与国家标准、行业标准和权威部门保持一致；如有现有约定的译法，应尽量采用。

第二，小句，即一个无动词结构并包含主谓关系的成分，要按其功能，结合上下文做出恰当的翻译转换（译作单句、从句还是其他某种形式）。

第三，在句子层，译者要注意英汉结构差异，必要时做出恰当转换，最终搭建起既符合译入语表达习惯又给予句中其他信息附着余地的句式结构。

第四，在段落层，译者要注意段落信息的完整性、话题的凸显性、句间关系的衔接性以及信息的推进性，使得译文段落如原文段落一样信息饱满，浑然一体，读来通畅。

第五，在篇章层，译者要按照译入语文本的架构模式安排译文，同时也要动态监控、调整以上各步骤信息的转换情形，尽量保证达到译文读者阅读译文如同原文读者阅读原作一样的效果。

3. 表达阶段

表达是理解的结果，但理解正确并不意味着必然能表达得正确。

（1）直译

在译文语言条件许可时，在译文中既保持原文的内容，又保持原文的形式。

1) 短语/词组直译

E.g. 纸老虎 paper tiger；一国两制 one country, two systems；"三个代表" the Three Represents theory；癌细胞 cancer cell；爱国统一战线 the patriotic united front；磕头 kowtow；荔枝 litchi；冷战 cold war；X光诊断 X-ray diagnosis；热线 hot line；黑市 black market；支柱产业 pillar industry；血浓于水 blood is thicker than water；斑马线 zebra crossing；版权 copyright；半封建半殖民地社会 semi-feudal and semi-colonial society；半信半疑 half believing, half doubting；本意 original meaning；被动吸烟 passive smoking；鼻音 nasal sound；比较文学 comparative literature；闭合电路 closed circuit；边防部队 frontier guards；边缘科学 frontier science；表面张力 surface tension

2)句子直译

E.g. Physics studies force, motion, heat, light, sound, electricity, magnetism, radiation, and atomic structure.

物理学研究力、运动、热、光、声、电、磁、辐射和原子结构。

(2)意译

直译无法执行时,通过变通的方法传达出原文的意思和精神。

1)短语/词组意译

E.g. 喉结 Adam's apple;乱七八糟 at sixes and sevens;半老徐娘 an attractive middle-aged woman;表里如一 think and act in one and the same way;串讲 explain a text sentence by sentence;彩霞 rosy clouds;残阳 the setting sun;长年累月 year in and year out;答谢宴 a return banquet;大不了 at the worst;大动肝火 fly into a rage;大写金额 amount in words;大雄宝殿 the precious Hall of a great hero;大烟鬼 opium addict;大爷作风 ways of the idle rich

2)句子意译

E.g. It's raining cats and dogs.

大雨滂沱。

E.g. Don't cross your bridges before you come to them.

不必担心过早/不必自寻烦恼。

E.g. Once the wife of a parson, always the wife of a parson.

嫁鸡随鸡,嫁狗随狗。

E.g. 说曹操,曹操就到。

Talk/Speak of the devil (and he will appear).

更多例子见表1.3。

表 1.3 词语的字面意思与实际意思

原　文	字面意思	实际意思
Queen's English	女王的英语	标准英语
small talk	小声说话	闲聊
sandwich man	卖三明治的人	上有老下有小之人
black sheep	黑羊	害群之马
home secretary	家庭秘书	(英国)内政大臣
wet paint	湿油漆	油漆未干
staff only	只有职员	员工通道 (若译为"闲人免进",表意不够客观)

4.校对阶段

为保证译文质量,校对是必不可少的阶段。校对工作可"自下而上"(即按照单词—词组—小句—句子—段落—篇章顺序)进行。在这个阶段,译者须对译文语言不断进行推敲、润色,对原文内容甚至风格在译文中的再现情况不断核实。

校对工作往往按照信息层次逐层、动态、多遍进行。参考步骤见表1.4（假如校对4遍）。

表1.4　校对的参考步骤

校对遍数	做　　法
第1遍	逐句、逐段进行校对，确保原文信息全部译入译文中（从大处着眼，确保信息的完整性）
第2遍	仔细检查译文中措辞的准确性、句式搭建的合理性以及逻辑推进的合理性（从细节处着眼）
第3遍	若英译汉，可删除汉语译文中可有可无的字（比如查看汉语关联词存在的必要性，能删则删），避免"……的……的……"现象；若汉译英，可检查用于明晰逻辑关系的关联词和语法手段的应用情形（这是英语语言的本质要求），还有各个信息位置安排的合理性，力求译文语言有美感。（从细节处着眼） 注：可参照本书第二章罗列的英语和汉语的差异情形，确保差异转换到位，译出地道的目的语语言的特点。具体来说，与汉语恰恰相反，英语是①"形合"语言；②"主语显著"语言；③被动语态多用的语言；④"物称"多见的语言；⑤"静态"语言；⑥"化零为整"的语言；⑦"先表态，后叙事"的语言
第4遍	抛却原文，将译文当作一句/段/篇文字阅读、检查甚至欣赏，在不改变意思的基础上，修正小到如措辞拗口的表达法、大到如逻辑推进不自然等不当之处，以求在内容上和形式上与原文保持一致，力求译文内容完整，自然推进，字正句顺

接下来我们一起看一个校对的例子。

【原文】

还有半年大学毕业时，我做了一个重要的决定：先不工作，用一年时间做公益。做这个决定出于两个原因：一是我在大学里就一直参与公益活动，这种实践对我的心智健全和人格完整帮助很大，我愿意去经受更多；二是我们服务的对象，是一个即将消失在历史中的边缘老年群体，我们是在和时间抢人。比起做决定所经历的一番挣扎，更困难的是怎样说服家里人同意。他们无法理解为什么辛辛苦苦供我读了十几年书终于毕业，我却不立即去工作赚钱，而是跑去做这种事。

(慕冬，《意林》，2018年第6期)

【某学生译文】

Half a year before I graduated from college, I made an important decision: not to work first, but to do①public welfare for one year. There were two reasons for this decision. One was that I have been participating in public welfare activities since I was in college ②. This practice has greatly helped my ③mental health and personality integrity. I am willing to ④go through more. The other reason is that ⑤the object of our service is ⑥a marginal group of elderly people who are about to disappear in history. We are ⑦robbing people of time.⑧It's more difficult to ⑨convince the family to agree than the struggle to make a decision. They had worked hard for more than ten years to let me go to school⑩. So they couldn't understand why I went to do ⑪it instead of working to make money immediately after ⑫graduating.

校对修改点(至少需将文中画线部分改为以下内容):

①处"public welfare"改为"charity work"。

②处". This practice"改为", which",将两句合为一句,提高英语的表达力。

③表意不充分。将原文"mental health and personality integrity"改为"sound mind and integral personality"。

④处"go through more"改为"experience more than before"。

⑤处"the object"改为"the target group"。

⑥要紧扣原文。这里"老年群体"应视作一个整体,将原文"a marginal group of elderly people"改为"the elderly, marginalized by society"。

⑦不可直译,将原文"robbing people of time"改为"racing against time in this work"。

⑧本句句首处添加"Actually",将"It's"改为"Actually, it's",以增强信息的连贯性。

⑨处"convince"改为"persuade"。

⑩处". So"改为", so",将前后两句连为一句,尽量写长句,将两个简单句变为一个并列句。

⑪处"it"改为"charity work"。

⑫处"graduating"改为"my graduation"。

练 习 题

一、英译汉练习

In college, as he was getting involved in protests against the apartheid government in South Africa, Barack Obama noticed, "that people had begun to listen to my opinions." Words, the young Mr. Obama realized, had the power "to transform": "with the right words everything could change—the lives of ghetto kids in South Africa or my own tenuous place in the world."

Much has been made of Mr. Obama's eloquence—his ability to use words in his speeches to persuade and uplift and inspire. But his appreciation of the magic of language and his ardent love of reading have not only endowed him with a rare ability to communicate his ideas to millions of Americans while contextualizing complex ideas about race and religion, they have also shaped his sense of who he is and his apprehension of the world.

Mr. Obama's first book, *Dreams from My Father* (which surely stands as the most evocative, lyrical and candid autobiography written by a future president), suggests that throughout his life he has turned to books as a way of acquiring insights and information from others—as a means of breaking out of the bubble of self-hood and, more recently, the bubble of power and fame. He recalls that he read James Baldwin, Ralph Ellison, Langston Hughes, Richard Wright and W. E. B. Du Bois when he was an adolescent in an effort to come to terms with his racial identity and that later, during an ascetic phase in college, he immersed himself in the works of thinkers like Nietzsche and St. Augustine in a spiritual-intellectual search to figure out what he truly believed.

(Michiko Kakutani,《英语学习》,2009 年 5 月)

二、汉译英练习

2018 年 5 月 5 日是卡尔·马克思的 200 周年诞辰。马克思可以算是中国人最熟悉的德国人,不过我们多是把马克思与抽象的政治理念和哲学思想联系在一起。当提起马克思时,首先浮现在脑海中的大多是那个严肃的哲人形象。2017 年的德国电影《青年马克思》,为观众展现了一个更加真实的马克思。

电影讲述了青年马克思 1843 年到 1848 年革命思想的形成和《共产党宣言》诞生的历史。在这段短暂但又风起云涌的时期,马克思和恩格斯彻底改变了人类历史进程。

(扣小米,《三联生活周刊》)

第二章 英汉比较

1898年,商务印书馆出版了马建忠编著的《马氏文通》(见图2.1)。这是我国第一部系统的汉语语法著作。该书以古汉语为研究对象,把西方的语法学成功地引进我国,创立了第一个完整的汉语语法体系,奠定了我国现代语言学的第一块基石。该书开启了汉语与英语的对比研究。

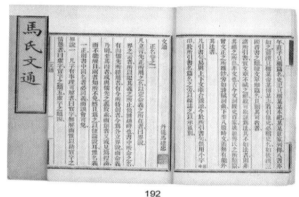

图 2.1 《马氏文通》封面及正文

一般来说,世界语言分为多个语系,如汉藏语系、印欧语系、阿尔泰语系、闪-含语系、乌拉尔语系、伊比利亚-高加索语系、马来-波利尼西亚语系、南亚语系、达罗毗荼语系等。汉语属于汉藏语系,英语属于印欧语系,我国学者对英汉语言对比做了较为深入的研究。部分研究成果如下。

一、词义不对等

词义不对等主要表现在以下3个方面。
1. 词义空缺
词义空缺指目的语中没有这样的表达法。
karaoke 卡拉OK
hippie 嬉皮士
GUCCI 古驰
Givenchy 纪梵希
brunch 早午餐〔即 breakfast(早餐)加上 lunch(午餐)的合成词,而早午餐并不是每天都有,通常只有在周日才吃,就餐时间也比平时长,通常从上午10时至下午3时〕
commuter 通勤者,经常乘公共车辆往返者(根据英文解释翻译成汉语)
busboy 餐馆工

肉夹馍 Chinese sandwich/hamburger

粽子 a pyramid-shaped dumpling made of glutinous rice wrapped in bamboo or reed leaves (eaten during the Dragon Boat Festival)

荔枝 litchi/lychee

旗袍 a close-fitting woman's dress with high neck and slit skirt; cheongsam; mandarin gown

阴 (in Chinese thought) yin, the feminine or negative principle in nature

阳 (in Chinese thought) yang, the masculine or positive principle in nature

清明 ①Pure Brightness—the 5th of the 24 solar terms; ②the day marking the beginning of the 5th solar term (traditionally observed as a festival for worshipping at ancestral graves, technically known as "grave sweeping")

我国的专有名词(指特定的或独一无二的人或物,如人名、地名、国家名、景观名、著作名等)也可归于此类。

孔子 Confucius

孙中山 Sun Yat-sen

陕西省 Shaanxi Province

中华人民共和国 the People's Republic of China

兵马俑 terra-cotta warriors

北京大学 Peking University

《红楼梦》*Dream of the Red Chamber*

2. 词义内涵不同

词义内涵不同,即原文表达法是真实存在的,但在更多场合用的并非字面意思,而是它的引申义(见表2.1)。

表2.1 词义内涵不同

英 文	字面意思	实际意思
a piece of cake	一块蛋糕	一件轻而易举的事
black tea	黑茶	红茶
black coffee	黑咖啡	清咖啡(既不加糖也不加牛奶的浓咖啡)
white coffee	白色的咖啡	加了牛奶的咖啡
black art	黑色艺术	妖术
black stranger	陌生的黑人	完全陌生的人
a bad sailor	一个坏水手	一个常晕船的人
blind date	盲目的约会	(由第三者安排的)男女初次见面
backseat driver	坐在后面的司机	因瞎指挥而坏事的人
dog ear	狗耳朵	书的折角
dead president	死了的总统	美钞

续表

英　文	字面意思	实际意思
dead shot	死的射击	神枪手
white elephant	白象	无用而累赘的东西
bring down the house	把房子推倒	博得满堂喝彩
call sb's name	叫某人的名字	辱骂某人
go Dutch	去荷兰	各自付款
face the music	面对音乐	承担后果或责任
lead a dog's life	过着狗的生活	过着贫困的生活
let the cat out of the bag	把猫从袋子里放出来	泄密

3. 风马牛不相及

在这里"风马牛不相及"指原文词条不能当错误的字面意思理解，唯一正确的真实意思与字面意思相去甚远（见表2.2）。

表2.2　风马牛不相及

英　文	字面意思	实际意思
American cloth	美国布	彩色防水布
English disease	英国病	软骨病
French gray	法国灰	浅灰色
Roman nose	罗马人的鼻子	高鼻梁鼻子、鹰钩鼻
Russian boot	俄罗斯的靴子	长筒靴
Spanish castle	西班牙的城堡	空中楼阁
Spanish potato	西班牙马铃薯	山芋
Turkish delight	土耳其的快乐	橡皮糖
Uncle Tom	汤姆大叔	逆来顺受的人

翻译时不可望文生义，要充分考虑信息逻辑、地道搭配、译文效果等因素，否则译文读来轻则令人费解，重则让人不知所云或产生误解。

E.g. 回家养病

to come back home on sick leave（"养病"不能译为 raise illness）

E.g. 邻居们纷纷赶去救火。

Neighbors around all rushed to fight the fire.（"救火"不能译为 save fire）

E.g. 消防工作责任重于泰山。

原译：The responsibility for fire prevention and fighting is as heavy as Mount Tai.

司马迁在给好友任安的《报任安书》中写道："人固有一死，或重于泰山，或轻于鸿毛。"这句话成为千古名句。英语读者如果没有汉语文化背景，读这个译文就不理解为什么只是"泰山"，为什么不是其他山？这里"消防工作责任重于泰山"中的"泰山"一词对于缺少我国文化背景的一般外国人来讲很难理解，甚至会导致误解。因此从信息通畅传播的角度讲，应将"泰山"泛化译为"a mountain"。

改译：The responsibility for fire prevention and fighting is as heavy as a mountain.

二、搭配不对等

英语与汉语分属不同语系，根植于迥异的文化语域，受地域、习俗、文化、宗教、社会制度等因素影响，在语言层面表现为搭配不对等的情形（完全对等是罕见的），即当我们将原文中约定俗成的某种说法译为目标语时，经常无法照字面意思直译（将构成原语词汇中的词各自直译，合成后无法生成能传递出原词意的地道译文）。

比如：at all costs 无论如何，不惜任何代价；at a loss 不知所措；on the contrary 相反；out of danger 脱离危险；by heart 牢记；for instance 例如；at intervals 不时；to the point 切中要害；at the mercy of 受……支配；on purpose 故意；at random 随意地；等等。

汉译英时，搭配不对等情形也有很多。比如以下几个例子。

重起炉灶 begin all over again；make a fresh start
出尔反尔 go back on one's word；contradict oneself
出伏 the hottest days of the year are over
德高望重 (of an old person) be of noble character and high prestige；enjoy high prestige and command universal respect
分庭抗礼 stand up to sb. as an equal；act independently and defiantly
好说歹说 use every possible argument to convince sb.
不忘初心 remain true to one's original aspiration
决一雌雄 fight to see who is stronger；fight it out
开荤 (esp. of a person with a religious belief) end a meatless diet
口是心非 say yes but mean no；say one thing but mean another
狼狈周章 terror/panic-stricken
雷霆万钧 as powerful as a thunderbolt
难兄难弟 two of a kind；birds of a feather
年富力强 in the prime of life
守正不阿 be strictly just and impartial

三、形合与意合

英语是语法型（形合）语言。英语重语法结构，其语义与语法形式密不可分，语言的意义通过形式表达出来。比如，各分句之间的关系大多是通过词汇纽带直接显示出来。英语注重以形显意，句子成分（包括单词、短语、分句）之间的逻辑关系靠关联词等显性连接手段直接标示。

汉语是语义型（意合）语言。在通常情况下，汉语各分句之间的联系主要是通过逻辑纽带或语序间接地表现出来，句子成分之间靠隐性连贯。

以下例句中，画线的词在译文中荡然无存，正是由于英汉语言在这方面的差异。

1. 英译汉

E. g. After the age of eighty she found she had some difficulty in getting to sleep, so she habitually spent the hours from midnight to 3 a.m. reading popular science.
过了八十以后,她常睡不着觉,从午夜到凌晨三点总要读些科普读物。

E. g. I do not believe that she ever had time to notice that she was growing old.
我认为她从来没有工夫去注意自己在日益衰老。

E. g. She was one of the founders of Girton College, and worked hard at opening the medical profession to women.
她曾是戈登学院的创办人之一,竭力向女性开放医学行业。

E. g. WE THE PEOPLES OF THE UNITED NATIONS DETERMINED to save succeeding generations from the scourge of war, which twice in our lifetime has brought untold sorrow to mankind, and to reaffirm faith in fundamental human rights, in the dignity and worth of the human person, in the equal rights of men and women and of nations large and small, and to establish conditions under which justice and respect for the obligations arising from treaties and other sources of international law can be maintained, and to promote social progress and better standards of life in larger freedom, AND FOR THESE ENDS to practice tolerance and live together in peace with one another as good neighbors, and to unite our strength to maintain international peace and security, and to ensure, by the acceptance of principles and the institution of methods, that armed force shall not be used, save in the common interest, and to employ international machinery for the promotion of the economic and social advancement of all peoples, HAVE RESOLED TO COMBINE OUR EFFORTS TO ACCOMPLISH THESE AIMS.

(出处:*Charter of the United Nations*,《联合国宪章》)

【参考译文】

我联合国人民同兹决心欲免后世再遭今代人类两度身历惨不堪言之战祸,重申基本人权、人格尊严与价值,以及男女与大小各国平等权利之信念,创造适当环境,俾克维持正义,尊重由条约与国际法其他渊源而起之义务,久而弗懈,促成大自由中之社会进步及较善之民生,并为达此目的力行容恕,彼此以善邻之道,和睦相处,集中力量,以维持国际和平及安全,接受原则,确立力法,以保证非为公共利益,不得使用武力,运用国际机构,以促成全球人民经济及社会之进展,用是发愤立志,务当同心协力,以竟厥功。

(作者不详,百度文库)

上段是《联合国宪章》第一段。本段中有大量表示信息之间关系的有形手段,如动词不定式、介词及介词短语、定语从句等。然而,在汉语译文中,这些有形连接手段不见了,这是由英语和汉语的本质特点决定的。

2. 汉译英

E. g. 学得有趣,效率就会高。
Learning is more efficient when it is fun.

E. g. 活到老,学到老。

One is never too old to learn.

It is never too late to learn.

We live and learn.

E. g. 到年底,扫尘、洗地、杀鸡、宰鹅,彻夜的煮福礼,全是一个人担当,竟没有添短工。

At the end of the year, she swept and mopped the floors, killed chickens and geese, and sat up to boil the sacrificial meat, all single-handed, so that they did not need to hire extra help.

E. g. 中国作为一个发展中的沿海大国,国民经济要持续发展,必须把海洋的开发和保护作为一项长期的战略任务。

As a major developing country with a long coastline, China must take exploitation and protection of the ocean as a long-term strategic task before it can achieve the sustainable development of its national economy.

E. g. 麒麟花在阳光照射下,鲜艳夺目,经久不凋,是很好的室内装饰盆花。

Under bright sunlight, the flowers of Euphorbia splendens are dazzling. Because it does not wilt and is long-lasting, it is the perfect potted plant for indoor decoration.

四、主语显著与话题显著

"主语显著"指的是主语和谓语是句子结构的最基本语法单位,而且句子一般都有主语和谓语两个成分。英语即属于这种语言。

现代英语基本句型可划分为五种,即:

①"主语+谓语",如"The river runs.";

②"主语+谓语+宾语",如"He painted a picture.";

③"主语+谓语+间接宾语+直接宾语",如"He gave me a medical handbook.";

④"主语+谓语+宾语+宾语补足语",如"They made him their team leader.";

⑤"主语+系+表语",如"He looks strong."。

话题显著指以"话题和评论"为句子结构基本单位的语言。汉语即属于这种语言,"话题+评论"这样的句式是汉语中常见的句式。

1. 英译汉:英语"主谓结构"转为汉语"话题+评论"结构

E. g. She has got a mellow, full voice.

她的嗓音柔和、饱满。

E. g. A telephone was fitted up in the pavilion.

亭子里装了一部电话机。

E. g. This pool of human resources has one of the highest mobility rates in China.

这些人力资源在中国的流动性最大。

2. 汉译英:把汉语"话题+评论"转为英语"主谓结构"结构

E. g. 今天食堂卖饺子。

Jiaozi are served in the canteen today.

E. g. 这件事只能搞好,不能搞砸。

    You must make the thing a sure success. It brooks no failure.

E. g. 弟弟学习比哥哥好。

    The younger brother studies better than the elder.

E. g. 他本事比你大。

    He is more capable than you.

E. g. 他的作文几乎没有语法错误。

    There are few grammatical mistakes in his composition.

E. g. 他的智力比弟弟低。

    He is intellectually inferior to his younger brother.

E. g. 开汽车没有方向盘不行。

    You can't drive a car without a steering wheel.

    It is never possible to drive a car without a steering wheel.

    The steering wheel is a necessary part of a car.

五、被动与主动

英语的被动语态去除了人的主观能动性,突出了动作承受者,这样表意更为客观。汉语通常从人的角度出发描写万物,往往很少直接用"被"来表示信息之间的动宾关系,而改用"于""受""遭受""受到""给""把"等词表示被动意义,表面上呈现主动形态。

英语的被动和汉语的主动之间的转换至关重要,转换不好就会破坏译文的流畅感。

1. 英译汉

E. g. Kissinger was alarmed by China's first atomic blast in October, 1964.

    1964 年 10 月,中国爆炸了第一颗原子弹,这把基辛格吓了一跳。

E. g. Are you clear what is expected of you?

    你清楚大家对你的期望吗?

E. g. If the chain reaction is not controlled, a big explosion will result.

    不控制连锁反应,就会引起一场大爆炸。

E. g. He was surrounded and asked a lot of questions.

    大家把他围住,向他提出一个又一个问题。

E. g. The president was assassinated in a theatre last night.

    这位总统昨晚在一家剧院遇刺。

2. 汉译英

E. g. 有很多问题亟待解决。

    Many problems have to be solved immediately.

E. g. 建议每位发言人的讲话不要超过五分钟。

    It is suggested that each speaker be allotted five minutes.

E. g. 这种反应需要能量,太阳光则能提供所需的能量。

    Energy is needed for the reaction and it is supplied by the light of the sun.

E. g. 当地政府已经采取或正在采取何种措施以减少空气污染?

What measures have been or are being adopted by the local government to reduce air pollution?

E. g. 必须指出,有些问题还待澄清。

It must be pointed out that some questions have yet to be clarified.

E. g. 物质既不能创造又不能消灭。

Matter can neither be created nor be destroyed.

六、物称与人称

汉语语言:习惯以人称视角为切入点,从人的角度来叙述客观事物,即采用能主动发出动作或有生命的东西,包括人类的组织形式,充当主语。翻译时,若能将人称主语改为物称主语,即可生成表意客观的英语译文。

英语语言:在选择主语时,往往用不能主动发出动作或无生命的事物词语。这种句式往往带有拟人化色彩,结构严密,言简意赅。这一倾向在书面语,尤其在新闻、科技论述、学术文献中尤为明显。翻译时,通常将物称主语变为人称主语。

1. 英译汉

E. g. His failure to observe the safety regulations resulted in an accident to the machinery.

他没有遵守安全规则,机器出了故障。

也可以说:

Because he failed to observe the safty rules, the machine broke down.

E. g. His personality is his only claim to remembrances.

人们能记起他的唯有他的品格。

也可以说:

People remember him solely for his character.

E. g. The sense of inferiority that he acquired in his youth still hasn't completely disappeared.

他在青少年时期留下的自卑感还没有完全消失。

E. g. It was with some difficulty that he found the way to his own house.

他费了不少劲儿才找到回家的路。

E. g. It was beyond his power to sign such a contract.

他无权签订这种合同。

E. g. An idea suddenly struck me.

我突然想到了一个主意。

E. g. American English owes a great deal to Noah Webster, an American lexicographer and writer.

美国词典编纂家及作家诺亚·韦伯斯特对美式英语做出了巨大的贡献。

E. g. My duty forbids me to fly from danger.

职责所在,我不能临阵脱逃。

2. 汉译英

E. g. 他一想到面试就十分担忧。

The thought of the interview filled him with apprehension.

E. g. 请本大厦各租户协助我们的工作。

Cooperation from all tenants in this building would be appreciated.

E. g. 敬请告知汇款的详细地址。

Details regarding your remittance address would be appreciated.

E. g. 有人笑出了声,但这笑声只是有人在绝望之中试图使气氛变得轻松一些。

There is laughter, but it's a laughter that comes from a desperate attempt to lighten the atmosphere.

E. g. 经过调查,我们得出了上述结论。

Investigation led us to the foregoing conclusion.

七、静态与动态

英语呈静态(static),有一种少用动词或用其他手段表示动作意义的自然倾向。

汉语呈动态(dynamic),动词十分丰富,应用广泛而自由,动词并无人称与数的限制,没有严格意义上的时态、语态、语气的变化,没有谓语动词与非谓语动词的区别,因而使用频率较高,常常大量采用连动式或兼语式的说法。

由于英语是静态语言,所以在英语文章中有很多动作概念用英语名词表达的例子,这在英文写作中是"动词的名词化"现象。

1. 英译汉——化静为动

E. g. This requires preparation and planning at both the business and IT levels.

这要求同时在业务层和IT层准备和规划。

E. g. Social development suggests universal exploration.

社会的进步促使人类探索宇宙。

E. g. The contamination of soil by crude oil is a growing problem as China accelerates its exploitation of oil reserves to meet rising energy demands.

随着中国加速开采其石油储备以满足日益增加的能源需求,原油污染土壤越来越成为一个问题。

E. g. The arrival of non-French companies in France and the loss of a considerable market share to foreign companies that do provide superior service is the major reason for this turnaround in opinion.

一些外国公司进入法国,相当一部分市场份额流失到一些确实能提供优质服务的外国公司,成为这种观念转变的主要原因。

E. g. Jos could not bear the sight of her pain.

乔斯不忍看她受苦。

英语为静态语言,即英文中存在大量的以静态(如名词、形容词、副词、介词等)形式表示动态(动作)概念的表达法。比如:put an end to(结束)、make preparations for(准备)、make an analysis(分析)、out of control(失去控制)、in a red shirt(穿一件红衬衫)、of great significance (有重大意义)等。这些是地道的英语表达法。

2. 汉译英——化动为静

E.g. 这能生产出大量的油,供人们食用。
It produces a great quantity of oil which can be made into food for human consumption.

E.g. 绝对不许违反这个原则。
No violation of this principle can be tolerated.

E.g. 只要仔细将它们比较一下,你就会发现不同之处。
Careful comparison of them will show you the difference.

E.g. 应当始终注意保护仪器,不使其沾染灰尘和受潮。
Care must be taken at all times to protect the instrument from dust and dampness.

E.g. 这次会议具有重大意义。
This meeting is of great importance.

E.g. 这项目正在讨论之中。
The project is under discussion.

八、"化整为零"与"化零为整"

英语广泛使用各种起连接作用的词(包括连词、关系代词、关系副词、连接代词、连接副词以及大量介词),把许多从句和短语组织起来,成为句中套句,环扣相嵌,盘根错节,结构紧凑的长句("化零为整")。

汉语的偏正复句之间没有一定的连接词,因此,不可能组织起来成为复合长句,往往彼此分立,形成并列的散句或分立的简单结构,相互间在形态上连接显松散("化整为零")。

1. 英译汉——化整为零

E.g. This is the cat that killed the rat that ate the cake that was put in the house.
这就是那只捕杀了老鼠的猫。老鼠偷吃了放在屋里的蛋糕。

E.g. The many colors of a rainbow range from red on the outside to violet on the inside.
彩虹有多种颜色,外圈红,内圈紫。

E.g. The number of the young people in the United States who can't read is incredible about one in four.
在美国,大约有四分之一的年轻人没有阅读能力,这简直令人难以置信。

E.g. He wished that he had asked her to dance, and that he knew her name.
他多么希望自己当时请她跳了舞,现在还知道她的芳名。那该有多好啊!

E.g. Chilly gusts of wind with a taste of rain well depeopled the streets.
阵阵寒风,带着雨意,街上冷冷清清,几乎没有什么人了。

E. g. A bankable actor is one with whose name a producer can raise enough money to make a film.

"摇钱树"型演员是这样的一类演员：制片人可借他们的大名筹措到足够拍一部电影的金钱。

2. 汉译英——化零为整

E. g. 他的学习一直很好，考试成绩在班里一直都是数一数二，可这一段时间不知什么原因，连前十名也进不去了。

As a very good student in class, he has always achieved the highest scores in the examinations, but somehow he has never ranked among the top ten.

E. g. 老栓正在专心走路，忽然吃了一惊，远远地看见一条丁字街，明明白白横着。（鲁迅《药》）

Absorbed in his walking, Old Shuan was startled when he saw the cross road lying distinctly ahead of him.

E. g. 她曾经多次访问中国，在离大城市不远的一些农村，就连上厕所都是个问题。

She visited China many times, where, in some villages near big cities, even going to the toilet became a problem.

E. g. 我访问了一些地方，遇到了不少人。要谈起来，奇妙的事儿可多着呢。

There are many wonderful stories to tell about the places I visited and the people I met.

E. g. 该生在学习过程中积极主动，认真踏实，取得了良好成绩，名列前茅。

In the course of his/her studies, the above-mentioned student is positive, conscientious, and pragmatic/practical. He/She gets good grades and ranks among the top students in the class.

E. g. 长江全长约 6 300 千米，比黄河（5 464 千米）长 800 余千米。

The overall length of the Yangtze River is about 6,300 kilometers, which is longer than the Yellow River (5,464 km) by more than 800 kilometers.

九、思维方式的转变

英语叙述时往往"表态在前，叙事在后"，而汉语往往"叙事在前，表态在后"。这是英语和汉语在思维上的差异导致的结果，翻译时要做出转换。

1. 英译汉

E. g. It is important for you to ask this question.

问这个问题对你很重要。

E. g. It is a truth universally acknowledged that a single man in possession of a good fortune must be in want of a wife.

凡是有钱的单身汉，总想要位太太，这已经是个举世公认的真理。

E. g. It does not matter whether he accepts my opinions or not.

他是否接受我的观点，我并不在乎。

E. g. It was a keen disappointment when I had to postpone the visit which I intended to pay to China in January.

我原来打算在一月访问中国，后来不得不推迟，我感到非常失望。

2. 汉译英

E. g. 爱迪生是位真正的天才，这是不容置疑的。

It is undeniable that Edison was a genius in the truest sense of the word.

E. g. 她觉得回复这封信，是她应尽的责任。

She felt it incumbent upon her to answer the letter at once.

E. g. 大多数年轻人都认为过轻松不用努力的生活是最好的，这是令人遗憾的事。

It is to be regretted that the majority of young people should look upon an effortless life as the highest good.

E. g. 在我们家，饭前洗手是每个人的习惯。

In our home it is a rigid rule for each person to wash his/her hands before eating.

练 习 题

一、英译汉练习

Chinese Premier Li Keqiang promised on Monday to give $100 million in additional humanitarian assistance for refugees as he attended a high-level summit in New York on Monday.

Li told the historic UN summit addressing large movements of refugees and migrants that the refugee crisis poses a political, social and security threat that created opportunities for terrorists to exploit.

Li said China would also "seriously consider setting aside the China-UN Peace and Development Fund to support development Fund to support developing countries in their effort to deal with the problem."

During the annual gathering of world leaders at the UN in September last year, China said it would establish a 10-year, $1 billion fund to support the UN's work. It also took a first step in fulfilling this pledge when it signed an agreement with the UN in May to pay $20 million annually for a decade to help fund peace, security and development.

At the sidelines of the summit, Li is expected to meet US President Barack Obama to address economic issues, even as thorny issues such as North Korea's nuclear agenda might be raised, analysts said.

"Li can't give Obama any promise on North Korea's nuclear issue; the US should be realistic when they talk to Premier Li," Ni Feng, deputy director of the Institute of American Studies at the Chinese Academy of Social Sciences, told the *Global Times* on Monday.

The US blamed China for not imposing serious sanctions on North Korea, but China said the US should start negotiations rather than launch military drills and deploy the Terminal High Altitude Area Defense (THAAD) system to provoke North Korea, said Jin Canrong, associate dean at the School of International Studies of Renmin University of China...

(Yang Sheng, *Global News*)

二、汉译英练习

随着"丹东一号"身份确认为致远舰,这也意味着为期两年的水下调查阶段结束,进入考古发掘阶段。《华西都市报》记者获悉,水下考古队在10月4日正式启动水下发掘工作,这也是致远舰身份确认后的第一次水下发掘行动。这意味着致远舰的考古工作进入一个新的阶段。

随着辽宁丹东港沉船被确认为致远舰,有更多文物陆续出水,比如发现了一枚印章,上面刻有"云中白鹤"四个字,专家认为其疑似邓世昌的私人物品。

在此前的打捞中,曾出水了诸多生活用品,包括以"竹林七贤"为主题花纹的青花碗,以及一些钥匙、锁和银锭,其中还有一枚当时的"港币"硬币。

(刘叶蓓,*中国青年网*)

第三章 遣词用字

在遣词造句方面,好的翻译如同写作,至少要做到字正句顺,译文信息忠实、饱满,行文流畅,读来通顺。对翻译初学者来说,他们在措辞上会时有错误。

一、词语搭配

在漫长的语言发展过程中,词汇层自然生成的搭配,即词汇搭配,是语言学习迈向应用的很重要的一个环节。每种语言中都有很多词语搭配。

汉语中的词语搭配。如生意兴旺、嗓音清脆、头脑清楚、性格文静、声音柔和、心情沉重、形象丰满、精力旺盛、技术高超、态度严肃、工艺精湛、目标明确、品质高尚、工作认真、生活美好、纪律严明、品格高尚等。

【美文赏析】

月光如流水一般,静静地泻在这一片叶子和花上。薄薄的青雾浮起在荷塘里。叶子和花仿佛在牛乳中洗过一样;又像笼着轻纱的梦。虽然是满月,天上却有一层淡淡的云,所以不能朗照;但我以为这恰是到了好处——酣眠固不可少,小睡也别有风味的。月光是隔了树照过来的,高处丛生的灌木,落下参差的斑驳的黑影,峭楞楞如鬼一般;弯弯的杨柳的稀疏的倩影,却又像是画在荷叶上。塘中的月色并不均匀;但光与影有着和谐的旋律,如梵婀玲上奏着的名曲。

这段文字选自朱自清的《荷塘月色》,文笔优美、想象丰富。作者通过叠词"静静""薄薄""淡淡""弯弯"等词将"月光""叶子""青雾""杨柳"等串联起来,描写了荷塘月色之美,抒发了自己沉郁的心情。

这样优美的文章是翻译学习者/工作者学习的典范。通过学习,不断实践,力求译文措辞准确、表意清晰,如若文字同时富有感染力,就再好不过了。

要注意学习英语中的词语搭配。如 come up with 提出/想出/赶上;join in 加入/参加;stay up 熬夜;interfere with 干涉/打扰;drop out 退学/从……当中退出;on average 平均,一般来说;on board 在船(车、飞机)上;as a rule 通常/照例;come/go into force 生效/实施;make friends 交朋友;hang on 抓紧不放/继续下去;make up 组成/补足/化妆/编造;mix up 混淆/拌和;out of breath 喘不过气/上气不接下气;follow up 跟踪/坚持完成/继续做某事。

1. 语法搭配

语法搭配,即符合语言法则的搭配,类似于固定搭配。比如:lead to 造成/引起;differ from 与……不同;qualify for 有……的资格;relevant to 与……相关的;furious about 对……感到愤怒;uneasy about 对……感到不安;pleased with 对……感到满意;dissatisfied with 对……不满意;content with 对……感到满意等。

2. 非语法搭配

非语法搭配,即搭配符合语言应用规则,但搭配词语可替换,非固定式。比如:做手术 perform/have an operation;做家务 do household chores/house work;犯错误 make a mistake 或 commit an error;犯心脏病 suffer from/have a heart attack;险胜 a narrow win/victory 或 win by a narrow margin;熟睡 fast/sound asleep;完全醒着 wide/fully awake。

二、选词用字

1.深刻理解语境

语境即言语环境,包括语言因素,也包括非语言因素。上下文、时间、空间、情景、对象、话语前提等与语词使用有关的都是语境因素。交际中的语句(不论在书面或口头上)都和语境作为一个不可分割的整体出现,是互相依存的关系。如果忽视这种相互依存的关系,人类的交际就无法实现。

(1)英译汉

1)complete

E. g. He will help you **complete** the task.

这项任务由他辅助你去**完成**。

E. g. 2,000 shoppers **completed** our questionaires.

2 000 名顾客**填写**了我们的调查表。

E. g. It's not too difficult, but I can't string together these words into a **complete** sentence.

不算太难,可我还是不能把这些单词连成一个**完整**的句子。

E. g. We have to live with the fact that this experiment is a **complete** failure.

我们得承认这次实验**彻底**失败了。

E. g. She says the recovery of the Gulf is far from **complete**.

她说墨西哥湾的恢复工作还远远没有**完成**。

E. g. Unlike with **complete** recovery, you have to restore all data files, instead of only the selected data files.

与**完全**备份不同,您必须恢复所有数据文件,而不只是选定的数据文件。

2)take

E. g. What did they **take** us for?

他们把我们**当成**什么了?

E. g. You should learn to **take** criticism.

你应该学会**接受**批评。

E. g. **Take** it to the kitchen.

把它**拿**到厨房去。

E. g. **Take** that picture off the wall.

把墙上那幅画**揭**下来。

E. g. **Take** ten drops every four hours.

每隔四小时**喝**十滴(药)。

E. g. She vowed that she would **take** the matter to court.
她信誓旦旦地说一定要把此事**告**到法庭。

3) hold

E. g. **hold** a meeting 开会/举行会议

　　hold one's attention 吸引某人注意

　　hold one's position 坚守阵地/坚持立场

　　hold one's view 坚持观点

　　hold somebody guilty 判定某人有罪

　　hold one's tongue 管住嘴

　　hold a baby in one's arms 抱孩子

　　hold one's drink 大量喝酒而不醉（指酒量大）

　　hold a pipe between the teeth 嘴里叼着烟斗

　　hold one's end up 做好分内的事；坚持到底

　　hold power 掌权

　　hold a leading post 担任领导工作

(2) 汉译英

在不同情形下，同一个词需译成不同的英语。

1) 辛苦

E. g. 翻译工作很**辛苦**。
　　　Translation is **hard work**.

E. g. 同志们**辛苦**了！
　　　You comrades have been **working hard**.

E. g. 路上**辛苦**了。
　　　You must have had a **tiring** journey. / You must be **tired** after the journey.

2) 发

E. g. 发短信 **send** a text message

　　　发警告 **issue** a warning

　　　发货 **dispatch** goods

　　　发光 **give out** light, shine

　　　发制服 **provide** staff with uniforms

　　　发工资 **pay** wages

　　　发月饼 **give** sb. moon cakes

3) 打

E. g. 打稻子 **thresh** rice

　　　打行李 **pack** one's luggage; pack up

　　　打硬仗 **fight** a hard battle

　　　打电报 **send** a telegraph

　　　打草鞋 **weave** straw sandals

　　　打一个问号 **make** a query

打鱼 **catch** fish

打蛔虫 take medicine to **get rid of** roundworms

打一盆水 **fetch** a basin of water

打灯笼 **carry** a lantern

打了800斤麦子 **harvest** 400 kilos of wheat

打手势 **make** a gesture

4）出

E.g. 出城 **go out of** town

出站 **come out of** the station

不出三年 **within** 3 years

球出了边线。The ball **went over** the sideline.

出杂志 **publish** a magazine

出证明 **issue** a certificate

出主意 **offer** advice；**supply** ideas；**make** suggestions

出布告 **post** an announcement；**put up** a notice

我们要多出人才。We must **cultivate** a greater number of qualified personnel.

这事出在30年前。It **happened** thirty years ago.

防止出事故 prevent accidents

2. 注意词语的色彩

词语有中性、褒义和贬义之分，翻译时需要特别注意。

1）slim 与 skinny

slim 为褒义词，用于描写身材时意为"苗条的/修长的"。

E.g. The young woman was tall and slim.

那个年轻女子个子高挑，身材苗条。

skinny 为贬义词，用于描写身材时意为"瘦骨嶙峋的"。

E.g. He was quite a skinny little boy.

他是个骨瘦如柴的小男孩。

2）famous 与 notorious

famous 为褒义词，意为"著名的"。

E.g. The town is famous for its cathedral.

这个城镇以大教堂著名。

notorious 为贬义词，意为"声名狼藉的/臭名昭著的"。

E.g. The bar has become notorious as a meeting-place for drug dealers.

作为毒品贩子接头的场所，这家酒吧已变得声名狼藉。

3）nourishing 与 fattening

nourishing 为褒义词，意为"有营养的/滋养多的"。

E.g. Most of these nourishing substances are in the yolk of the egg.

这些营养物质大部分在蛋黄里。

fattening 为贬义词，意为"使人发胖的"。

E. g. To get your weight down, you must keep off fattening foods.
要使体重下降,你一定不能吃让人发胖的食物。

4)"政治家"与"政客"

政治家(statesman)是指那些在长期的政治实践中涌现出来的具有一定政治远见和政治才干、掌握着政党或国家权力并对社会历史发展起着重大影响作用的领导人物;政客(politician)就是以政治活动为职业,为了本阶级、本集团或个人某种政治需要而搞政治投机、玩弄政治权术的人。

E. g. He is a statesman of great eminence.
他是个声名显赫的政治家。

E. g. 就如政客们常说的,这关乎我们的血汗和财富。
It is, as politicians like to say, about our blood and treasure.

3. 熟语、新词的翻译

当今世界发展异常迅速,国际交流日趋频繁,信息传播更加便捷。在几乎各个领域,新词不断涌现,如"打酱油""浮云""裸婚"等。这些新词凝聚了人民群众的智慧,形象生动,感情鲜明,内涵丰富,具有很强的时代色彩,一定程度上丰富了我们民族的语言和文化。

随着中国加速融入世界,世界渴望了解中国的方方面面情况。这些新词的翻译给翻译工作者提出了新的要求。

(1)英译汉

自李大钊等人提倡新文化运动以来,外来语越来越多地出现在汉语中而成为汉语语言和文化的一部分。

比如:beer(啤酒);coffee(咖啡);chocolate(巧克力);egg tart(蛋挞);ice cream(冰淇淋);sandwich(三明治);hamburger(汉堡);brandy(白兰地);cheese(芝士);curry(咖喱);hot dog(热狗);whisky(威士忌);soda(苏打);pudding(布丁);pizza(比萨饼);salad(色拉);Coca Cola(可口可乐);Sprite(雪碧);Simmons(席梦思);sofa(沙发);poker(扑克);hula loop(呼啦圈);valve(阀);jeep(吉普车);engine(引擎);tyre(胎);cement(水泥);shampoo(香波,即洗发水);CD,Compact Disc(激光唱片);Benz(奔驰);telephone(电话);taxi(的士);vitamin(维他命);jazz(爵士);angel(天使);romantic(罗曼蒂克);salon(沙龙);hysteria(歇斯底里);humor(幽默);logic(逻辑);model(模特);carnation(康乃馨);card(卡片);neon(霓虹);dacron(的确良);cashmere(开司米);nylon(尼龙);algebra(代数);geometry(几何);lurch(趔趄);talk show(脱口秀);shock(休克);cool(酷);fee(费);club(俱乐部);system(系统);bungee(蹦极);mosaic(马赛克);Shangeri-La(香格里拉);cartoon(卡通);montage(蒙太奇);marathon(马拉松);bikini(比基尼);democracy(民主);science(科学);copy(拷贝);Nikon(尼康);click(点击);Safeguard(舒肤佳);Mcdonald's(麦当劳);KFC,Kentucky Fried Chicken(肯德基);DINK,Double Income No Kids(丁克家族);party(派对);Internet(互联网);topology(拓扑)等。

由以上例子可看出,对于外来语,汉语译文主要采用音译法。

(2)汉译英

这些年,随着我国国力不断增强,很多国家开始向我国学习经验。表现在语言层面上,就是越来越多的汉语词汇出现在英语中,多见于英语俚语词典中。

比如:关系(guanxi);中国宇航员(taikonaut);枸杞(goji);饺子(jiaozi);少林寺(Shaolin Temple);气功(qigong);武术(wushu);锅贴、煎饺(potsticker);功夫(kung fu);西安人/的(Xi'aner/Xi'anese);拼音(Pinyin);茅台(Maotai);人民币(Renminbi);旗袍(cheongsam);中式英语(Chinglish);北京烤鸭(Beijing Roast Duck);秧歌(yangko);馄饨(wonton)等。

由以上例子可看出,对外传播汉语新词,主要采用拼音法/拼音＋改造法。

此外,对于习语、谚语等的翻译,还有其他译法。

E. g. 说曹操,曹操就到。
Speak/Talk of the devil (and he will appear)。（对应法）

E. g. 鱼和熊掌不可兼得。
You can't have your cake and eat it。（对应法）

E. g. 一个和尚挑水吃,两个和尚抬水吃,三个和尚没水吃。
One boy is a boy, two boys half a boy and three boys no boy。（对应法）

E. g. 三个臭皮匠,赛过诸葛亮。
Three cobblers with their wits combined equal Zhuge Liang the mastermind。（增译法）

E. g. 好心当作驴肝肺
take an honest man's heart for a donkey's liver and lungs—take sb.'s good will for ill will（直译＋释义法）

E. g. 横挑鼻子竖挑眼
Find fault in a petty manner. 或 pick holes in sth. 或 nitpick（释义法）

4. 选词用字常用方法

(1)通过词典查询词义

通过词典查询词义是外语学习者最常见的做法。时下,各种网络词典不断出现,常用的词典有《有道词典》(完美结合了互联网在线词典和桌面词典的优势)、《金山词霸》(完整收录柯林斯词典,唯一完整解析牛津高阶词典的软件)、《灵格斯词霸》(一款简明易用的词典与文本翻译软件,支持全球超过80多种语言的词典查询)、《星际译王》(Linux下知名的完全免费的开源词典软件,上百万人在使用,拥有上千本词典供用户使用)等。很多网络词典的翻译质量都是不错的。

对于句子以上的语言单位,一般译者会用"翻译"模块,有时会查到网络词典中内嵌的句子,但是很多时候是该词典生硬的译文,译者要根据源语和目的语的语言和文化知识学会识别、修正错误,甚至还需润色译文。例如《有道词典》译:

我是一位中国人。I am a Chinese.

我是一位帅气的中国人。I am a handsome Chinese.

我是一位个子高大、长相帅气的中国人。

I am a tall, handsome, the Chinese people.

改译:I am a tall and handsome Chinese（man）。

当原文信息量大、信息之间关系复杂时,网络词典的翻译就令人失望了(实际上目前很多网络词典都是这样)。

如:(原文) Elizabeth Economy, C. V. Starr senior fellow and director for Asia studies at the Council on Foreign Relations

《有道词典》译:Elizabeth Economy C. V. 斯塔尔高级研究员和亚洲研究主管对外关系委员会

这时,译者要发挥主观能动性,厘清原文信息之间的逻辑关系,按照一定的规范(如此处所需的译名规范),合理译出原文信息。

编者译:伊丽莎白·伊科诺米,C. V. 斯塔尔高级研究员,对外关系委员会亚洲研究主管

又如:(**原文**)James Steinberg, former deputy secretary of state and currently dean of social science, international affairs and law at the Maxwell School of Citizenship and Public Affairs, Syracuse University

《有道词典》译:前副国务卿詹姆斯·斯坦伯格和目前社会科学学院院长,国际事务和法律麦克斯韦公民与公共事务学院,锡拉丘兹大学

编者译:詹姆斯·斯坦伯格,美国前副国务卿,现任雪城大学公民权利与公共事务麦斯威尔学院社会科学、国际事务与法律系主任

(2)通过互联网查询词义

现在是互联网的天下,互联网让偌大的地球变成了一个"村庄"。译者可以利用这个强大的工具为自己所用(尤其是当词典查不到的时候)。

1)一带一路

《有道词典》的"网络释义"上给了以下译法:One Belt And One Road;One Belt One Road;OBOR;One Belt 等。到底应该采用哪种译法呢?

查询互联网得知,2015年9月在"一带一路"提出两周年之际,国家发改委会同外交部、商务部等部门对"一带一路"英文译法进行了规范,在对外公文中,统一将"丝绸之路经济带和21世纪海上丝绸之路"的英文全称译为"the Silk Road Economic Belt and the 21st Century Maritime Silk Road","一带一路"的英文简称译为"the Belt and Road",英文缩写用"B&R"。由此,我们得知"the Belt and Road"是"一带一路"最权威的英文表述方式了。

2)Scientists Stalk Mammoth Clone

这是一篇英文文章的标题,文章出自2000年10月版的《英语学习》。文章指出,科学家在西伯利亚的冻土中意外地发现了已经灭绝数万年之久的猛犸象遗体,然后挖掘出来,移至实验室研究,试图克隆猛犸象。

将"Scientists Stalk Mammoth Clone"输入到《有道词典》中,我们得到译文:科学家跟踪猛犸象克隆体。stalk 作为及物动词,其汉语意思是"追踪,潜近;高视阔步"。我们将这个标题输入搜索引擎中,仔细查看搜索结果,发现《英语学习》杂志提供了"科学家探究猛犸克隆"的中文翻译,契合文章内容。为使标题意思更清晰,我们可以将标题改为"科学家探究猛犸象克隆"。

(3)通过文本中的逻辑关系判断词义

词义可分为概念义(词语本身所表达的意义,即词语的本义,它是词义的核心)和联想义(通过此物进而联想到彼物所产生的意义),联想义又可分为内涵意义、文体意义、情感意义和搭配意义。

内涵意义:一个词基本意义之外的含义。比如英语动词 take 一词,在《有道词典》上的释义为"*vt.* 拿,取;采取;接受(礼物等);买,花费;耗费(时间等)"。除了基本意思"拿,取"之外,其他的释义皆可视作 take 的内涵意义。

文体意义:具有文体特征的词语在不同语境下产生的意义。文体特征,如词语有"正式""非正式""俚语""方言"等之分。

情感意义:当语言使用者通过语言表达其情感和态度时传递出的意义,即人们主观评价时所表达的意义,或喜爱,或憎恶,或肯定,或否定,或赞许,或贬斥等。

搭配意义:由一个词从与他相结合的其他的词的意义中所获得的各种联想构成的,是一种必须与别的意义搭配在一起才能产生的意义。

很多时候,译者需要结合上下文,厘清信息间的逻辑关系,才能译出地道的译文。

1) hot

E. g. When the oil is **hot**, add the sliced onion.

　　油**热**之后,加入切好的洋葱。

E. g. It took **hot** competition from abroad, however, to show us just how good our product really is.

　　然而,正是来自国外的**激烈**竞争让我们看到自己的产品有多好。

E. g. His **hot** temper was making it increasingly difficult for others to work with him.

　　他**暴躁的**脾气使得别人越来越难与他一起工作。

E. g. **Hot** girls are always popular.

　　性感的女孩总是受人欢迎。

E. g. Ray was getting very **hot** and bothered about the idea.

　　雷为这个想法感到**焦虑不安**。

2) 情况

E. g. **情况**不明。

　　The **situation** is not clear.

E. g. 这种**情况**必须改变。

　　This **state of affairs** must change.

E. g. 前面有**情况**,做好战斗准备。

　　There is **enemy activity** ahead. Prepare for combat.

E. g. 他们的**情况**怎么样?

　　How are they now?

　　How do **matters** stand with them?

E. g. 我们可能去那儿,那得看**情况**而定。

　　We may go there, but that **depends**.

(4) 通过平行文本(parallel text)确定词义

平行文本原指并排放在一起、可以逐句对照阅读的原文及其译文。广义的平行文本也包括与原文内容相似的译出语资料,主要用于更深入地理解原文。简单来说,平行文本就是与原文内容接近的任何参考资料。

理想的状态是,译者是"万事通",应该无所不知,然而现实情况并非如此。对于不熟悉的内容,译者有时可以通过平行文本解决翻译时遇到的问题。

E. g. "阿人主导、阿人所有"的和解进程

这是笔者曾遇到的一个翻译片段,翻译时遇到问题。《有道词典》上没有译文,在互联网上也没有查到译文。一个偶然的机会,笔者在一篇外交新闻中看到了"阿人主导、阿人所有"的我国官方的英文说法是"Afghan-led,Afghan-owned",所以"'阿人主导、阿人所有'的和解进程"可翻译为"Afghan-led,Afghan-owned" reconciliation process。

以下为我国外文局审定的部分时政术语英译蓝本(见表3.1),供大家学习,可从中感悟一下翻译的奥妙。

表 3.1　部分时政术语的英语译文

汉语原文	英语译文
高举中华民族大团结旗帜	to uphold the great unity of the Chinese nation
集中力量办大事	to concentrate strength for major undertakings
坚持和完善支撑中国特色社会主义制度的根本制度、基本制度、重要制度	to uphold and improve the fundamental, basic and important systems that underpin the system of socialism with Chinese characteristics
着力固根基、扬优势、补短板、强弱项	to solidify the foundation, leverage our strengths and tackle areas of weaknesses
党的全面领导制度	the system of overall leadership by the Communist Party of China
新型政党制度	a new model of political party relations
民族区域自治制度	the system of regional ethnic autonomy
国之重器	national pillars/major projects (or weapons)
人民是我们党执政的最大底气。	The people's support is the strongest foundation for our party's governance.
共和国勋章	the Medal of the Republic
发展才是硬道理。	Development is what really matters to all.
农业农村优先发展	to prioritize the development of agriculture and rural areas
站起来、富起来到强起来。	China has stood up, become prosperous and is growing strong.
不获全胜,决不收兵。	Never call retreat until a complete victory.
共和国是红色的。	The People's Republic of China has a revolutionary tradition.
市场准入负面清单制度	a negative list for market access
理论武装	to arm ourselves with theory
依宪治国、依宪执政	Constitution-based governance
中国特色社会主义法制道路	the path of law-based governance under Chinese socialism

第三章 遣词用字

练 习 题

一、请将下列英语句子翻译成汉语，注意粗体字的正确译法

1. If you upend the box, it will **take** less space.
2. When that bomb explodes, it'll **take** everyone with it!
3. She vowed that she would **take** the matter to court.
4. **Take** whatever measures you consider best.
5. **Take** ten drops every four hours.

二、请将下列汉语句子翻译成英语，注意粗体字的正确译法

1. 她会**打**篮球，也会**打**网球。
2. 他砰砰**打**门，一直到她开门让他进去为止。
3. 这个木制的东西是用来**打**鸡蛋的。
4. 你如果有黑桃牌，就必须**打**出来。
5. 他们的衣服在衣箱里放的时间这么长，都**打**褶了。
6. 他们**打**桥牌消遣。

三、英译汉练习

The crown of "greatness" never sat easily on the snowcapped head of John Updike, one of the great writers of the 20th century, who died from lung cancer at the age of 76. He grew up a clever, stuttering child in small-town Pennsylvania and went to college at Harvard, where he served as head of the *Lampoon*, the campus humor magazine, rather than its storied literary magazine, *the Advocate*. He dabbled in cartooning, and his first published work in the *New Yorker* consisted of light verse.

But he was a novelist at heart, and it was with the novel, along with the short story, that he would have his lasting, lifelong romance. This appears to have dawned on Updike slowly, but it was abundantly clear by the publication of his second novel, *Rabbit, Run*, the first volume of five that chronicled the life of Rabbit Angstrom, Updike's great hero. Rather than a fictional alter ego, Angstrom was a vulgarian, a crass, lusty, middle-class salesman, through whom Updike anatomized and dramatized the great American spiritual and cultural crises of his generation.

Updike's hallmark was his glittering, gloriously vivid style. His talent for spotting detail, for capturing in prose the slightest shift in light or in a character's mood was unmatched. It was not the most fashionable of gifts. While his contemporaries practiced the rock-ribbed realism of Hemingway and Carver or the high-concept contraptions of the metafictionists, Updike conducted his pursuit of eloquence and wit almost alone. Ironically, it was sometimes held against him, and he was tagged a lightweight.

(Lev Grossman,《英语学习》,2009 年 5 月)

四、汉译英练习

10 月 4 日,马云的第一幅油画作品《桃花源》在香港的苏富比以 3 300 万元被拍卖。拍卖会现场异常疯狂,经过 40 多次的加价,最终以高价拍出。期间,甚至有人直接从 360 万元加价到 500 万元,随后又有人从 900 万元加价到 1 800 万元。

《桃花源》是马云与中国艺术家曾梵志携手,为桃花源生态保护基金会筹款创作的。马云说,第一次画画,与梵志一起画画,他深感荣幸,这也是他第一次用油画画画,感觉挺好。据悉,这幅画拍卖所得将捐给桃花源生态保护基金会。

曾梵志被认为是当代中国较具代表性和国际影响的艺术家之一。

(崔江,《华西都市报》)

第四章 句子翻译

一、翻译常用方法

1. 音译

音译,顾名思义,就是根据翻译对象的发音译出译文。这种方法广泛地用于人名、地名、货币、公司名、商标名、化学元素名等的翻译中。

(1)人名、地名

Bernard Shaw 萧伯纳;Michigan 密歇根州;Washington 华盛顿;New York 纽约;Chamberlain 张伯伦;Wilde 王尔德;Marx 马克思;Yeats 叶芝;Liszt 李斯特;Petöfi 裴多菲;Jude 裘德;Keats 济慈;Chopin 肖邦;Schopenhauer 叔本华;Rick Santorum 李三多;Chaucer 乔叟;Kissinger 基辛格;Louisiana 路易斯安那州;西安 Xi'an;咸阳 Xianyang;上海 Shanghai;新疆 Xinjiang。

但是也有例外情形。如:孔子 Confucius;孟子 Mencius;孙中山 Sun Yat-sen;蒋介石 Chiang Kai-shek;李小龙 Bruce Lee;清华 Tsinghua 等。

(2)货币

世界货币翻译。如:Krona 克朗(瑞典等);Krone 克朗(丹麦、挪威);Kwacha 克瓦查(赞比亚等);Kwanza 宽札(安哥拉);Kyat 元(缅甸);Lira 里拉(意大利等);Loti 洛蒂(莱索托);Pound 英镑(英国);Mark 马克(德国);Euro 欧元(欧盟中多个国家的货币);Kina 基那(巴布亚新几内亚);Kip 基普(老挝);Koruna 克朗(捷克等);Metical 梅蒂尔卡(莫桑比克);Naira 奈拉(尼日利亚);Ngultrum 努扎姆(不丹);Ouguiya 乌吉亚(毛里塔尼亚);Peseta 比塞塔(西班牙)。

(3)商标名

如:Bally 百利;Dunhill 登喜路;Escada 埃斯卡达;Fendi 芬迪;GUCCI 古驰;Givenchy 纪梵希;Cartier 卡地亚;Chanel 香奈尔;Calvin Klein 卡文·克莱;Christian Dior 克里斯汀·迪奥;Comme des Garcons 川久保玲;Anna Sui 安娜·苏;立白 Liby(洗洁精);奇瑞 Chery(汽车);新科 Shinco(电器);茅台 Maotai(酒);鄂尔多斯 Erods(羊毛衫);容声 Ronshen(电器);李宁 LI-NING(运动用品);康佳 KONKA(电器);青岛 Qingdao(啤酒);华为 Huawei 等。

(4)化学元素名(不全是音译,见表 4.1)

表 4.1 部分化学元素名中英文对照

英文名称	Hydrogen	Helium	Lithium	Beryllium	Boron	Carbon	Nitrogen	Fluorine
汉语名称	氢	氦	锂	铍	硼	碳	氮	氟

2. 增译

增译,是根据英汉两种语言不同的思维方式、语言习惯和表达方式,在翻译时增添一些词、短句或句子,以便更准确地表达出原文所包含的意义。

(1)增加原文中省略的信息

  E. g. Matter can be changed into energy, and energy into matter.
    物质可以转化为能量,能量也可以转化为物质。

  E. g. Tom has already been to Britain, so has Jack.
    汤姆曾去过英国,杰克也曾去过英国。

  E. g. Are you ready? Yes, I am.
    你准备好了吗? 我准备好了。

  E. g. I was taught that two sides of a triangle are greater than the third.
    我学过,三角形的两边之和大于第三边。

  E. g. He wanted to swim across the river but I warned him not to.
    他想从河这边游到河那边去,我劝告他不要这么做。

  E. g. I am looking forward to the holidays.
    我在盼望着假期的到来。

  E. g. What if he should fail?
    万一他失败了,那该怎么办?

  E. g. 扒车 climb onto a slow-moving train.

  E. g. 白旗 white flag (a signal of surrender or truce)

  E. g. 白字 a character misused or mispronounced through confusion with one that sounds or looks like it

  E. g. 百花齐放,百家争鸣 let a hundred flowers blossom and a hundred schools of thought contend (a policy set forth by Mao Zedong for promoting the progress of the arts and the sciences and the development of a flourishing socialist culture)

  E. g. 中国有13亿人口,占全球的五分之一。
    China has a population of 1.3 billion, accounting for one-fifth of the population of the world.

  E. g. 上海的优势在于科技实力。
    The advantage of Shanghai lies in its advanced scientific and technical strength.

(2)增加关联词

  E. g. Heated, water will change into vapor.
    水如受热,就会变成水蒸气。

  E. g. Having answered the letter, she went on to read an English novel.
    她写完回信后就去读英文小说了。

  E. g. Some books are to be tasted, others to be swallowed, and some few are to be chewed and digested.
    书有可浅尝者,有可尽食者,少数则需咀嚼消化。

  E. g. Baihe, one of China's largest online dating and matchmaking websites, is no stranger to legal disputes.

百合网是中国最大的在线约会和相亲网站之一，但法律纠纷不断。

E.g. 1917年，俄国发生了十月革命，建立了世界上第一个社会主义国家。
In 1917, the October Revolution took place in Russia, and the first socialist state in the world was established.

E.g. 西安有的路很短，短到不足300米。
Some roads in Xi'an are so short that they are even not 300 meters long.

E.g. 手写会耗费很多时间，并容易出错，阻碍了文化的发展。
Writing by hand took much time and it was easy to make mistakes, which impeded the progress of culture.

E.g. 传说古时候有一个叫作"年"的怪兽，每到腊月三十晚上就出来吃人。
There is a legend that in ancient times, a monster called Nian went out to eat people every New Year's Eve (lunar calendar) in the evening.

(3) 其他增译情形

E.g. Either of them can stay to take care of this sick cat.
他们两人中任一人都可以留下来照顾这只病猫。（增加 either 内涵义）

E.g. Avoid using this computer in extreme cold, heat, dust or humidity.
不要在过冷、过热、灰尘过重、湿度过大的情况下使用此电脑。（增加原文中省略的信息）

E.g. ladies and gentlemen
女士们，先生们（增加复数概念词"们"）

E.g. 诸葛亮 Zhuge Liang, a statesman and strategist during the period of the Three Kingdoms (220—280AD), who became a symbol of resourcefulness and wisdom in Chinese folklore（增加背景信息）

E.g. 鲁班 Lu Ban, a master craftsman of the Spring and Autumn Period (770—476 BC), since deified as the patron saint of carpenters（增加背景信息）

E.g. 蔡锷 Cai E, a leader of the Revolt Against the Restoration of Monarchy in 1915（增加背景信息）

E.g. 蚯蚓是一种有益的动物。
The earthworm is a useful animal.（增加表示类别的词"the"）

3. 省译

省译法是与增译法相对应的一种翻译方法，即删去不符合目标语思维习惯、语言习惯和表达方式的词，以避免译文累赘。

(1) 省略代词

E.g. Anyone who does not recognize this fact is not a materialist.
不承认这个事实就不是唯物主义者。

E.g. During their stay in Beijing, they visited some old friends of theirs.
在北京逗留期间，他们拜访了一些老朋友。

E.g. She laid her hand gently on his arm as if to thank him.

她轻轻地把手放在他的胳膊上,好像表示感谢。

(2)省略原文中的关联词

英语是形合语言(靠有形手段将信息连接起来),汉语是意合语言(不需要外在手段,而靠信息内在的逻辑连接信息),所以英译汉时存在大量的省略。

E. g. When I was home in Britain on holiday last summer, I spent an evening looking at photos my father had taken.

去年夏天,我回到英国老家度假,花了一个晚上看父亲拍的照片。

E. g. Because of her lovely personality and excellence in studies, she is elected the president of her sorority called Delta Nu and voted homecoming queen of the year.

她性格可爱,学习优异,当选"德耳塔·努"女生联谊会主席和返校节女王。

E. g. She has a very smart and handsome boyfriend named Warner Huntington, a famous senator's son.

她的男友华纳·亨廷顿,聪明过人,英俊潇洒,是一位著名参议员的儿子。

(3)省略的其他情形

E. g. Every day the earth is rotating while it is revolving around the sun.

每天,地球自转的同时也在绕着太阳公转。(省略冠词)

E. g. Smoking is prohibited in public places.

公共场所不许吸烟。(省略介词)

E. g. 我们必须培养分析问题、解决问题的能力。

We must cultivate the ability to analyze and solve problems.

(省略原文重复出现的词"问题")

E. g. 那些是美味佳肴。

Those are delicious food.

("美味"和"佳肴"为重复信息,英语要避免重复)

4. 词类转换

词类转换,即在翻译过程中,为使译文语义饱满,读来通顺、流畅,而改变词汇类别。因为英汉在词法、句子结构、逻辑、表达方式等方面有差异。所以,词类转换在翻译过程中使用非常频繁。

E. g. He gave every indication of being a fool.

他处处显出自己是个傻瓜。(名词→动词)

E. g. This is the most definite indication that the project is a purely technological one.

这最明确地表明,该项目完全是个技术项目。(名词→动词)

E. g. The application of electronic computers greatly increases labor productivity.

使用计算机可以大大提高劳动生产率。(名词→动词)

E. g. I think that, as far as the database course is concerned, Mr. Brown is a better teacher than I am.

我认为,就数据库这门课而论,布朗先生比我教得好。(名词→动词)

E. g. Are you for or against me?

你支持我还是反对我?(介词→动词)

E. g. The pavements are designed to provide easy access for people in wheelchairs.
设计人行道是为了让使用轮椅的人能方便进出。(形容词→副词)

E. g. Understanding how the animals acquire and make good use of these new genes could have implications for medicine.
理解这些动物如何获得并好好利用这些新基因可能对医学有启发。(形容词→副词)

E. g. The design aims at automatic operation, easy regulation, simple maintenance and high productivity.
译文1:该设计的目的在于实现自动操作、方便调节、简单维护及高生产率。(动词→名词)
译文2:该设计旨在实现自动操作、方便调节、简单维护及高生产率。(保留动词词类,因为汉语是动态语言,动词使用频繁。)

E. g. 人们常用剪纸美化居家环境。
译文1:People often beautify their homes with paper cuttings.(动词→介词)
译文2:Paper cuttings are often used to beautify homes.(动词词类没有变化)(更好)

E. g. 四大发明经由各种途径传至西方,对世界文明发展史也产生了很大的影响。
The Four Great Inventions have had a great effect on the history of world civilization since their introduction in various ways to the west.(动词→名词,英语是静态语言)

E. g. 我荣幸地告诉您,您的请求已得到批准。
I have the honor to inform you that your request is granted.(副词→名词)

E. g. 河流下游的情况是多种多样的。
The lower stretches of rivers show considerable variety.(形容词→名词)

5. 结构调整

英汉两种语言句子结构特点不同。英语句子(尤其是长句)中往往有较多的修饰语,一个修饰语还可以被另一个修饰语所修饰,用不同的关联方式有机连接。这样,句子似乎可以不断延伸,因此句式结构显得冗长、复杂却又主次分明,条理清晰,被称为"树状形结构"。

汉语句子往往按照自然事理的发展顺序和客观的因果关系而展开,呈现方式多为"话题+评价"模式,修饰语较短,句子由一个个分句构成,分句与分句、短语与短语之间有语义联系,但是几乎不用关联词,主谓结构不是很明显,所以汉语句子结构显得松散,短句多,句子意思主要靠时间和逻辑顺序明晰,被称为"波浪形结构"。因此,英汉互译时,关键就是变换句子结构。

E. g. My uncle passed away in hospital at 2:30 a. m. on September 12, 1999.
我的伯父于1999年9月12日凌晨2点30分在医院逝世。

英语句子多呈现"主语+最重要信息+'废话'(其他信息)"模式,而汉语句子多呈现"主语+'废话'(其他信息)+最重要信息"。所以,在翻译过程中要做结构上的调整,不然读来不畅,甚至无法表意。

E. g. We can gain some time if we cut across this field.

我们如果抄近路穿过这片田野可以省下一些时间。

E. g. 分子受热时速度就会增加。
The speed of the molecules is increased when they are heated.

E. g. 在西雅图,一位九岁男孩带枪上学,结果枪支在背包中意外走火,造成一名同学受重伤。
In Seattle, a 9-year-old boy brought a gun to school which seriously injured a classmate when it was accidentally discharged in his backpack.

E. g. As was cleared up some time later, the news came from distant source that an earthquake was felt the very day the little copper ball fell.
远方传来了消息:就在小铜球坠落的当天发生了地震。过了一段时间,这一切才得以澄清。(根据时间做出调整)

E. g. It's horrifying to think that institutions could be a place of injury or even death.
一想到学校可能是带来伤害甚至致人死亡的地方,人们就会不寒而栗。(这种调整是源于英汉思维上的差异。英语先表态,后叙事,而汉语恰恰相反。)

E. g. 柯灵,生于1909年,浙江省绍兴人,中国现代作家,1926年发表第一篇作品,叙事诗《织布的妇人》。
Ke Ling is a modern Chinese writer who was born in Shaoxing, Zhejiang Province in 1909. His first writing, a narrative poem, *the Woman Weaver*, came out in 1926.

6. 其他翻译方法

(1) 直译与意译

直译是在译文语言条件许可时既保持原文内容又保持原文形式的翻译方法。一般来说,这是译者倾向的一种翻译做法,也是最理想的一种翻译方法。

E. g. Deoxyribonucleic acid＝DNA＝de＋oxy＋ribo＋nucleic acid 脱氧核糖核酸;stem cells 干细胞;optical drive 光驱;satellite antimissile observation system 卫星反导弹观察系统;anti-armored vehicle missile 反装甲车导弹;power transmission relay system 送电中继系统;dark horse 黑马;安全玻璃 safety glass;安全帽 safety helmet;小天鹅 Little Swan;红蜻蜓 Red Dragonfly;自然美 Natural Beauty;自由鸟 Free Bird;三鹿 Three Deer;双星 Double Star;蜂花 Bee & Flower;金星 Kingstar;长城 the Great Wall

E. g. 搬起石头砸自己的脚 pick up a stone only to drop it on one's own feet

北大西洋公约组织 the North Atlantic Treaty Organization (NATO)

三教九流 the three religions and the nine schools of thought

四书五经 the Four Books and the Five Classics

参考书 a reference book

直译＋注释。有时候,为了更清晰表意,需要注释信息。如:

E. g. 白区 White area (the Kuomintang-controlled area during the Second Revolutionary Civil War, 1927—1937)

E. g. 巴黎公社 the Paris Commune (the world's first dictatorship of the proletariat, established by the French working class after smashing the old state machine in 1871)

E. g. 北朝 the Northern Dynasties (386—581), namely, the Northern Wei Dynasty(北魏，386—534), the Eastern Wei Dynasty(东魏，534—550), the Western Wei Dynasty(西魏，535—556), the Northern Qi Dynasty(北齐，550—577) and the Northern Zhou Dynasty(北周,557—581)

(2)顺译与倒译

顺译,即顺应着原文信息顺序翻译。

E. g. For a little child, it's difficult to memorize so many words in such a short period of time.
对一个小孩来说,很难在这么短时间内记住这么多字。

E. g. It is certain that most engineering materials are partly elastic and partly plastic.
可以肯定,大多数工程材料都有几分弹性和塑性。

E. g. Different forms of energy can all be used to do work.
不同形式的能都可用来做功。

E. g. As you would be our guest, we would of course meet all your expenses.
您是我们的客人,我们当然会为您支付全部的费用。

E. g. 一般认为元宵节始于汉代。
It is generally recognized that the Lantern Festival began in the Han Dynasty.

E. g. 秦国历时10年,先后灭了韩、赵、魏、楚、燕、齐,于公元前221年统一了中国。
Within only ten years, the Qin vanquished the Han, Zhao, Wei, Chu, Yan and Qi one after another, and united the whole of China in 221 BC.

E. g. 香港一名妇人失踪17天,昨天(2017年2月22日)有人在一条干涸山涧内发现了她。
In Hong Kong, a woman was missing for 17 days until yesterday (February 22, 2017) when she was found in a dried-up mountain stream.

倒译,即从句末向句首方向翻译。

E. g. Don't be careless with your work because you are pressed for time.
不要因为时间紧迫就马马虎虎。

E. g. 受梵蒂冈派遣,他远渡重洋,到日本传教,已有二十多年时间了。
It was more than twenty years since the Vatican dispatched him all the way across the ocean to Japan as a missionary.

E. g. 他俩能在地里找口粗茶淡饭,完全是靠丈夫起早贪黑的耕作。
It was only by the husband's incessant labor that they could draw a meager living from their land.

E. g. It is by mechanical means that a float switch is usually used to turn off the burner or shut off fuel to the boiler to prevent it from running once the water goes below a certain point.

当水位低于某个点位时,使用浮控开关关掉燃烧器或断开锅炉的燃料供应,防止锅炉继续运行,这是一种机械手段。

(3)合译与拆译

合译,是指将并列句或复合句合为更长句子的译法,使得译文更符合目的语的表达方法,与拆译正好相反。

E. g. Clarence Saunders was an American grocer who first developed the modern retail sales model of self service. His ideas have had a massive influence on the development of the modern supermarket.

美国杂货商克拉伦斯·桑德斯最先建立了现代自助式零售模式,其思想对现代超市的发展影响巨大。(合译)

E. g. Now he is teaching at Beijing Foreign Studies University as a foreign expert. He concentrates on graduate courses in American Culture Studies and a new course entitled Western Civilization with Chinese Comparisons.

现在,作为一名外国专家,他在北京外国语大学教书,主要教授美国文化研究和中西方文明比较(新课程)等研究生课程。(合译)

E. g. 毕昇(生卒年未详),北宋布衣。湖北英山县人。

Bi Sheng (the years of his birth and his death unknown) was a commoner who lived in Yingshan County, Hubei Province, during the Northern Song Dynasty. (合译)

E. g. 近年来,为进入海外大学读书而参加雅思考试(IELTS)的学生人数不断增加。雅思考试的组织者们也相应增加了考试次数来满足需求。

Recently, an explosion in the number of students sitting for the International English Language Testing System (IELTS) required for entry into overseas universities to study has forced IELTS organizers to increase the frequency of the exam. (合译)

E. g. This is the cat that killed the rat that ate the cake that lay in the house that Jack built.

这就是那只捕杀了老鼠的猫。老鼠偷吃了放在屋里的蛋糕。屋子是杰克盖的。(拆译)

[评价]千万不能译成"这就是那只捕杀了偷吃了放在杰克修建的房间里的蛋糕的老鼠的猫",要避免"……的……的……"不停的现象。

E. g. Newton invented a paper lantern illuminated by a candle which he carried with him to light his way to school on dark winter mornings.

牛顿发明了一只用蜡烛点亮的纸灯笼。在冬天漆黑的早晨,他打着灯笼上学。(拆译)

E. g. I looked left, right and behind me. Nothing. Not a car, no suggestion of headlights, but there I sat, waiting for the light to change, the only human being for at least a mile in any direction.

我环顾四周,什么也没看到,没有一辆汽车,连车灯的影子也没有。尽管如此,我还是一直端坐着,等待指示灯转换。至少在周围一英里范围内,就我一人。(拆译)

E.g. 活字印刷术具有一字多用、重复使用、印刷多且快、省时省力、节约材料等优点,比雕版印刷术有了质的飞跃,对后世印刷术乃至世界文明的进步,有着巨大而深远的影响。

Movable-type printing makes use of multi-purpose engraved characters which can be used repeatedly to produce high efficiency printing in large quantity, thus saving time, effort and materials. This represented a qualitative leap, compared with wood block printing and has had an enormous, far-reaching impact on later printing as well as on the progress of world civilization. (拆译)

[评价]原文中包含2个概念:①活字印刷术的特点;②活字印刷术带来的影响。

E.g. 对于生长生活在北京的我来讲,根本没有家乡的概念,总是被老公称为"没有家乡的人"。

Considering that I grew up in and live in Beijing, I really don't have a concept of home at all. Because of this, my husband always refers to me as "a person without a hometown". (拆译)

二、从句的翻译

若按照词性,英语从句可分为名词性从句(包含主语从句、宾语从句、表语从句和同位语从句)、形容词性从句(即定语从句)和副词性从句(状语从句)。

汉语无从句之说,汉语句子分单句和复句。单句是由短语或单个的词构成的句子,独立地表达一个相对完整意思的句子。复句由两个或两个以上意义紧密联系、结构相互独立的单句即分句组成。汉语复句分为联合复句和偏正复句。联合复句中各个分句之间是平等关系,没有主从之分,包括并列复句、承接复句、递进复句、解说复句和选择复句。偏正复句由正句和偏句两部分组成,有主次之分。其中,正句承担了复句的基本意思,是基本的、主要的;偏句修饰或限制主句,是辅助的、次要的。根据正句和偏句之间的关系,偏正复句可以分为因果复句、条件复句、假设复句、转折复句、让步复句和目的复句。

1. 英语从句的翻译方法

(1)保持原位

E.g. <u>Whatever he saw and heard on his trip</u> made a deep impression of him.
<u>此行所见所闻</u>都给他留下了深刻的印象。(主语从句)

E.g. I understand that he is well qualified, but I feel <u>that he needs more experience</u>.
我明白他工作很称职,但我觉得<u>他需要积累更多的经验</u>。(宾语从句)

E.g. Things are not always <u>as they seem to be</u>.
事物并不总是<u>如其表象</u>。(表语从句)

E.g. I have no idea <u>when he will be back</u>.
我不知道<u>他什么时候回来</u>。(同位语从句)

(2)译为前置定语(一般仅限部分定语从句)

当构成定语从句的词不超过 8 个,一般要将定语从句译为前置定语。

E. g. Is he the man who wants to see you?
　　　他就是想见你的那个人吗?

E. g. The package which/that you are carrying is about to come unwrapped.
　　　你拿的包快散了。

E. g. Is this the reason why (for which) he refused our offer?
　　　这就是他拒绝我们帮助他的理由吗?

E. g. He is unlikely to find the place where he lived forty years ago.
　　　他不大可能找到他四十年前居住过的地方。

但是也有例外情形。

E. g. I told the story to John, who told it to his brother.
　　　我把这件事告诉了约翰,约翰又告诉了他的兄弟。

翻译时要注意表达效果:忠实+通顺。

(3)译为另一单句

当构成定语从句的词超过 8 个时,一般译为另一单句。

E. g. English majors, who are looking for jobs based on their language skills, face pressure from all sides.
　　　英语专业学生正在运用所掌握的语言技能寻找工作,他们面临来自方方面面的压力。

E. g. Her father, Bill Heslop is a failed politician who always blames his family for his failure.
　　　她的父亲比尔·赫斯洛普是一个失意的政治家,总是将他的失败归咎于他的家人。

(4)译为其他类型从句

E. g. The thought came to him that maybe the enemy had fled the city.
　　　他突然想起敌人可能已经逃出城了。(同位语从句译为宾语从句)

E. g. You must grasp the concept of "work" which is very important in physics.
　　　你必须掌握"功"这个概念,因为这个概念在物理学中很重要。(定语从句译为状语从句)

E. g. I've come from Mr. Wang with a message that he won't be able to see you this afternoon.
　　　我从王先生那里来,他让我告诉你他今天下午不能来看你了。(同位语从句译为宾语从句)

2. 汉语复句的翻译技巧

翻译汉语复句的关键在于抓住句子的重心,将主要信息译为英语的主句,其余部分视情况可分别用分词、动名词、不定式、介词短语等来处理。与英语相比,汉语句子较为简短、零散,词序也较为固定,翻译时应注意句子的合并、语序的调整。

E. g. 我访问了一些地方,遇到了不少人,要谈起来,奇妙的事儿可多着呢。
　　　There are many wonderful stories to tell about the places I visited and the people I

met.

E.g. 只有这样,才能使我们具备对中国社会问题的最基础的知识。

Only in this way can we acquire an elementary knowledge of Chinese society.

E.g. 与其治标,不如治本。

We should effect a permanent cure rather than a temporary one.

E.g. 冯玉祥一面与武汉来的这些人应付,一面宣布他要去徐州会蒋介石。

Dealing with the people from Wuhan, Feng Yuxiang announced that he would go to Xuzhou to meet Chiang Kai-shek.

三、长句的翻译

翻译长句时,首先要分析原文的句法结构,弄懂整句的中心意思,厘清信息层次及信息之间的逻辑关系,然后根据信息之间的相互逻辑关系(因果、条件、让步、时空顺序等),按照目的语的特点和表达方式,正确地译出原文。

长句的翻译分5步进行。

第一步:划清句子成分。根据英语词汇在英语句子中的地位和作用,英语句子的成分可分为主语、谓语、宾语、宾语补足语、表语、定语、状语、同位语及独立成分等。现代汉语里一般的句子成分有八种,即主语、谓语、宾语、动语、定语、状语,补语和中心语。

第二步:弄懂整句的中心意思。

第三步:厘清信息层次及信息之间的逻辑关系。

第四步:逐一翻译每句信息。

第五步:对译文进行调整、组合,然后检查、修改、润色,完成译文。

E.g. Human beings have distinguished themselves from other animals, and in doing so ensured their survival, by their ability to observe and understand their environment and then either to adapt to that environment or to control and adapt it to their own needs.

第一步:划清句子成分。

Human beings(主语) have distinguished(谓语) themselves(宾语) from other animals(状语), and in doing so(状语) ensured(谓语) their survival(宾语), by their ability to observe and understand their environment and then either to adapt to that environment or to control and adapt it to their own needs(状语).

第二步:弄懂整句的中心意思。英语句子的中心意思往往在主句。本句的主句是"Human beings have distinguished themselves from other animals, and in doing so ensured their survival",其意思是:"人类将自己与其他动物区别开来,这样也确保自己生存下来"。

第三步:厘清信息层次及信息之间的逻辑关系。通过主句和状语的逻辑关系得知,该状语应表示原因,整句信息呈现因果关系。

第四步:逐一翻译每句信息。

原译:人类把自己和其他动物区别开来。人类具有观察和了解周围环境的能力;他们要么适应环境,要么控制环境,或根据自身的需要改造环境。就这样,人类一代代生存了下来。

[评价]笔者认为,若将主句语义完整、连贯的信息"Human beings have distinguished themselves from other animals, and in doing so ensured their survival"割裂开来,处理不妥,译文读来不够通畅。

第五步:对译文进行调整、组合,然后检查、修改、润色,完成译文。

改译:人类能够观察和了解周围环境,然后要么适应环境,要么控制环境并根据自身的需要改造环境。就这样,人类把自己和其他动物区别开来,一代代生存下来。

汉语写作往往状语先行,将表示原因、条件、让步、方式等信息的状语置于主句之前。

E.g. The saga of the White Star Liner *Titanic*, which struck an iceberg and sank on its maiden voyage in 1912, carrying more than 1,500 passengers to their death, has been celebrated in print and film, in poetry and song.

先划清句子成分。

The saga(主语) of the White Star Liner *Titanic*(后置定语,修饰 saga), which struck an iceberg and sank on its maiden voyage in 1912, carrying more than 1,500 passengers to their death(后置定语,修饰 Titanic), has been celebrated(谓语) in print and film, in poetry and song(状语).

划清句子成分后,该句的中心意思、其他信息及其关系一目了然。

原译:白星公司客轮"泰坦尼克"号在1912年的处女航中因撞上冰山而沉,致使船上1 500多名乘客罹难。此后关于它的轶事传闻就一直成为各种书刊、电影、诗歌、歌曲的内容而广为流传。

[评价]汉语故事型写作往往按照"时间—地点—人物—事件—经过—结果—意义"顺序展开。汉语是意合语言,写作时作者应尽量不用关联词。该译文中关联词"因""致使"其实可以省略。"成为各种书刊、电影、诗歌、歌曲的内容"的表述显得生硬。整句读来不够通畅。

改译:1912年,白星公司客轮"泰坦尼克"号在其处女航中撞上冰山沉没了,船上1 500多名乘客罹难。此后,该客轮的轶事传闻在各种书刊、电影、诗歌、歌曲中广为流传。

E.g. Behaviorists suggest that the child who is raised in an environment where there are many stimuli which develop his or her capacity for appropriate response will experience greater intellectual development.

行为主义者认为,一个孩子如果生长在有很多刺激因素的环境里,而这些刺激因素促进了其应变能力的发展,那么这个孩子在心智上就会取得更大的发展。

E.g. Aluminum remained unknown until the nineteenth century, because nowhere in nature is it found free, owing to its always being combined with other elements, most commonly with oxygen, for which it has a strong affinity.

直到19世纪铝才为人类所发现,因为铝有很强的亲和力,通常和其他元素(往往是氧)结合,在自然界找不到游离态的铝。

E.g. Television, it is often said, keeps one informed about current events, allowing one to follow the latest developments in science and politics, and offers endless series of programs which are both instructive and entertaining.

人们常说,通过电视可以了解时事,追踪科学和政治的最新发展动态,还可观看层出不穷既有教育意义又有娱乐性的节目。

E. g. What should doctors say, for example, to a 46-year-old man coming in for a routine physical check-up just before going on vacation with his family who, though he feels in perfect health, is found to have a form of cancer that will cause him to die within six months?

比如,一名46岁的男子,在与家人外出度假前来进行常规体检,虽然他感觉身体状况良好,医生却发现他患了某种癌症,生命只剩下6个月的时间。这时,医生该怎么对他说呢?

E. g. 他回到家乡后,尽管一个月只有千余元收入,仍然奢侈无度,挥金如土。

After he returned to his hometown, he was still extravagant, spending money like water, though he earned no more than ¥1,000 each month.

[评价]该句的中心意思是"仍然奢侈无度",具体表现为"挥金如土"。汉语原句既有时间状语——"他回到家乡后",又有让步状语——"尽管一个月只有千余元收入",为保持英语句子的平衡感,2个状语以主句为中心一前一后放置。

E. g. 我初次上课时提问了一个还未讲到的问题,本来没有抱太大的期望有学生可以回答出来。

In my first class, I asked a new question that I did not expect anyone would be able to answer.

E. g. 西安,古称"长安",位于关中平原中部,北临渭河,南依秦岭,是举世闻名的世界四大文明古都之一,是中国历史上建都时间最长、建都朝代最多、影响力最大的都城,先后有21个王朝和政权建都于此,是13朝古都,中国历史上四个鼎盛的朝代周、秦、汉、唐均在西安建都。

Xi'an, called "Chang'an" in the past, is located in the middle of the Guanzhong Plain, next to the Weihe River to the north, with the Qinling Mountains to the south. It is world renowned as one of the four greatest ancient cities. As a capital city, it lasted for the longest time and had the largest number of dynasties, thus exerting the greatest influence in Chinese history. It served as the capital city of 21 kingdoms and regimes in total. It was the ancient capital city of 13 dynasties, including the four most prosperous, namely, the Zhou, Qin, Han and Tang.

练 习 题

一、英译汉句子练习

1. If you use the Internet regularly, your activities are likely spread out all over the Web.

2. Opiates have long been used by doctors to ease the pain of seriously ill or severely injured people.

3. In an engineering design, safety factors and economy can never be neglected.

4. China's planned launch of *Shenzhou VI* vessel, its second manned space mission, signals that the country has begun to carry out aerospace experiments with real-human participation, said a senior space engineer here on Sunday.

5. Clearly, cool temperatures slow down the action of bacteria.

6. Steel is widely used in industry because it possesses a great number of useful properties.

7. The reader might speak into a telephone where the information is transduced from patterns of compressed air molecules traveling at the speed of sound into electronic pulses traveling down a copper wire close to the speed of light.

8. Changing attitudes among all voters, and especially Democratic voters, made support for same-sex marriage an article of faith for anyone seeking to lead the party.

9. The Republicans shifted their views from 2007 through 2011, the early years of the Obama presidency.

10. Five years ago, Michael Preysman swore that his online clothing company, Everlane, would never have a bricks-and-mortar store.

11. Given the widespread closures around the country—more than 7,000 stores have shuttered so far this year—landlords and shopping centers are more willing to forge flexible arrangements, including monthly or yearly leases, with niche brands.

12. The yield of apples in this region has increased by 2 times as compared with that of 2017.

13. Price is a main factor distinguishing wired- and wireless-technology options in a business.

14. As we have mentioned above, coal production and use is accompanied by serious environmental problems.

15. People tend to idealize the past; they imagine a group of family and friends entertaining themselves by playing games and telling stories around a warm fireplace, but I do not think that TV can be blamed for the lack of communication among family and friends.

二、汉译英句子练习

1. 造纸术是中国的四大发明之一,是中华民族对世界文明的杰出贡献。
2. 预计到2050年,全国将有三分之一的人口超过60岁。
3. 提到中国体育不能不说乒乓球。
4. 西湖位于浙江省省会杭州,水域面积超6平方公里。
5. 那时起他在中国游历17年,访问了中国的许多城市。
6. 本文论及语法上的衔接,涉及照应、替代、省略、连接四个方面。
7. 友谊路,对于老西安人来说,具有不一般的意义。
8. 西安很多的道路,两旁都有参天的大树。

9. 西安,古称"长安""镐京",是陕西省省会。
10. 不用去西藏,西安也有一条美爆了的环山路。
11. 秦国历时10年,先后灭了韩、赵、魏、楚、燕、齐,于公元前221年统一了中国。
12. 在教授该课程时,我比较注重对学生运用基本理论和基础知识分析和思考问题的能力及实际计算和操作能力的培养。
13. 药品生产企业供应商发生变更的,企业在变更后15个工作日内将变更情况报市、州食品药品监督管理局备案。

三、英译汉练习

America: Still Paradise for New Immigrants?

Like Alice following the white rabbit, thousands of immigrants to the U.S. are trapped in the confusing and all-powerful legal net of recently enacted harsh laws, which the Immigration and Naturalization Service (INS) is required to administer. These Federal statutes do riot comport with due process standards or the fundamental fairness inherent in the American justice system that protect our citizens. Clearly, there is a double standard for immigrants.

For example, about the time the controversy over Elian Gonzalez—the six-year-old boy plucked from the coastal waters off Florida after an escape attempt from Cuba took the lives of his mother and several others—first reached fever pitch, a young Chinese girl captured while trying to enter the U.S. after she fled her homeland, appeared at a review hearing. She was unable to understand English and terribly frightened, and, as tears rolled uncontrollably down her cheeks, she could not wipe them away because her arms were chained to her waist. She must have been in terror, having fled only to be jailed and hauled in chains before strangers, where she understood nothing. She faces deportation.

Moreover, consider the compelling stories of two mothers also subject to deportation. The first is a young German woman who was adopted and brought to Georgia. Now the mother of two, she recently applied for citizenship. Instead, she was ordered deported because, as a teenager, she had entered a guilty plea to charges stemming from pulling the hair of another girl over the affections of a boy.

The second, a young mother faces deportation and separation from her children because she called the police after being brutally beaten by her husband. Instead of coming to her defense, police arrested her because she bit her husband as he sat on her and repeatedly hit her. Incredibly, both mothers face deportation, while their children—all born here—can remain.

How can a hair-pulling or biting incident be grounds for deportation? Equally important, how has the U.S. become a country that tears apart families or denies due process to those trying to obtain freedom, safety, and prosperity for themselves and their families?

(William G. Paul,《英语学习》,2000 年 10 月)

四、汉译英练习

对长期处于象牙塔内、只对社会进行有限接触的学生来说,不知道毕业后要从事什么工作,对人生未来的取舍一片模糊,是再正常不过的了。

但你说"我希望首先能正确认识自己",这就有问题了。

试想从今天起,大家每天起床后给自己树立目标,花更多时间思考、认识自己,坚持一年后,就能更清楚地了解自己吗?

答案是否定的。认识自我不能靠空想来完成,它需要一个人离开舒适区,走出宿舍和校门,去不断尝试、不断试错,不断否定自己的上一个想法,调整和优化下一次尝试。

(温言,《职业规划的三种误区》)

第五章 篇章翻译

一、篇章的定义、特点及布局模式

1. 篇章的定义

所谓篇章,即在交际功能上相对完整和独立的、通常是大于句子的一个语言片段。篇章可以短到一则通知、一首小诗,可以长到系列小说。篇章将译者的视野从词、句扩展到句群、段落和篇章层面。

2. 篇章的主要特点

第一,有中心思想,论述可以从不同角度和层面展开,但始终不能离开这个中心。

第二,各段落要有段落大意。

第三,信息的一致性(内容上,甚至风格上)。

第四,信息的连贯性。

3. 篇章(以文章为例)的布局模式。

- 主题(中心思想)

Ⅰ. 简介

Ⅱ. 主要观点1

  A. 从属观点1

    1. 阐明观点的细节

    2. 进一步拓展信息(方法:举例、作比较、打比方、列举、引用等)

  B. 从属观点2

    1. 阐明观点的细节

    2. 进一步拓展信息(方法同上)

Ⅲ. 主要观点2

  A. 从属观点1

    1. 阐明观点的细节

    2. 进一步拓展信息(方法同上)

  B. 从属观点2

    1. 阐明观点的细节

    2. 进一步拓展信息(方法同上)

  C. 从属观点3

    1. 阐明观点的细节

    2. 进一步拓展信息(方法同上)

Ⅳ. 结论

假如翻译一篇文章,在很多情况下,译者提供的译文是"总—分—总"模式,只是语言是目的语。实际上,这是很多不同篇幅文章呈现的模式。

E. g. 大学英语四、六级范文

The Irish countryside is very beautiful. There is a popular Irish song which says that there are 100 different shades of green in the Irish landscape, and this is no exaggeration. Thanks to generous rainfall, much of the countryside is covered in rich green vegetation, which is why Ireland is also known as the Emerald Isle. It also has a varied landscape with dramatic mountains, rocky coastlines and rolling hills.

这段文字有中心句(第1句),然后有拓展句(第2～4句)。信息呈典型的"总—分"英语写作模式展开。

E. g. 大学英语四、六级作文

Nowadays, the Internet is playing an increasing important role in our life. We can use it for different kinds of purposes. The advantage of Internet which we can take of can be listed as follows.

To start with, the Internet can provide us with a variety of news and information. It keeps us informed of the news from home and abroad conveniently. We can get almost all kinds of information needed. Besides, we can use it for communication. For instance, not only can we use it to send e-mail, but also we can call others through Internet if we have not a telephone on hand. Moreover, Internet is also a means of entertainment. For instance, we can enjoy music, watch sport matches and play chess or cards.

Last but not the least, there are so many on-line schools and on-line books on the Internet packed with lots of information that we can read them without even leaving our home...

In a word, the Internet has made our life more colorful and convenient as well.

信息呈"总—分—总"模式布局。

E. g. 英语专业八级范文

In many countries it is common for teenagers to take part-time jobs while they are still in high school, while in other societies this is virtually unheard of. In the latter situation, students are expected to spend all of their time on their studies and consider schoolwork their "job". In my opinion, students benefit more from a more balanced lifestyle, which may include working at a part-time job. Therefore, I believe that it is a good idea for students to work while studying. (观点)

While it is true that a student's most important goal must be to learn and to do well at his studies, it does not need to be the only goal. In fact, a life which consists of only study is not balanced and may cause the student to miss out on other valuable learning experiences. In addition to bringing more balance to a student's life, part-time work can broaden his range of experience...(原因)

For all of these reasons, I firmly believe that most students would benefit from taking a part-time job while they are in high school. (重申观点) Of course, they must be careful not to let it take up too much of their time because study is still their primary responsibility. In sum, living a balanced life is the best way to be successful.

信息呈"总—分—总"模式布局。

4. 汉语的思维顺序基本遵循的三个原则

(1) 时序原则

时序原则即按照事情发生的先后顺序进行陈述。

话说天下大势,分久必合,合久必分。周末七国分争,并入于秦。及秦灭之后,楚、汉分争,又并入于汉。汉朝自高祖斩白蛇而起义,一统天下,后来光武中兴,传至献帝,遂分为三国。推其致乱之由,殆始于桓、灵二帝。桓帝禁锢善类,崇信宦官。及桓帝崩,灵帝即位,大将军窦武、太傅陈蕃,共相辅佐。时有宦官曹节等弄权,窦武、陈蕃谋诛之,机事不密,反为所害,中涓自此愈横……

(罗贯中,《三国演义》)

(2) 因果原则

因果原则即先陈述原因,后给出结果,或者先说条件,后说结果。

当有殿头官喝道:"有事出班早奏,无事卷帘退朝。"只见班部丛中,宰相赵哲、参政文彦博出班奏曰:"目今京师瘟疫盛行,伤损军民甚多。伏望陛下释罪宽恩,省刑薄税,祈禳天灾,救济万民。"天子听奏,急敕翰林院随即草诏:一面降赦天下罪囚,应有民间税赋悉皆免除;一面命在京宫观寺院,修设好事禳灾……

(施耐庵,《水浒传》)

(3) 范围原则

范围原则即汉语习惯从总体到细节,从背景环境到具体情况,从外围因素到内部因素进行陈述。在语言表达上,汉语习惯把次要的信息安排在靠近句首位置,将重要内容后置,英语往往恰恰相反。

又行了半日,忽见街北蹲着两个大石狮子,三间兽头大门,门前列坐着十来个华冠丽服之人。正门却不开,只有东西两角门有人出入。正门之上有一匾,匾上大书"敕造宁国府"五个大字。黛玉想道:这必是外祖之长房了。想着,又往西行,不多远,照样也是三间大门,方是荣国府了。却不进正门,只进了西边角门。那轿夫抬进去,走了一射之地,将转弯时,便歇下退出去了。后面的婆子们已都下了轿,赶上前来……

(曹雪芹、高鹗,《红楼梦》)

二、篇章翻译的过程

1. 英译汉

【原文】

In many Western countries, a considerable number of parents have removed their children from school and are teaching them at home. Such children do all their normal lessons at home, often under the guidance of a parent. The first thing to consider is whether this is legal or not. In most countries it is, so long as parents can prove that their children are receiving an adequate education, equal to that provided by their state educational system. The next consideration is whether the parents have the time, self-discipline, intelligence and patience to teach their own child week after week, day in and day out, for hours on end. Then there is the problem of what will be taught, and how.

翻译步骤：

第一步：通读全文，把握段落话题和主要信息点。段落话题往往在第一/二句（有可能第一句是过渡句，第二句才是主题句），其他句子往往为扩展句，进一步阐明话题/主题句信息。

本段主题句在第一句："In many Western countries, a considerable number of parents have removed their children from school and are teaching them at home."。

第二步：标记、翻译生词、短语等。

In many Western countries, a <u>considerable</u> number of parents have <u>removed</u> their children from school and are teaching them at home. Such children do all their normal lessons at home, often under the guidance of a parent. The first thing to consider is whether this is legal or not. In most countries it is, so long as parents can prove that their children are receiving an adequate education, equal to that provided by their <u>state educational system</u>. The next consideration is whether the parents have the time, <u>self-discipline</u>, intelligence and patience to teach their own child week after week, day in and day out, for hours <u>on end</u>. Then there is the problem of what will be taught, and how.

第三步：分析长、难句（分析逻辑关系，划分句子成分）。

<u>In most countries</u>（状语）it is (legal)（主＋系＋表），<u>so long as parents can prove that their children are receiving an adequate education</u>（条件状语从句），<u>equal to that provided by their state educational system</u>（后置定语，修饰 education）.

第四步：逐句翻译，注意以下 3 点。

1）信息的整体性和一致性。

2）信息调整（因英汉表意差异）。

如原文中"week after week, day in and day out, for hours on end"可译为"连续数小时，日复一日，周而复始"。

3）译文忠实（于原文）、通顺、流畅。

第五步：调整、润色、改进译文。

【参考译文】

在西方很多国家，已有相当多的家长把孩子从学校带回家自己教。这些孩子通常是在一位家长的指导之下在家里学习所有的标准课程。（让孩子在家学习）首先要考虑的是这样做是否合法。在多数国家，这样做是合法的，只要家长能证明孩子受到的教育与国家教育体制提供的教育相当。其次要考虑的是家长是否有时间、自制力、学识和耐心,可以连续数小时、日复一日、周而复始地教自己的孩子。然后要看教什么、怎么教。

2. 汉译英

【原文】

雅思(IELTS),全称为国际英语测试系统,是著名的国际性英语标准化水平测试之一。IELTS 于 1989 年设立,由英国文化协会、剑桥大学考试委员会和澳大利亚教育国际开发署(IDP)共同举办,其中剑桥大学负责有关学术水平试题内容,而 IDP 及英国文化协会负责于世界各地定期举办考试。考生可以选择学术类测试和培训类测试。雅思成绩被英国、澳大利亚、加拿大、新西兰、南非等英联邦的许多教育机构,以及越来越多的美国教育机构及各种各样的专业组织接受。雅思考试成绩的有效期限为两年。

第一步:通读全文,把握段落话题和主要信息点。

因为我们的母语是汉语,所以理解原文一般不成问题。

第二步:标记、翻译生词、短语等。

如原文中"国际性英语标准化水平测试"(international standardized English proficiency test)、"英国文化协会"(the British Council)、"剑桥大学考试委员会"(Cambridge English Language Assessment)、"IDP"(全称为 International Development Program)、"澳大利亚教育国际开发署"(IDP Australia)、"共同举办"(co-organize)、"学术类测试和培训类测试"(academic and general training)、"英联邦"(the Commonwealth of Nations)等信息需要标记、翻译。

第三步:分析长、难句(分析逻辑关系,划分句子成分)。

原文中,"IELTS 于 1989 年设立,由英国文化协会、剑桥大学考试委员会和澳大利亚教育国际开发署(IDP)共同举办,其中剑桥大学负责有关学术水平试题内容,而 IDP 及英国文化协会负责于世界各地定期举办考试"明显是长句。

仔细阅读后可知,本句包含 2 个意思:①雅思设立的时间和相关负责机构;②不同机构的职责范围。所以,为了明晰关系,英译时需断为两句分别翻译。

第四步:逐句翻译。

第五步:调整、润色、改进译文。

【参考译文】

IELTS, short for the International English Language Testing System, is one of the well-known international standardized English proficiency tests. Established in 1989, it is now co-organized by the British Council, Cambridge English Language Assessment and IDP Australia. Specifically, the University of Cambridge is responsible for test content at the academic level, while the IDP and the British Council are in charge of examinations regularly held worldwide. The examinations, which fall into two categories, namely, academic and general training, are provided for examinees to choose from. The IELTS score, which is valid for two years, is accepted by a growing number of educational institutions in the Commonwealth of Nations, such as Britain, Australia, Canada, New Zealand, South Africa, and by more and more American educational institutions and various professional organizations.

三、篇章翻译译文的评判标准

在本书的第一章,笔者罗列了翻译界大家、学者总结出的多种翻译标准。总的来说,这些标准都有一定的道理。影响最大的翻译标准莫过于100多年前严复提出的"信""达""雅"了。对于一般题材和体裁的文章来说,翻译标准也可用于译文评价标准,因为越来越多的学者认为"翻译是目的语写作",一般的写作要求也是译文要达到的要求。那么,具体来说,篇章(大于句子单位的文本)翻译译文评价标准是什么呢?

(1)信息的完整性

语篇层面原文信息具有完整性,译文理应也具有完整性。

(2)信息的衔接和连贯性

篇章语言学认为,衔接和连贯是语篇的重要特征。衔接是外在表现,连贯是内在要求,两者相辅相成。

(3)语篇功能明显

一般来说,一个语篇文本具有一个以上的语篇功能。比如,散文中可能会有记叙的成分,议论文中会有说明的成分,但是总体来看往往其中某个功能突出,翻译时要体现这一功能,做到"翻啥像啥"。比如,翻译新闻,译文要符合一般的目的语新闻的措辞和行文模式。

练 习 题

一、英译汉练习

Muriel Heslop is a large, big-boned young woman from a dysfunctional family in New York. Her father, Bill Heslop is a failed politician who always blames his family for his failure, and who often publicly tells his children that they are useless. Muriel's mother, Betty Heslop, is an unhappy housewife who is silently drowning in an ocean of dirty laundry and unwashed dishes. Muriel's siblings are couch potatoes who sit around staring at the television all day long.

Muriel often hangs around a group of friends from middle school, Tania, Nicole and other girls. Tania and her group are all slim, tanned young women who are madly in love with themselves. They see Muriel's company as an insult, because she is fat, ugly, unemployed and never dressed properly. She listens to the 70's music and is not mad enough to fit into their image of party animals. In her unhappy moments, Muriel often retreats to her bedroom and blocks out the reality with ABBA songs.

Muriel can hardly believe her luck when Tania's wedding bouquet falls right into her hands. But before she can indulge herself in the prospect of being the next one to get married, Tania and her group force her to give it up to another girl, as they believe she will be the last woman in the world to get married, if she ever gets married at all. To rub salt into her wound, her eye-catching leopard-skin dress, which is so out of place at the wedding reception, is spotted by a shop detective who works in the shop where Muri shoplifted it. Muriel is arrested in the middle of the wedding reception and a police car delivers her home for the receipt of the dress. As she cannot produce the receipt, Bill bribes the two policemen with a case of beer and saves her from being arrested…

(李又文，《英语学习》)

二、汉译英练习

周子阳是个感性的人，这点从他很爱哭可以证明。有一次和制片方一起看完《老兽》这部影片后，周子阳独自躲在房间里酣畅地流泪；在等待台湾金马奖领奖的间歇，他突然悲喜交集，又是一阵哭泣。

作为一个非科班出身的年轻导演，周子阳倾十年之力，终于拍成自己的首部电影《老兽》。影片 2016 年在第 11 届 FIRST 青年电影展上甫一亮相即大受好评，斩获 3 个奖项，并在第 54 届台湾金马奖上获得最佳原著剧本、最佳男主角和金马奖国际影评人费比西奖 3 个奖项。

(张嘉，《北京青年报》)

第二部分 实践篇

第六章　新闻语篇的翻译

一、新闻语篇的语言特点

新闻语篇是在新闻学、传播学、社会学、政治学、经济学等多种学科和语体的综合影响下所形成的一种语体。当今世界，迅速及时地报道国内外发生的时事新闻无疑是新闻传媒的首要任务，新闻语篇也自然成了当今社会生活中一种极其重要的大众传播媒介和载体。

1. 英语新闻语篇的语言特点

（1）标题特点

标题主要具有以下 2 个特点。

第一，省略。

为了起到言简意赅、突出重要内容的效果，标题中常常省略某些语法成分或词语，尤以虚词为主，如冠词、连词、人称关系代词、系动词等。

  E. g. 37 Killed in Italian Plane Crash（省略了 be 动词）

    意大利一飞机坠毁 37 人遇难

  E. g. Three Dead After Inhaling Oven Gas（省略了 be 动词）

    炉灶煤气泄露 3 人中毒身亡

  E. g. China to Acquire Overseas Stake for Second time（to 前省略了 is；Second 前省略了 the）

    中国将再次从海外购买股份

  E. g. Apple CEO Confident of Prospects Despite Naysayers（省略 be 动词）

    尽管有反对者，苹果首席执行官对前景充满信心

  E. g. Export Skills Key to Further Growth of Foreign Trade（省略 be 动词）

    改进商品出口技巧是对外贸易进一步发展的关键

  E. g. China's Oldest, Longest Bridge Found in Xi'an（省略 and）

    西安发现中国最古老长桥

  E. g. Major Projects Well on Track in the Capital（省略 be 动词）

    首都主要建设项目进展顺利

但是，近年来从我国政府官网、权威报刊和杂志的英文报道来看，英语句子形式的标题越来越普遍。以下例子来自我国外交部英文网站。

  E. g. Chinese Government Sends Medical Team of COVID-19 Experts to Sudan

中国政府向苏丹派遣新冠肺炎专家医疗队

E. g. President Xi Jinping Speaks with Palestinian President Mahmoud Abbas on the Phone

习近平主席同巴勒斯坦总统马哈茂德·阿巴斯通电话

E. g. Xi Jinping meets with visiting World Health Organization（WHO）Director-General Tedros Adhanom Ghebreyesus

习近平会见来访的世界卫生组织总干事谭德塞

E. g. Chinese and Russian Foreign Ministry Spokespersons Held Consultations and Agreed to Cooperate in Combating Disinformation

中俄外交部发言人进行了磋商,双方同意在打击虚假信息方面进行合作

第二,时态和语态。

新闻标题中常见的动词形态有三种:一般现在时、一般将来时和现在进行时。

新闻报道的时间大多发生在过去,但是为了让读者有身临其境感和新鲜感,感到新闻之"新",英文报刊在报道过去发生的事实时,往往在标题中广泛地使用动词的一般现在时。

E. g. UK's Oldest Person Dies at 115

英国第一寿星谢世,享天年 115 岁

E. g. Annan Reaches Bagdad in Last-Minute Peace Bid

安南抵达巴格达做最后一刻的和平努力

E. g. Sino-US Venture Expands Biz in China

中美合资企业扩大在中国业务

E. g. Six Die in Moscow Bomb Blast

6 人在莫斯科炸弹爆炸中死亡

E. g. Tremor Rocks Ecuador, Peru

厄瓜多尔和秘鲁发生地震

英语新闻若报道正在发生的事或动作,新闻标题通常采用现在进行时"be＋V-ing"这一形式,其中"be"通常省略;若报道将来发生的事情,除用一般将来时的"will＋动词原形"外,更多的还是采用"be＋to"结构,其中不定式前的"be"通常省略,以节省标题字数。既有主动语态,又有被动语态。

E. g. Deposits,Loans Rising in HK

香港储蓄与贷款额节节攀升

E. g. Moscow's Food Price soaring

莫斯科食品价格飞涨

E. g. Buenos Aires "Close" to deal on fresh IMF loan

布宜诺斯艾利斯与国际货币基金组织新一笔贷款协议"接近"成交

第六章 新闻语篇的翻译

（2）词汇特点

新闻涵盖范围广泛，内容丰富，如总统庄严的声明、民众轻松的谈话、各学科的术语、各领域的行话、风土人情甚至市井俚语，无所不包。用词呈现以下3个特点。

第一，用词简明扼要（可用"＝"前词语代替"＝"后表达法）。

如 hurry＝walk hurriedly；outcome＝final outcome；as a rule＝as a general rule；visible＝visible to the eye；consensus＝consensus of opinion；destroyed＝totally destroyed；cut＝reduce；probe＝investigate；deal＝bargain/transaction。

E. g. The company will cooperate with any government probe in the matter as well. (probe＝investigate)

该公司还将全力配合任何政府部门对该事件的调查。

E. g. Other countries appropriated the profits from the deal. (deal＝bargain/transaction)

其他国家从这项交易中侵吞了利益。

第二，新词层出不穷。

这跟新闻性质有关，新闻经常报道新鲜信息。

如 down payment（分期付款中的）头期款；maglev train 磁悬浮列车；cyber love 网恋；eco-friendly car 环保车；selling points 卖点；suicide bomber 人体炸弹；big city ills 都市病；blue collar 蓝领；white collar 白领；bright collar 亮领（电脑及通讯专业人员）；open collar 开领（在家用电脑上班一族）；COVID-19 新冠病毒。

以下为"十八大"以来出现的部分新词。

如生态文明体制改革 reform for promoting ecological progress；河长（管理河流保护/治理的官员）制 river chief；海绵城市 sponge cities；全域旅游 all-for-one tourism；蓝天保卫战 make our sky blue again；绿色发展、循环发展、低碳发展 Green, circular and low-carbon development；党内监督 intra-Party supervision；拍蝇打虎 hunting tigers, swatting flies；裸官 naked officials；关键少数 critical minority；天网行动 Sky net；八项规定 the eight-point guidelines；打铁还需自身硬 To be turned in iron, the metal itself must be strong；"三严三实" Three Stricts and Three Honests。

第三，大量使用缩略语。

为节省篇幅，新闻报道中大量使用缩略语。

E. g. Members' Close Ties Emphasized Ahead of SCO Summit（SCO＝Shanghai Cooperation Organization，上海合作组织）

上海合作组织开峰会前，强调成员国之间的密切联系

US seeks MIAs（MIA＝Missing in Action，作战失踪人员）

美国寻找作战失踪人员

CIA wary on Iranian N-arms（CIA＝Central Intelligence Agency，中央情报局）

中情局谨慎对待伊朗的核武器问题
Long-Term Plan to TCM（TCM＝Traditional Chinese Medicine,中医）
中医药长远规划
PCM（Pulse Code Modulation）脉冲编码调制
WAP（Wireless Application Protocol）无线应用协议
IP（Internet Protocol）互联网协议
HTTP（Hypertext Transport Protocol）超文本传输协议
OTG（USB On-The-Go）一健拷贝
RMC（Repeater Management Controller）天线信道控制器

2.汉语新闻语篇的语言特点

(1)具体（内容具体）

如实地记叙具体人、具体事、具体时间、具体地点、具体经过，也要求具体形象的现场描写、细节描写等。

(2)准确（准确鲜明）

新闻必须准确，不能含糊其词，不能模棱两可，不能夸大也不能缩小。

(3)简练（简洁明快）

新闻要求快，要求迅速及时。这就决定了新闻语言要简明扼要、开门见山、直截了当。

(4)通俗（通俗易懂）

考虑到人民大众的新闻接受度，新闻语言要通俗易懂，明白晓畅。

人民网5月22日波哥大电（记者 吕鸿 王骁波）当地时间21日下午，李克强总理在总统府与哥伦比亚总统桑托斯举行会谈时说，中哥经济互补性强，合作前景广阔，中方愿同哥方扩大相互投资，推进产业对接。会后，两国领导人见证了产能、基础设施、金融、教育文化等一系列合作协议的签署。

上例是人民网一则简短的新闻报道，措辞严谨、准确，信息推进自然，表意清晰，这是新闻写作的典范。

翻译是目的语写作。同理，汉语新闻英译时自然要体现英语新闻的语言特点，让读者阅读英语译文时感受到内容的自然流畅。

【参考译文】

As reported by *people. com. cn* in Bogota on May 22（reporters Lv Hong and Wang Xiaobo）, Chinese Premier Li Keqiang held talks with Colombian President Juan Manuel Santos at the presidential palace on the afternoon of May 21（local time）, during which he observed that China and Colombia enjoy strong economic complementarity as well as broad prospects for cooperation and that China is willing to expand mutual investment and promote joint industrial development with Colombia. After the meeting, the leaders of the two countries witnessed the signing of a series of cooperation agreements on production capacity, infrastructure, finance, education and culture.

二、新闻语篇翻译实例

1. 英译汉

【原文】

Mali holds state funeral for ex-president Toure

Malian President Bah N'Daw arrives at the funeral of former President of Mali Amadou Toumani Toure in Bamako on November 17, 2020. Former President Amadou Toumani, who passed away at the age of 72, is known for having led the transition after overthrowing the government of Moussa Traoré in 1991 and for being democratically elected President of Mali in 2002 and 2007. (Photo by MICHELE CATTANI / AFP)

Mali held a state funeral on Tuesday for former president Amadou Toumani Toure, an emblematic figure who steered the troubled nation to free elections and led it for a decade before being ousted in a coup.

Toure, sometimes called Mali's "soldier of democracy", died on November 10 at the age of 72 after he had been transferred to Turkey for medical care following heart surgery.

A coffin draped in the national flag and borne by six soldiers was slowly carried into the center of a square in the capital of Mali for ceremonies attended by the leaders of the country's latest putsch and by foreign dignitaries.

"A great man has fallen," the master of ceremonies declared. "It is an incalculable loss for Mali. He came bringing the breath of life, he leaves with the wind of hope."

Those in the VIP stand included Bah N'Daw, a former military officer who is currently president of Mali's transitional government, and the vice president, Assimi Goita, who led the August 18 coup.

Niger and Guinea-Bissau were represented by their prime ministers, and other countries in the region sent their envoys.

Ceremonies were to conclude with a parade by troops and aircraft, according to the programme.

Toure, a former soldier, first took charge of the country for a year in 1991. He helped overthrow the iron-fisted regime of Moussa Traore, who had been in power since 1968. He then took the helm of a transitional committee, exercising the duties of head of state and steering the country to elections.

These were won in 1992 by Alpha Oumar Konare—the first democratically-chosen president in Mali's post-independence history.

Universally known by his initials as ATT, Toure won presidential elections in 2002 and again in 2007.

His presidency was abruptly curtailed in 2012 by rebel troops who accused Toure of failing to support their battle against Tuareg and jihadist insurgents in the north of the country.

Toure fled to Senegal, only returning from exile in 2017. The chaos that followed his downfall wrecked Mali's poorly-equipped and demoralized army.

The jihadists swiftly overran the north of the country before being forced out in 2013 by French intervention.

They regrouped and advanced into central Mali, a flashpoint region where they ignited ethnic conflict, and then headed into neighbouring Burkina Faso and Niger.

Thousands have died and hundreds of thousands have fled their homes...

(AFP, *The Guardian*)

从标题可以看出，这是一则关于为马里前总统杜尔举行葬礼的新闻。

翻译操作步骤：

1) 词汇层

① 专有名词（译法须与官方译法保持一致）

Mali 马里共和国（西非国家）；Amadou Toumani Toure 阿马杜·图马尼·杜尔；Bah N'Daw 巴·恩多；Bamako 巴马科（马里共和国的首都）；Assimi Goita 阿西米·戈伊特；Niger 尼日尔（非洲中西部国家）；Guinea-Bissau 几内亚比绍（西非国家）；Moussa Traore 穆萨·特拉奥雷；Alpha Oumar Konare 阿尔法·奥马尔·科纳雷；Tuareg 图阿雷格部族（西撒哈拉和中撒哈拉的柏柏尔人）；Senegal 塞内加尔（非洲国家）；Burkina Faso 布基纳法索（非洲国家）

② 其他词汇

state funeral 国葬；emblematic 标志的；oust 罢免/革职；coup 政变；heart surgery 心脏手

术;drape 用布帘覆盖;bear 运送;putsch 叛乱(政变);dignitary 高官/显要人物;envoy 使者;iron-fisted regime 铁腕政权;helm 领导地位;curtail 剥夺……特权等;jihadist insurgent 圣战叛乱分子;exile 流放;downfall 垮台;wreck 破坏;overrun 占领(领土);flashpoint 危险即将爆发的地点

2)句子层

E. g. Mali held a state funeral on Tuesday for former president Amadou Toumani Toure, an emblematic figure who steered the troubled nation to free elections and led it for a decade before being ousted in a coup.

本句较长,信息层次分明,表意清晰。在本句中,主干信息为"Mali held a state funeral","an emblematic figure"为"Amadou Toumani Toure"的同位语,起补充和说明作用,"who steered the troubled nation to..."为定语从句,修饰其前的"an emblematic figure"。

汉语常用短句表意,一个个主谓结构信息表面呈现并列状态。所以,英译汉时,译者须将英语原文环环相扣的句子信息拆为一个个主谓结构,按照时序、因果、范围等原则合理安排信息顺序,尽量不用关联词,一一呈现即可。本句可译为:周二,马里为前总统阿马杜·图马尼·杜尔举行国葬。杜尔是马里的标志性人物,曾带领这个动荡不安的国家进行自由选举,领导该国长达 10 年,后来在一场政变中被推翻。

E. g. A coffin draped in the national flag and borne by six soldiers was slowly carried into the center of a square in the capital of Mali for ceremonies attended by the leaders of the country's latest putsch and by foreign dignitaries.

本句为另一个长句,含有"draped""borne""carried"和"attended"四个表示被动意思的过去分词,翻译处理得当与否直接决定着汉语译文流畅与否。这是因为中高级英语多用被动句(这样表意客观),而汉语甚少使用"被"字表意。鉴于此,英译汉时,译者须尽最大努力消除汉语译文中的"被"字,以确保译文结构简约(合理断句后,汉语译文改用短句表意),读来流畅。本句可译为:六名士兵抬着国旗覆盖的棺材,缓缓步入马里首都(即巴马科)的一个广场中心。最近参与政变的马里领导人和外国政要出席了这一仪式。

E. g. His presidency was abruptly curtailed in 2012 by rebel troops who accused Toure of failing to support their battle against Tuareg and jihadist insurgents in the north of the country.

本句为文中又一个漂亮长句。其中,主句为"His presidency was abruptly curtailed in 2012 by rebel troops",为被动句,含动作发出者(rebel troops)、动作本身(curtailed)和动作承受者(His presidency)。根据英汉差异(英语多被动,汉语多主动),翻译时应尽量调整为主动句。这个主句可调整为"反对派军队突然剥夺了杜尔的总统职位"。

笔者曾讲过英译汉时定语从句的处理方法:当构成定语从句的单词不超过 8 个时,一般把定语从句翻译为汉语的前置定语,放在被修饰语前;当构成定语从句的单词超过 8 个时,一般应将定语从句译为汉语单句。根据这一原则,本句中的定语从句"who accused Toure of failing..."应该译为汉语单句。本句可译为:2012 年,反对派军队突然剥夺了杜尔的总统职位。他们指责杜尔,说他不支持他们在该国北部与图阿雷格部族和圣战叛乱分子作战。

E. g. They regrouped and advanced into central Mali, a flashpoint region where they ignited ethnic conflict, and then headed into neighboring Burkina Faso and Niger.

— 73 —

本句中的"a flashpoint region"为"central Mali"的同位语,"where they ignited ethnic conflict"为定语从句,修饰"region"。正确翻译并罗列这些信息是保证汉语译文质量的关键。汉语表意时,常出现表面上的主谓结构信息并列情形。所以,正确理解信息之间关系、合理安排信息顺序就显得至关重要。根据信息之间的逻辑关系,本句可译为:圣战分子重新集结,进入危险一触即发的马里中部地区,点燃种族冲突之火,然后前往邻国布基纳法索和尼日尔。

【参考译文】

马里为前总统杜尔举行国葬

2020年11月17日,马里总统巴·恩多在巴马科出席前总统阿马杜·图马尼·杜尔(享年72岁)的葬礼。1991年,阿马杜·图马尼推翻了穆萨·特拉奥雷的政府统治,领导过渡政府,2002年和2007年通过民主选举当选马里总统。(法新社/米歇尔·卡塔尼摄)

周二,马里为前总统阿马杜·图马尼·杜尔举行国葬。杜尔是马里的标志性人物,曾带领这个动荡不安的国家进行自由选举,领导该国长达10年,后来在一场政变中被推翻。

有时,人们把杜尔称为马里的"民主战士"。在接受心脏手术后,他被转移到土耳其接受治疗,11月10日去世,享年72岁。

六名士兵抬着国旗覆盖的棺材,缓缓步入马里首都(即巴马科)的一个广场中心。最近参与政变的马里领导人和外国政要出席了这一仪式。

葬礼主持人致辞:"一位伟人倒下了,这对马里造成了不可估量的损失。他带着生命的气息来到这里,乘着希望之风离开了我们。"

在贵宾席上就座的有马里前军官、过渡政府现任总统巴·恩多,以及领导了8月18日政变的副总统阿西米·戈伊塔。

尼日尔和几内亚比绍两国总理代表各自国家,该区域其他国家派出特使,共同出席了这一葬礼仪式。

根据安排,仪式将以军队检阅和飞机表演的形式结束。

杜尔曾是一名军人,1991年第一次掌管国家,为期一年。他帮助推翻了自1968年以来一直执政的穆萨·特拉奥雷铁腕政权。然后,他领导过渡委员会,行使国家元首职权,领导国家进行选举。

1992年,阿尔法·奥马尔·科纳雷赢得了选举。科纳雷是马里独立历史上第一位民选总统。

众所周知杜尔全名的首字母缩写是ATT。2002年和2007年,他均赢得总统选举。

2012年,反对派军队突然剥夺了杜尔的总统职位。他们指责杜尔,说他不支持他们在该国北部与图阿雷格部族和圣战叛乱分子作战。

杜尔逃到了塞内加尔,直到2017年才流亡归来。他下台后出现的混乱局面摧毁了马里装备简陋、士气低落的军队。

圣战分子迅速占领了该国北部地区,直到2013年,在法国的干预下才被迫从这里退出。

接着,圣战分子重新集结,进入危险一触即发的马里中部地区,点燃种族冲突之火,然后前往邻国布基纳法索和尼日尔。

数千人已死亡,数十万人逃离了家园。

2. 汉译英

【原文1】

李克强"大数据词典":共享、开放、安全

人民网记者 杨芳

2014年7月25日,李克强考察山东浪潮集团时,企业负责人向总理大胆"提要求":"希望您像支持中国高铁一样,支持国产'云计算'关键应用主机走向海外。"李克强当场承诺,今后出访不仅会推销中国高铁、中国核电,也会向全球市场推荐中国的"云计算"。

作为被诸多经济学家和企业家热捧的时髦词汇,"大数据"也在中国总理李克强的"词典"里占有一席之地。

自2014年3月将"大数据"首次写入《政府工作报告》以来,李克强总理在多个场合提及这一"热词"。今年年初在贵州考察北京·贵阳大数据应用展示中心时,他指出大数据为政府决策提供第一手科学依据,实现"人在干,云在算"。在他今年主持召开的国务院常务会议上,"大数据"被部署了5次。

昨天召开的常务会议上通过了《促进大数据发展的行动纲要》,这意味着我国大数据发展迎来顶层设计。李克强总理强调,制定大数据行动纲要,要突出围绕"政府大数据建设"和"创造健康发展的大数据环境"这两项核心内容展开。总理的讲话重点凸现了共享、开放和安全这三大关键词。

从标题可知,本文的中心意思是"李克强'大数据词典':共享、开放、安全"。

翻译操作步骤:

1)词汇层

浪潮集团 Inspur Group

云计算 cloud computing

关键应用主机 key-application consoles

时髦词汇 buzz words

《政府工作报告》 *the Government Work Report*

2)标题的翻译

汉语文章的标题一般不是以句子形式出现。本文标题即如此——"李克强'大数据词典':共享、开放、安全"。英语写作时,须明示信息之间的逻辑关系。那么,这个标题"李克强'大数据词典':共享、开放、安全"中如何明晰冒号前后关系呢?英文中列举信息前,一般会有一个概括性表达概念。"共享、开放、安全"和"李克强'大数据词典'"之间的关系可以理解为:"共享、开放、安全"是"李克强'大数据词典'"中的重要词汇。可将标题译为:Key Words from Premier Li Keqiang's "big data dictionary": Sharing, Openness & Security.

3)句子层

E.g. 2014年7月25日,李克强考察山东浪潮集团时,企业负责人向总理大胆"提要求":"希望您像支持中国高铁一样,支持国产'云计算'关键应用主机走向海外。"

汉语写作往往状语先行,即将状语置于主句前。本句时间状语有两个:"2014年7月25

日"和"李克强考察山东浪潮集团时"。英语句式呈现模式：主语＋最主要部分＋"废话"（相对而言不太重要的信息），这样可尽可能突出主要信息。从英文新闻写作角度看，可将"2014年7月25日"置于句首，像汉语一样指明新闻发生时间，将另一时间"李克强考察山东浪潮集团时"弱化处理。故此，本句可译作：On July 25, 2014, the director of Shandong Inspur Group, made a bold "demand" to premier Li Keqiang inspecting there, "I hope you can support the export of key-application consoles, to which domestic 'cloud computing' is applied, as you do to China's high-speed railway."

E.g. 作为被诸多经济学家和企业家热捧的时髦词汇，"大数据"也在中国总理李克强的"词典"里占有一席之地。

翻译本句时，译文句式的搭建不难，因为"作为……"不能作主句，主句就只能从逗号后的"'大数据'也在……"中产生。将逗号后信息缩至最短，即"'大数据'……占有一席之地"可直译为"have a place"。

本句中"热捧"不易翻译，若直译为"receive heated extolling"（受到热烈的赞颂），似乎过了火。那么，"诸多经济学家和企业家热捧的时髦词汇"中"热捧"到底该怎么理解呢？笔者将其理解为"多次引用"，因为"人热捧词汇"，一个具体的表现为"人会在（多个场合）多次引用该词"，逻辑上完全通畅，所以这种译法可行。另外，"时髦词汇"不可望文生义地译为"fashionable words"！有这种词汇吗？哪些词汇不fashionable呢？碰到这样经不起推敲的译法，译者须查词典、网络或专业书籍解决。"时髦词汇"正确的译法是"buzz word(s)"。本句可译为："Big data", the buzz words, cited by many economists and entrepreneurs many times, has also its place in the "dictionary" of China's premier Li Keqiang.

E.g. 李克强总理强调，制定大数据行动纲要，要突出围绕"政府大数据建设"和"创造健康发展的大数据环境"这两项核心内容展开。

动笔翻译前，译者通过词层（准确措辞）、句子层（搭建译文句子结构）和篇章层（合理安排信息顺序，做到信息层层推进，话题凸显）的"转换"，要做到对译文了然于心。

搭建本句译文句子结构比较容易，整句结构是："李克强总理强调……"译出英语应该是"主语＋谓语＋宾语从句"结构。"……制定大数据行动纲要，要突出围绕……"这部分逗号前后关系是什么？通过进一步分析，"制定大数据行动纲要"可解读为"要突出围绕……这两项核心内容展开"的目的。故此，本句可译作：Premier Li stressed that, in order to enact the outlines of action, two core contents must be centered: "governmental construction of big data" and "creating the healthily-developing environment of big data".

【参考译文】

Key Words from Premier Li Keqiang's "big data dictionary": Sharing, Openness & Security

Yang Fang (a journalist from People.cn)

On July 25, 2014, the director of Shandong Inspur Group, made a bold "demand" to premier Li Keqiang inspecting there, "I hope you can support the export of key-application consoles, to which domestic 'cloud computing' is applied, as you do to China's high-speed railway." Li promised on the spot, that from the next overseas visit on, he will not only promote China's high-speed railway and nuclear power, but also recommend China's "cloud computing" to global markets.

"Big data", the buzz words, cited by many economists and entrepreneurs many times, has also its place in the "dictionary" of China's premier Li Keqiang.

Since "big data" was first written in *the Government Work Report* in March, 2014, premier Li Keqiang mentioned this "hot phrase" on several occasions. At the beginning of this year, when visiting the Beijing Guiyang Big Data Application and Exhibition Center, he said that big data provides the first-hand scientific basis for government decision-making, having achieved the idea of "men are doing while the cloud is computing". "Big data" is deployed 5 times when he chaired a state council executive meeting this year.

Yesterday at the executive meeting, *the Outlines of Action for Promoting the Development of Big Data* was passed. This means that the nation's top leaders have begun to develop China's big data. Premier Li stressed that, in order to enact the outlines of action, two core contents must be centered: "governmental construction of big data" and "creating the healthily-developing environment of big data". Li's speech highlights 3 keywords—sharing, openness, and security.

【原文 2】

如果你觉得苹果在过去这两年里已经大动作不断了，那 2017 年将会再一次刷新你的认知。

2014 年发布的 iPhone 6 和 iPhone 6 Plus 帮助苹果一举成为世界上最赚钱的技术公司，而次年的 iPhone 6s 和 6s Plus 则更加引人关注。但在 2016 年，iPhone 的销量却出现了自 2007 年问世以来的首次下滑。

对于苹果而言，2016 是改进产品的一年，但 2017 年的情况可能会完全不同。全新设计的 iPhone、升级版 iPad、新的产品类型……根据之前曝光的这一系列传闻，明年将会成为苹果历史上最重要的一年。

（肖恩，腾讯网）

以上文字虽然以新闻形式出现，但是可以视作苹果公司另一种形式的广告语。

翻译操作步骤：

1）词汇层

大动作 big move, great action, dramatic shift；刷新 refresh, refurbish；刷新认知 refresh knowledge, surpass expectation；赚钱的 profitable, lucrative, remunerative；销量 volume of sales, sales；问世 found, set up, establish；下滑 fall, decline, go down

2）句子层

这里句子不长，只要明晰信息之间的逻辑关系，逐句翻译，做到"字正句顺"就可以了。

E. g. 全新设计的 iPhone、升级版 iPad、新的产品类型……根据之前曝光的这一系列传闻，明年将会成为苹果历史上最重要的一年。

根据上下文，"全新设计的 iPhone、升级版 iPad、新的产品类型……"应是"一系列传闻"的具体内容。所以,翻译时要做出调整,明晰关系。整句可译为:According to previous rumors regarding newly-designed iPhones, upgraded iPads and other new devices, 2017 will be the most important year in the history of Apple.

【参考译文】

If you think Apple has already made big moves over the past two years, in 2017 the company will once again surpass all expectations.

The release of iPhone 6 and iPhone 6 Plus both in 2014 helped Apple become the world's most profitable technology company, and the following year's iPhone 6s and iPhone 6s Plus attracted even more attention. However, sales in 2016 have fallen for the first time since the founding of Apple in 2007.

For Apple, 2016 is the year for improving its products, but next year, the situation could be completely different. According to previous rumors regarding newly-designed iPhones, upgraded iPads and other new devices, 2017 will be the most important year in the history of Apple.

练 习 题

一、英译汉练习

Rex Tillerson faces tough task in Moscow as Syria tension rises

The US secretary of state's visit to Russia promised a push for closer ties.

A huge red carpet was rolled out on the tarmac of the Moscow airport where Rex Tillerson's plane touched down, but it was unlikely Russia would similarly welcome his calls for it to stop backing Bashar al-Assad in Syria.

While the US secretary of state's decision to skip a Nato summit and visit Moscow initially seemed to highlight the White House's desire for better relations with Russia, expectations shifted after Donald Trump launched cruise missile strikes on a Syrian airbase last week, a move condemned by the Kremlin.

The days when Russian politicians talked about better relations and state television trumpeted Trump as a "real man" were clearly over.

As Tillerson began his meetings in Moscow on Wednesday, the question was not so much whether he could reach an agreement on Syria, but whether he could start any sort of dialogue at all. His first meeting with Sergei Lavrov, the Russian foreign minister, at February's G20 summit in Germany began with an apparent disagreement over the presence of journalists. Their interaction seemed cold compared to the fellow feeling between Lavrov and the former US secretary of state John Kerry.

Putin's spokesman Dmitry Peskov said on Tuesday that a meeting with Tillerson was not on Vladimir Putin's schedule "for now", and the US embassy said it had no information about a potential meeting.

Putin would probably meet with Tillerson only if the sit-down with Lavrov were relatively cordial and productive, Russian analysts said. "If they remain totally opposed and are only talking about America putting forward an ultimatum, and Russia refuses, then a meeting [with Putin] is meaningless," said Alexei Makarkin, a political analyst.

The mood music before the visit was not promising. In light of the chemical attack that killed more than 70 people in Syria last week, Tillerson said on Tuesday Russia had "failed to uphold" its 2013 promise to destroy Assad's chemical weapons, adding that Washington saw "no further role" for Assad as the country's leader, a harsher line on him than it had taken before.

In response, Putin doubled down on his support for Assad, comparing western accusations that the regime was responsible for the chemical attack to the false assertions that Iraq had weapons of mass destruction before the US invasion in 2003. He called for a United Nations investigation into the attack, while claiming that nefarious forces were "planning to again plant some substance and accuse the Syrian authorities of using chemical weapons"…

(作者不详，*The Guardian*，2017)

二、汉译英练习

访美期间，习近平主席与奥巴马总统就阿富汗问题深入交换意见，决定就阿富汗问题保持沟通与合作，以支持阿富汗和平重建和经济发展，支持"阿人主导、阿人所有"的和解进程，并促进中美阿三边对话。

日前，第四届"美中合作培训阿富汗外交官美方培训班"开班仪式在美国举行。中国外长王毅表示，中美合作培训阿外交官项目增进了中美阿三方的相互了解，体现了国际社会支持阿和平重建的共同努力，是中美在第三国合作的成功范例。中美两国还在纽约联合主持阿富汗重建与区域合作高级别会议，为阿富汗政府和地区经济合作继续提供强有力的国际支持。

(韩显阳，光明网，2015)

第七章　旅游语篇的翻译

一、旅游语篇的特点

旅游语篇的功能是提供信息和建议,带有很强的感召意向。旅游资料包罗万象,大致可以分成两大类:文化内涵丰富的材料与一般性材料。

这两类又可以细分为七种类型:
(1)介绍景点与旅游目的地地理位置与旅游价值的小册子(见图7.1);
(2)景区画册;
(3)景区风景明信片;
(4)旅游地图;
(5)旅游杂志;
(6)详细介绍单个景点的资料;
(7)游客须知/告示。

图7.1　旅游小册子

不同的旅游语篇有不同特点。
1. 汉语旅游语篇的文化内涵极其丰富,语言华丽
E.g.
泰山古称岱山,又称岱宗。位于山东省中部,为中国五岳(泰山、华山、衡山、嵩山、恒山)之一。因地处东部,故称东岳。泰山总面积426平方千米,主峰玉皇顶海拔1 532.8米,山势雄伟壮丽,气势磅礴,名胜古迹众多,有"五岳独尊"之誉。孔子有"登泰山而小天下"之语;唐代诗

人杜甫有"会当凌绝顶,一览众山小"的佳句。泰山在人们的心目中,已成为伟大、崇高的象征。

E. g.

景区内有七星岩,是桂林经典"三山两洞"之一洞,雄伟壮观,气势磅礴,自古以来就有"第一洞天"之美誉,它以那美轮美奂的洞中奇景,诠释了岩溶洞穴的瑰丽。大自然这位独一无二的艺术家,以他巧妙的鬼斧神工,为你雕琢了这似幻似真的奇妙景观,七星岩导游独特的知识性讲解,让你感受到的不仅仅是七星岩的美丽……

(桂林七星公园介绍)

2. 英语旅游语篇语言风格简约,平实易懂,描述客观

E. g.

Wall Street is the name of a narrow street in lower Manhattan in New York City, running east from Broadway downhill to the East River. Considered to be the historical heart of the Financial District, it was the first permanent home of the New York Stock Exchange. The phrase "Wall Street" is also used as a metonym to refer to American financial markets and financial institutions as a whole. Most New York financial firms are no longer headquartered on Wall Street, but elsewhere in lower or midtown Manhattan, Fairfield County, Connecticut, or New Jersey.

(美国华尔街简介)

E. g.

Liberty Enlightening the World, known more commonly as the Statue of Liberty, is a statue given to the United States by France in 1885, standing at Liberty Island in the mouth of the Hudson River in New York Harbor as a welcome to all visitors, immigrants, and returning Americans. The copper statue, dedicated on October 28, 1886, commemorates the centennial of the United States and is a gesture of friendship between the two nations. The sculptor was Frederic Auguste Bartholdi. Gustave Eiffel, the designer of the Eiffel Tower, engineered the internal structure...

(美国自由女神像简介)

在翻译实践中,旅游语篇英译汉时除尽可能保持原始信息外,还要做到语言风格的调整和译文信息的连贯性。

二、旅游语篇翻译实例

1. 英译汉

【原文】

5 OUTDOOR ACTIVITIES AT THE BARCELONETA BEACH

Good weather is approaching and outdoor activities begin to be on top of our to-do list. One of the best places to practice outdoor activities is the beach, and one of the most beautiful beaches in the world is the Barceloneta. Now you can travel to Barcelona with the super fast Renfe-SNCF en Coopération trains and enjoy a pleasant and relaxing trip to the beautiful Barcelona. And once there, you can do these outdoor activities to enjoy the most of your visit to Barcelona.

The Barceloneta is one of the oldest neighborhoods in the city and has an atmosphere of its own that you will not find anywhere else. It still retains the essence of the fishing village it once was. And all this without giving up the nightlife, the fun and the huge and beautiful beaches that characterize the city of Barcelona.

Take a bike tour around Barcelona (Fig. 7.2)

图 7.2　Bike Tour

A bike tour is a fun outdoor activity that will also allow you to know the different corners of the city of Barcelona. The Barceloneta beach is the starting point of the Born Bike Tours. A guide will accompany your group through hidden streets, great squares and paradisiac beaches while they tell you all the secrets of the city of Barcelona. The routes are designed to pass through bike lanes, pedestrian zones and streets with speed restriction for cars. In this way you get a fun outdoor activity that is both safe and suitable for people of all ages.

See Barcelona from a Segway

Another outdoor activity you can practice in Barcelona and at the same time get to know the city is a Segway ride. If the bike is not your thing, you can hire a two-hour Segway ride through Barcelona. The tour begins in the center, at the Roman wall, takes you through the Gothic quarter and the most representative places of the city, and ends in the neighborhood of the Barceloneta.

Learn how to surf at the Barceloneta beach (Fig 7.3)

图 7.3　Surf at the beach

If you like surfing or want to learn to do it in Barcelona, Pukas is for you. This surf school offers different water and outdoor activities. Among them there are classes for children and newbies, surfboard rides to see the sunrise from the Barceloneta beach or paddle surf. You can even rent a paddle surf board which seats eight people. Enjoy with friends or family the waters of the Barceloneta and practice your favorite outdoor activities in Barcelona.

And don't forget to visit the Michelin Stars restaurants in Barcelona, as this is one of the gastronomic capitals of Spain and Europe. And unmissable opportunity!

Relax with outdoor yoga

If Zen philosophy teaches that contact with the earth is essential for mind balance, what better way to practice yoga than on the beach of the Barceloneta. For this reason, the last of our suggestions for outdoor activities is yoga Ashtanga Vinyasa with Annabel Caravaca. You can find the Beach Yoga Barcelona group on Facebook and also on the Barceloneta beach every Thursday from the last week of May. Outdoor yoga can be the perfect end to a long visit around Barcelona or a good day enjoying the beach of the Barceloneta.

A different point of view from the Barceloneta cableway (Fig 7.4)

图 7.4　The cableway

One of the most special outdoor activities you can do in Barcelona is climbing the Montjuïc hill with the cable car from the Barceloneta beach. It is a journey of almost a mile in the air that offers wonderful views of the whole city at your feet. Nowadays the cable car is restored, although it retains the look it had in the year 1933. For 11 € the one way trip and 16.50 € the round trip, you can climb up to 100 meters above the ground and feel the greatness of the city of Barcelona.

本篇旅游文本介绍巴塞罗那巴塞洛内塔海滩上的5项户外活动(由标题即可看出)。语言朴实,明白易懂,所以翻译起来困难不大。

翻译操作步骤:

1)词汇层

Renfe 西班牙国家铁路;SNCF 法国国营铁路公司;en Coopération 在合作中;Renfe-SNCF en Coopération trains 西法两国联营火车;Barceloneta 巴塞洛内塔;characterize 使成

为……的特点;paradisiac 天堂的;pedestrian zone 步行街;paddle surf board 划桨冲浪板;Zen philosophy 禅宗哲学;Montjuïc hill 蒙特惠奇山;cable car 缆车

2) 句子层

E. g. And all this without giving up the nightlife, the fun and the huge and beautiful beaches that characterize the city of Barcelona.

本句可译为:此外,这里的夜生活、娱乐活动以及巨大而美丽的海滩是巴塞罗那城市的特色。

翻译本句时注意措辞。without giving up 属于双重否定,在这里宜译成肯定说法;characterize 是该句的谓语,不宜直译为"使成为……的特点"。

E. g. A guide will accompany your group through hidden streets, great squares and paradisiac beaches while they tell you all the secrets of the city of Barcelona.

本句可译为:导游会告诉你巴塞罗那市所有的秘密,陪同你们一行人通过隐蔽的街道、大广场和天堂似的海滩。

翻译本句没有什么难点,但要按照英语信息主次调整中文译文信息顺序。

【参考译文】

巴塞洛内塔海滩上的5项户外活动

好天气即将来临,户外活动开始出现在我们的待办事项清单之首。开展户外活动最好的地方是海滩,西班牙巴塞洛内塔海滩是世界上最美丽的海滩之一。现在,您可以乘坐超级快速的西法两国联营火车前往美丽的巴塞罗那,享受一次愉快、轻松的旅行。到了那里,您可以开展户外活动,度过在巴塞罗那的大部分时光了。

巴塞洛内塔是这座城市最古老的街区之一,拥有您不会在其他地方感受到的独特氛围。这里依然保留作为渔村的本质特性。此外,这里的夜生活、娱乐活动以及巨大而美丽的海滩是巴塞罗那的特色。

骑自行车环游巴塞罗那

骑自行车是一项有趣的户外活动。骑上自行车您会看到巴塞罗那这座城市不同角落的风景。巴塞洛内塔海滩是"博恩"自行车之旅的起点。导游会陪同你们一行人通过隐蔽的街道、大广场和天堂似的海滩。在这些地方,巴塞罗那市的秘密尽在眼前。路线是这样设计的:先通过自行车道,再进入步行街,然后上有车速限制的街道。这样,您会觉得这项适合所有年龄段人参与的户外活动既有趣又安全。

骑"赛格威"电动车看巴塞罗那

在巴塞罗那,您可以骑"赛格威"电动车来了解这座城市,这是您可以体验的另一项户外活动。您若不喜欢骑自行车,可租两小时的"赛格威"电动车穿越巴塞罗那城。从罗马墙所在的市中心出发,穿过哥特区,参观该城最具代表性的地方,最后到达巴塞洛内塔海滩附近结束骑行旅程。

在巴塞洛内塔海滩学会冲浪

如果您喜欢冲浪,或想在巴塞罗那学习冲浪,普克珠贝学校欢迎您。该校提供不同的水上和户外活动,包括开设儿童和新手班,教会他们从巴塞洛内塔海滩出发,通过冲浪或划桨去看日出。您甚至可以租一个能容纳8人划桨的冲浪板。与朋友或家人尽情地在巴塞洛内塔水域玩吧,在巴塞罗那开展您最喜欢的户外活动。

巴塞罗那是西班牙和欧洲的美食首都之一,别忘了在巴塞罗那米其林星级餐馆就餐。机不可失,时不再来!

在户外做瑜伽,放松身心

如果禅宗哲学告诉我们,与大地接触是保持心理平衡必不可少的,那么还有什么地方比巴塞洛内塔海滩更适合练习瑜伽的呢。因此,就户外活动而言,我们最后建议您与安娜贝利·卡拉瓦卡团队成员一起练习阿斯汤伽瑜伽。您可以在脸书上找到沙滩瑜伽巴塞罗那团队。从五月最后一个星期开始,每周四在巴塞洛内塔海滩,您也可以找到这个团队。在巴塞罗那游览久了或在巴塞洛内塔海滩玩了一天后,您可在海滩上做瑜伽,放松身心。

坐巴塞罗那缆车看不一样的风景

您可以在巴塞洛内塔海滩乘坐缆车爬上蒙特惠奇山,这是您在巴塞罗那能参与的最特别的一项户外活动了。坐缆车行程大约1英里,整个城市的美景尽收眼底。如今,缆车已修复,尽管还是1933年时的样子。花费11欧元(单程)或16.5欧元(往返),您就可以爬升到距离地面100米高的地方,感受巴塞罗那的锦绣风光了。

2. 汉译英

【原文1】

卢沟桥在北京市西南约15千米处,丰台区永定河上。因横跨卢沟河(即永定河)而得名,是北京市现存最古老的石造联拱桥。桥身结构坚固,造型美观,具有极高的桥梁工程技术和艺术水平,充分体现了古代汉族劳动人民的聪明才智和桥梁建造的辉煌成就。卢沟桥为华北最长的古代石桥。1937年7月7日,日本帝国主义在此发动全面侵华战争。宛平城的中国驻军奋起抵抗,史称"卢沟桥事变"(亦称"七七事变")。中国抗日军队在卢沟桥打响了全面抗战的第一枪。

这段文字介绍了卢沟桥的地理位置、历史地位、特点和"卢沟桥事变"。
翻译操作步骤:
1)词汇层
横跨 span;石造联拱桥 multi-arch stone bridge;体现 reflect;侵华战争 war of aggression against China;奋起抵抗 rise up in resistance;卢沟桥事变 the Lugou Bridge Incident;七七事变 the July Seventh Incident;全面抗战 the war of total resistance

2)句子层
E. g. 卢沟桥在北京市西南约15千米处,丰台区永定河上。
汉语是意合语言,信息之间的关系隐藏在字里行间;英语是形合语言,信息之间关系需要明示。本句中,逗号前后关系该如何明示呢?这句汉语表明卢沟桥的地理位置,有1个主语"卢沟桥",2个谓语。英语句子表达往往是以一个"主+谓"结构为中心,让其他信息设法附着在这个"主+谓"结构上。相对于第一个地点概念"在北京市西南约15公里处"而言,也许第二个地点"丰台区永定河上"更重要。所以可将这句译为:The Lugou Bridge, located about 15 kilometers southwest of Beijing, spans the Yongding River in the Fengtai District.

E.g. 桥身结构坚固,造型美观,具有极高的桥梁工程技术和艺术水平,充分体现了古代汉族劳动人民的聪明才智和桥梁建造的辉煌成就。

这句反映了汉语典型的行文模式:话题+评价。鉴于该句信息较多,句子较长,为了展示英语旅游文本简约、平实的风格和句式不长的表达特点,翻译本句时已从"充分"前的逗号处断为2句,并明示关系。可译为:With its solid structure and beautiful design, it reflects a very high level of both bridge construction technology and artistic achievement. Moreover, it gives full expression to the intelligence and skill of the Han Chinese workers and to the impressive achievement of ancient Chinese bridge construction.

【参考译文】

The Lugou Bridge, located about 15 kilometers southwest of Beijing, spans the Yongding River in the Fengtai District. Taking its name from the Lugou River (also known as the Yongding River), it is now the oldest existing multi-arch stone bridge in Beijing. With its solid structure and beautiful design, it reflects a very high level of both bridge construction technology and artistic achievement. Moreover, it gives full expression to the intelligence and skill of the Han Chinese workers and to the impressive achievement of ancient Chinese bridge construction. The Lugou Bridge, the longest ancient stone bridge in North China, is the spot where on July 7, 1937, the Imperialist Japanese army launched a full-scale war of aggression against China. In response, Chinese army stationed in Wanping Town immediately rose up in resistance. This event is known in history as the Lugou Bridge Incident (also the July Seventh Incident). It was here at the Lugou Bridge that the Chinese army fired the first shots of the war of total resistance.

【原文2】

冲浪运动

冲浪运动起始于澳大利亚。由于澳大利亚四面环海,气候温暖,多日照而少阴雨,有利于水上运动的发展,故而澳大利亚人特别喜爱冲浪运动。关于冲浪的起源还有一种说法:冲浪起源于20世纪60年代末世界冲浪胜地夏威夷群岛,1970年6月由美国一位冲浪爱好者电脑技师修万斯(Fix Vans)设计制造出世界第一条带有万向节的帆板,并获专利权,此后在当地很快兴起帆板热,不久便流传到欧洲、澳洲和东南亚一带,兴于澳大利亚。

(adamswww,百度知道)

这段文字简述了冲浪运动的起源和发展情况。
翻译操作步骤:
1)词汇层
冲浪运动 surfing;起始于 begin in, originate from;四面环海 encircled/surrounded by

seas, seagirt；阴雨 overcast and rainy；有利于 conducive to, make for；冲浪胜地 surfing spot；夏威夷群岛 the Hawaiian Islands；冲浪爱好 surfing enthusiast；电脑技师 computer mechanic/technician；万向节 universal joint；帆板 sailboarding；冲浪板 sailboard；专利权 patent；兴于 flourish in

2）句子层

E.g. 由于澳大利亚四面环海，气候温暖，多日照而少阴雨，有利于水上运动的发展，故而澳大利亚人特别喜爱冲浪运动。

本句有2个意思：澳大利亚水上运动发展较好的原因；澳大利亚人特别喜爱冲浪运动。翻译时宜断为2句。

E.g. 关于冲浪的起源还有一种说法：……

此处"说法"一词不宜照字面译为"statement""wording"等，因为冒号后讲了一个故事，所以应译为"story"。

E.g. 冲浪起源于20世纪60年代末世界冲浪胜地夏威夷群岛，1970年6月由美国一位冲浪爱好者电脑技师修万斯（Fix Vans）设计并制造出世界第一条带有万向节的帆板，并获专利权，此后在当地很快兴起帆板热，不久便流传到欧洲、澳洲和东南亚一带，兴于澳大利亚。

本句较长，包含2层意思：冲浪起源的"说法"；冲浪"热"。所以翻译时要断为2句，并注意明确不同层面的信息关系。

【参考译文】

Surfing

Surfing originated in Australia. Because Australia is surrounded by the sea, the climate, which is warm and sunny with few overcast or rainy days, is conducive to the development of water sports. As a result, Australians are quite keen on surfing. How surfing began is related to the following story according to which it originated in the late 1960s on the Hawaiian Islands, a world-famous surfing spot. In June of 1970, Fix Vans, a computer technician and surfing enthusiast in the U.S., designed and made the world's first sailboard with a universal joint for which he later obtained a patent. Thereafter, sailboarding soon became a local craze which subsequently spread to Europe, Southeast Asia and Australia, where it flourished.

【原文3】

西安是著名的丝绸之路的起点，同时拥有着深厚的历史文化积淀和浩瀚的文物古迹遗存，西安享有"天然历史博物馆"的美誉。

西安市内有着众多的闻名世界的重点文物保护单位，其中国家级重点文物保护单位89处，陵墓8 822处，古遗址5 700余处，文物点21 100余个。

1981年，联合国教科文组织把西安确定为"世界历史名城"，是国务院公布的国家历史文化名城之一。

西安有着优美的自然环境,历史上的八水绕长安是指渭、泾、沣、涝、潏、滈、浐、灞八条河流在西安城四周穿流,养育着西安的乡亲。

在西安碑林,有一块清代碑石记录了以西安为中心的关中八处著名的风景名胜,它们被称为"关中八景",又称"长安八景"。这八景分别是:华岳仙掌、骊山晚照、灞柳飞雪、曲江流饮、雁塔晨钟、咸阳古渡、草堂烟雾、太白积雪。这八景涵盖了西安周边著名的美景,成为西安面向世界的一张名片。

具有浓郁陕西特色的戏曲——秦腔,同样具有悠久的历史,它高亢嘹亮的唱腔,浓墨重彩的脸谱,无一不体现出西安人豪爽、热情的性格。田间地头吼一声秦腔,八百里秦川顿时豪情万丈。

西安,是一座独特地将历史与现代完美融合的城市,既依托着深厚的文化底蕴,传承中华五千年的历史,又与世界接轨,使现代西安逐步迈进国际大都市的行列。这样独特的一座城市,怎么能使人不流连忘返呢?

这是网上一篇介绍西安这座旅游城市的文章。
翻译操作步骤:
1)词汇层

历史文化积淀 cultural and historical significance;浩瀚的文物 abundant relics and sites;重点文物保护单位 key cultural relics sites under protection;名片 business card, travel card;高亢嘹亮的唱腔 loud, sharp singing;浓墨重彩的脸谱 heavily-colored mask;深厚的文化底蕴 profound cultural background;传承中华五千年的历史 five thousand years of China's heritage;迈进国际大都市的行列 become an international metropolis;流连忘返 linger

2)句子层

E.g. 西安是著名的丝绸之路的起点,同时拥有着深厚的历史文化积淀和浩瀚的文物古迹遗存,西安享有"天然历史博物馆"的美誉。

这句包含2个意思,翻译为英语时须从第一个逗号后断成2句。所以可以译为:Xi'an is the starting point of the famous Silk Road. Its cultural and historical significance, as well as the abundant relics and sites, help itself enjoy the laudatory title of "Natural History Museum".

E.g. 西安市内有着众多的闻名世界的重点文物保护单位,其中国家级重点文物保护单位89处,陵墓8 822处,古遗址5 700余处,文物点21 100余个。

这句包含2个意思,需从"89处"后的逗号处断开。翻译这句时要注意信息层次和信息关系的明示方法。可将这句译为:Here are many world-famous key cultural relics sites under protection, 89 of which are under state-level protection. There are 8,822 tombs, 5,700-odd ancient ruins, and more than 21,100 cultural relics.

E.g. 西安有着优美的自然环境,历史上的八水绕长安是指渭、泾、沣、涝、潏、滈、浐、灞八条河流在西安城四周穿流,养育着西安的乡亲。

本句包含2个意思,应从"历史上"之前断开。"八水绕长安"中"绕"可译为"run around",这样"水"和"长安"的逻辑关系即刻变通畅。"八水"的名字按照规范的译法是:河流名字用拼音,不管几个汉字,写在一起,第一个字母大写,后跟功能词"River"("河流"属于专有名词,第一个字母大写),前加"the"用以特指。比如,"渭"可译为"the Weihe River"。这也是"长江"(the Changjiang River,亦称 Yangtze River)译法模仿的结果。"八水"的谓语为"绕",为译出多样的句式,可将"养育……"译作状语。本句可译为:Xi'an has a beautiful natural environment. In its history, the eight waters that ran around Chang'an specifically are the Weihe River, the Jinghe River, the Fenghe River, the Laohe River, the Yuhe River, the Haohe River, the Chanhe River and the Bahe River, nurturing folks in this city.

E.g. 这八景分别是:华岳仙掌、骊山晚照、灞柳飞雪、曲江流饮、雁塔晨钟、咸阳古渡、草堂烟雾、太白积雪。

"八景"是专有名词,翻译时除按规范书写外,还须尽可能保留汉语原文意思,使英文读来有画面感。本句可译为:They are Huayue Palm, Sunset on Lishan Mountain, Baliu Flying Snow, Qujiang Stream, Morning Belling at Wild Goose Pagoda, Xianyang Ancient Ferry, Caotang Smoke, Taibai Snow.

E.g. 具有浓郁陕西特色的戏曲——秦腔,同样具有悠久的历史,它高亢嘹亮的唱腔,浓墨重彩的脸谱,无一不体现出西安人豪爽、热情的性格。

这句包含2个意思:秦腔历史悠久;秦腔的特点和西安人的性格。所以翻译为英语时要断成2句。这句逗号较多,翻译时要注意明晰、明示逗号前后信息关系。可将这句译为:Qin Opera, strongly characteristic of Shaanxi Province, also has a long history. It is characterized by loud, sharp singing and a heavily-colored mask, both showing the personality of generous and enthusiastic people in Xi'an.

【参考译文】

Xi'an is the starting point of the famous Silk Road. Its cultural and historical significance, as well as the abundant relics and sites, help itself enjoy the laudatory title of "Natural History Museum".

Here are many world-famous key cultural relics sites under protection, 89 of which are under state-level protection. There are 8,822 tombs, 5,700-odd ancient ruins, and more than 21,100 cultural relics.

In 1981, Xi'an was identified as "the World's Historical City" by UNESCO, one of the national famous historical and cultural cities announced by the State Council.

Xi'an has a beautiful natural environment. In its history, the eight waters that ran around Chang'an specifically are the Weihe River, the Jinghe River, the Fenghe River, the Laohe River, the Yuhe River, the Haohe River, the Chanhe River and the Bahe River, nurturing folks in this city.

In Xi'an Beilin Museum, one hearstone of the Qing Dynasty records eight famous scenic spots around Xi'an, known as eight sights in Guanzhong Plain, also called Chang'an Eight Sights. They are Huayue Palm, Sunset on Lishan Mountain, Baliu Flying Snow, Qujiang Stream, Morning Belling at Wild Goose Pagoda, Xianyang Ancient Ferry, Caotang Smoke,

Taibai Snow, covering famous scenic spots around Xi'an. They have become a travel card of Xi'an to the world.

Qin Opera, strongly characteristic of Shaanxi Province, also has a long history. It is characterized by loud, sharp singing and a heavily-colored mask, both showing the personality of generous and enthusiastic people in Xi'an. It seems that if someone in the farming field sings one line of Qin Opera, all people in the vast Qinchuan stretch will echo.

Xi'an is a unique city, both historical and modern. Its profound cultural background, five thousand years of China's heritage and integration with the world, help itself gradually on the way to becoming an international metropolis. How can't we linger in such a unique city?

练 习 题

一、英译汉练习

My First Trip to Sweden（Ⅱ）

"See that blind man crossing the street? The cars stop for him to get across."

We went sightseeing in Stockholm. Stephen, one of our hosts, accompanied us. We had just been to the King's Island and we were going to the ferry. Suddenly Stephen said to me, "See that blind man crossing the street? The cars stop for him to get across." "But how do the drivers know that a blind person is crossing the street? How does he signal the drivers?" I asked. "There is a button on the pole at the crisscross. The blind can press the button to give special signals to the drivers." He answered. I was deeply moved. The small device is the sign of consideration of the public for the disabled. City management can be very humane if the government cares for the people.

The Meeting in the Town Hall

As arranged, Eva, the mayoress of Linkoping was to meet the delegation. Deputy mayor of Changchun would hold a friendly talk with her and discuss the possibility of establishing sister cities between the two cities. Early in the morning we went to the Town Hall.

When we got near, we saw the Chinese national flag and the Swedish national flag flying over there. The mayoress waited at the gate with her assistant. She shook hands with each of us and led us in. She introduced her city to us with pictures and graphs in fluent English. It was a mystery to me that every Swede I came across spoke good English. I was told that the English language is taught as a compulsory course throughout every child's school years. That is, children begin to learn English when they start school and keep it until they graduate from high school.

"What are they doing with that fresco?"

Some people were transferring an old fresco inside the church of Linkoping to Malmo. "But how can they do that without damaging the picture?" I began to wonder. "Let's go and have a look!" we were suggested. When we entered the church, there was a group of people busy with the picture on the wall. It was an old picture telling a story of the Christian religion. There was some equipment I had no idea of, and two computers. On the screen of one computer, there was the part of picture already scanned. On the other computer was the sight of the destination in Malmo. Both groups of people in Linkoping and Malmo talked and exchanged ideas via the computers. They were transferring the picture via the Internet.

Different Hospitality

There were several occasions when we were invited to dinner by the hosts: the mayoress and the executives of the factories and companies we visited. These dinners were working lunches rather than the dinners like what we hold domestically in honor of our guests. Each of the guests and hosts had a plate for himself or herself, and there was no leftover. There was nobody who had nothing to do with the visit or the project. No persuasion to drink alcohol. No noise. The presiding host addressed his guests briefly and the guests gave an answering speech. All of us had a toast to the health of each other, then talked quietly over the meals. It was in an atmosphere of goodwill and friendliness.

"It's the law."

We were traveling in Malmo one evening. Stephen, the driver stopped at the red light at a crisscross. I could see no cars on the other street and no police car hanging around, so I asked Stephen, "Why don't you drive on? There is no other car, and it is getting late." But he said nothing and waited until the green light was on. When he drove on, he said to me, "It's the law." Before the visit to Sweden, I read about this kind of stories from magazines and I supposed they must have been exaggerated. But now, I really believe that they obey the law unconditionally.

(陈小君,《英语学习》,2002年10月)

二、汉译英练习

泰山古称岱山,又称岱宗。位于山东省中部,为中国五岳(泰山、华山、衡山、嵩山、恒山)之一。因地处东部,故称东岳。泰山总面积426平方千米,主峰玉皇顶海拔1 532.8米,山势雄伟壮丽,气势磅礴,名胜古迹众多,有"五岳独尊"之誉。孔子有"登泰山而小天下"之语;唐代诗人杜甫有"会当凌绝顶,一览众山小"的佳句。泰山在人们的心目中,已成为伟大、崇高的象征。

(Itum5165K,360回答)

第八章 科技语篇的翻译

一、科技语篇的特点

从广义上讲，科技语篇不仅涵盖自然科学领域的科学技术内容（如化工、机械、医学、计算机等），而且涉及社会科学领域的人文社会学科（如哲学、政治学、经济学、法学、历史学、伦理学、教育学等）。此外，广告、说明书、公文、契约等实用型文本也可归入科技语篇的范畴。

1. 科技语篇的特点

（1）周密、准确

周密指句子之间合乎逻辑，这样语言也就周密了，而语言周密来自对客观事物正确的观察。

（2）明朗、规范

语言明朗即语言的表达要清楚明白，让人读了能够理解。规范是指用词和语法规则正确，包括用词、语序和句子成分等方面的规范使用。

（3）平实、简要

平实就是自然朴素，不求粉饰，做到"文约而旨丰"，"文简而理周"。语言要精雕细琢，言简意深。

2. 科技英语语篇常见的语言特点

（1）大量使用被动语态

使用被动语态写作，可以去除人的主观能动性，表述更为客观。翻译成汉语时，为保证汉语译文阅读通畅，译者要尽可能去除"被"字眼。

E. g. The motors are engaged as pumps, building pressure in an accumulator tank to slow the car.

如同泵一样，这些马达工作时会给蓄电池箱增压以降低车速。

E. g. The decrease in intensity due to absorption is called damping and a wave whose intensity decreases for this reason is called a damped wave.

由于吸收而引起的强度减弱（特性）叫作阻尼，而由于吸收造成强度减弱的波叫作阻尼波。

E. g. How often observations are made, and how widely they are spaced, depend on the scale of the atmospheric events about which information is desired.

隔多久进行一次观测，这些观测站点彼此相距多远，取决于想要获得信息的大气事件的规模。

（2）非谓语动词多

非谓语动词包括动词不定式、动名词、现在分词和过去分词，是英文写作时除从句外将句子拉长的另一有力"武器"。科技语篇文本逻辑严密,环环相扣,非谓语动词有利于明晰信息之间的关系,文本句式也显得多样化。

E. g. Electrical energy can be stored in two metal plates separated by an insulating medium. Such a device is called a capacitor, or a condenser, and its ability to store electrical energy capacitance. It is measured in farads.

电能可储存在由绝缘介质隔开的两块金属极板内。我们把这样的装置称为电容器,其储存电能的能力称为电容。电容的测量单位是法拉。

E. g. Long regarded by elementary particle physicists as a costly nuisance, synchrotron radiation is now recognized as a valuable research tool.

过去很长时间内,基本粒子物理学家把同步加速器辐射当作费钱的废物,而现在人们认为同步加速器辐射是宝贵的研究工具。

E. g. Using a computer, we composed a series of synthetic songs by shuffling natural syllables into different patterns.

我们用计算机把音节组织成种种不同的结构模式,合成了一系列曲子。

E. g. Today, the electronic computer is widely used in solving mathematical problems having to do with weather forecasting and putting satellites into orbit.

今天,电子计算机广泛地用于解决与天气预报和把卫星送入轨道有关的数学问题。

(3)英语动词的名词化

英语动词的名词化,即英语语篇中一些表动作概念的词以名词形式出现,这是因为英语是静态语言,汉语是动态语言。翻译时要将表动作概念的名词译为汉语动词。

E. g. Archimedes first discovered the principle of displacement of water by solid bodies.

阿基米德最先发现固体排水的原理。

E. g. All substances will permit the passage of some electric current, provided the potential difference is high enough.

只要有足够的电位差,电流便可通过任何物体。

E. g. Television is the transmission and reception of images of moving objects by radio waves.

电视通过无线电波发射和接收各种活动物体的图像。

书面英语动词名词化例子见表 8.1。

表 8.1 书面英语动词名词化

口头语(动词)	书面语(名词化)	汉语意思
prepare	make preparation	准备
arrange	make arrangement	安排
plan	make planning	计划
emphasize	lay emphasis on	强调
end	put an end to	结束

续表

口头语（动词）	书面语（名词化）	汉语意思
leave	take one's leave	离开
support	in support of	支持
consider	take...into consideration	考虑
prioritize	take priority to	优先考虑

二、科技语篇翻译实例

1. 英译汉

【原文 1】

Scientists Stalk Mammoth Clone

It was the single, strangely spiraled tusk that first alerted scientists. Sticking out of the ice-covered Siberian soil, like an ivory tombstone, it revealed the presence of a true scientific wonder: underneath lay the frozen body of a Mammoth.

The discovery has presented researchers with an unprecedented opportunity—to move to a laboratory, a mammoth's entire, undisturbed body where it can be analyzed at leisure and its biological secrets revealed.

Last week, scientists completed the first stage of this remarkable transfer, using a helicopter to lift a 23-ton block of ice and mammoth to a new site where defrosting can be started.

As one of the team, Dutch paleontologist Dick Mol, put it, "It's very exciting. I've been working on mammoths for more than 25 years, and this was a dream for me—to find the soft parts and touch them and even smell them."

本文节选自 2000 年 10 月出版的《英语学习》上的一篇长文，讲述了在西伯利亚的冰原上，科学家发现了冰冻体猛犸象，计划克隆出活体猛犸象的故事。

翻译操作步骤：

1) 标题

根据文章内容，标题"Scientists Stalk Mammoth Clone"中"stalk"不宜直译为"跟踪"，要改变说法，可译为"科学家探究猛犸象克隆"。

2) 词汇层

stalk 追踪；mammoth 猛犸象，一种古代长毛象，已灭绝了几万年；spiraled tusk 螺旋形长牙；alert 使警觉；Siberian soil 西伯利亚土地；ivory tombstone 象牙墓碑；unprecedented 空前的，无前例的；Dutch paleontologist 荷兰古生物学家

3) 句子层

E.g. It was the single, strangely spiraled tusk that first alerted scientists.

这个句子不长,句式为英语强调句型:"主语+be+被强调部分+that/who 引导的从句"。一般情况下,当构成定语从句的词不超过 8 个时,要将定语从句译为前置定语。比如:

God helps those who help themselves.

自助者,天助也。

Those who make most people happy are the happiest in the world. (Karl Marx)

能使大多数人幸福的人是世界上最幸福的人。(卡尔·马克思)

但是这个句子例外。被强调部分"tusk"前已经有四个修饰词:"the single, strangely spiraled",如果把定语从句再译为前置定语就显得修饰语太累赘,而且定语显得"……的……的……"太啰唆。所以,要做到译文"信""达"和"雅",就要调整措辞。本句可译为:这个呈螺旋形奇怪形状、迄今为止发现的唯一的长牙第一次引起了科学家的注意。其中,"迄今为止发现的"属于增译,增加信息为的是将信息表达透彻。

E.g. I've been working on mammoths for more than 25 years, and this is a dream for me—to find the soft parts and touch them and even smell them.

这个句子属于口头英语,措辞简单,没有翻译困难。任何时候,译者翻译时须评估译文接受度(acceptability)。翻译时,要合理安排语言信息顺序,措辞准确,语句通畅,语义清晰。本句可译为:我研究猛犸象已经超过 25 年了。对我来说,找到猛犸象的软组织,用手抚摸甚至用鼻子闻闻,这是一个梦想成真的时刻。

【参考译文】

科学家探究猛犸象克隆

这个呈螺旋形奇怪形状、迄今为止发现的唯一的长牙第一次引起了科学家的注意。这个长牙伸出冰雪覆盖的西伯利亚大地,就像一个象牙墓碑,揭示了一个真正的科学奇迹:一头冰冻的猛犸大象躺在这块地下。

这一发现给研究人员提供了一个前所未有的机会:将整个保存完整的猛犸象骸骨搬到实验室,从容地加以分析,以揭示生物界的秘密。

上周,科学家使用直升机抬起重达 23 吨的猛犸冰块,运至一个新的地方开始解冻,完成了举世瞩目的第一阶段工作——转移猛犸象骸骨。

正如荷兰古生物学家迪克·摩尔(团队成员之一)所说:"这是令人振奋的事情。我研究猛犸象已经超过 25 年了。对我来说,找到猛犸象的软组织,用手抚摸甚至用鼻子闻闻,这是一个梦想成真的时刻。"

【原文 2】

The Dangers of Air Conditioning

About two-thirds of the world's population is expected to live in cities by the year 2020, and according to the United Nations, approximately 3.7 billion people will inhabit urban areas some ten years later. As cities grow, so do the number of buildings that characterize them: office towers, factories, shopping malls and high-rise apartment buildings. These structures depend on artificial ventilation systems to keep clean and cool air flowing to the people inside. We know these systems by the term "air-conditioning".

Although many of us may feel air-conditioners bring relief from hot, humid or polluted outside air, they pose many potential health hazards. Much research has looked at how the circulation of air inside a closed environment—such as an office building—can spread disease or expose occupants to harmful chemicals.

One of the more widely publicized dangers is that of Legionnaire's disease, which was first recognized in the 1970s. This was found to have affected people in buildings with air-conditioning systems in which warm air pumped out of the system's cooling towers was somehow sucked back into the air intake, in most cases due to poor design. This warm air was, needless to say, the perfect environment for the rapid growth of disease-carrying bacteria originating from outside the building, where it existed in harmless quantities. The warm, bacteria-laden air was combined with cooled, conditioned air and was then circulated around various parts of the building. Studies showed that even people outside such buildings were at risk if they walked past air exhaust ducts. Cases of Legionnaire's disease are becoming fewer with newer system designs and modifications to older systems, but many older buildings, particularly in developing countries, require constant monitoring.

(Robi Stauber,《英语学习》)

这是一篇科普文章,讲述空调的危害。相对于纯自然科学文本,科普文章易于理解,易于翻译。

翻译操作步骤:

1)词汇层

relief 缓解;pose hazard 造成危害;occupant 居住者;Legionnaire's disease 军团菌病(一种由嗜肺军团杆菌所致的急性呼吸道传染病);bacteria-laden air 携带细菌的空气;air exhaust duct 排气管

2)句子层

E. g. As cities grow, so do the number of buildings that characterize them: office towers, factories, shopping malls and high-rise apartment buildings.

本句是倒装句。"as"引导的伴随状语从句宜套用汉语"随着……",这样动词"grow"宜译为名词"发展"。"that characterize them"中"characterize"本意为"描绘……的特性;具有……的特征",但是经常不能直译,否则造成译文语句不流畅。通常要结合上下文灵活处理。本句可译为:随着城市的发展,写字楼、工厂、商场和高楼公寓等这些城市标志建筑物会越来越多。

E. g. This was found to have affected people in buildings with air-conditioning systems in which warm air pumped out of the system's cooling towers was somehow sucked back into the air intake, in most cases due to poor design.

本句为长句,是一个复合句,含主句和定语从句。翻译时,译者要按照目的语(汉语,是表意语言)重新罗列信息顺序。本句可译为:研究人员发现,空调系统压缩机排出的热气不知怎么地(大多由于设计不当)被吸入进气口,会影响建筑物中人们的健康。

【参考译文】

空调的危害

到 2020 年时,世界上大约三分之二的人将在城市居住。联合国统计数据表明,约十年后,大约有 37 亿人将在城市地区居住。随着城市的发展,写字楼、工厂、商场和高楼公寓等这些城市标志建筑物会越来越多。这些建筑物依靠人工通风系统来保持清洁,让建筑物中的人享受到清凉空气。我们知道这些系统是"空调"系统。

虽然很多人觉得空调可以缓解酷热、潮湿或受污染的外部空气对人的影响,但是空调也会带来许多潜在的健康危害。已有很多研究关注封闭环境中空气流通的方式。比如,办公大楼中空气流通会传播疾病,或置楼内人员于有害化学物品环境中。

一个广为人知的危害是军团菌病,这在 20 世纪 70 年代首次得到证实。研究人员发现,空调系统压缩机排出的热气不知怎么地(大多由于设计不当)被吸入进气口,会影响建筑物中人们的健康。不用说,这些温暖的空气为携带疾病的细菌提供了快速增长的完美环境。这些细菌来自外部建筑,以无害的形式大量存在。温暖的、携带细菌的空气与调节后制冷的空气混合在一起,然后在建筑物的不同地方循环流通。研究显示,即使建筑物外的行人经过排气管道也有健康危害。随着新系统设计改进和旧系统设施改造,军团菌病病例愈加少见,但是还需要持续监控很多老旧楼房,尤其是在发展中国家。

2.汉译英

【原文1】

物理学

物理学是研究物质世界最基本的结构、最普遍的相互作用、最一般的运动规律及所使用的实验手段和思维方法的自然科学。物理学是人们对无生命自然界中物质的转变知识做出规律性总结。现在,物理学已成为自然科学中最基础的学科之一。物理理论通常是以数学的形式表达出来。经过大量严格的实验验证的物理学规律被称为物理定律。然而如同其他很多自然科学理论一样,这些定律不能被证明,其正确性只能靠着反复的实验和观测来检验。

物理学是一种自然科学,主要研究的是物质,在时空中物质的运动,和所有相关概念,包括能量和作用力。更广义地说,物理学是对于大自然的研究分析,目的是要明白宇宙的行为。

物理学是最古老的学术之一。在过去两千年,物理学与哲学、化学等经常被混淆在一起,相提并论。直到十六世纪科学革命之后,才单独成为一门现代科学。

在物理学的领域中,研究的是宇宙的基本组成要素:物质、能量、空间、时间及它们的相互作用;借由被分析的基本定律与法则来完整了解这个系统。物理在经典时代是由与它极相像的自然哲学的研究所组成的,直到十九世纪物理才从哲学中分离出来成为一门实证科学。

本文介绍了物理学的定义、范围、发展历史、组成要素等内容。文字平实、质朴,逻辑严密,概念清晰。

翻译操作步骤：

1）词汇层

相互作用 interaction；无生命自然界 the inanimate natural world；物理定律［物］physical law；相提并论 bracket...together；组成要素 component；实证科学 empirical science

2）句子层

E.g. 物理学是研究物质世界最基本的结构、最普遍的相互作用、最一般的运动规律及所使用的实验手段和思维方法的自然科学。

汉语句子架构结构往往是"话题＋评价"，表现为"主语＋'废话'（相对不重要的信息）＋重要信息"这样的行文模式。本句是这一模式的典型例子。然而，英语句式经常表现为"主语＋重要信息＋'废话'（相对不重要的信息）"这样的模式。汉译英时，译者须抓住汉语原文的核心信息，知晓大小信息间的逻辑关系，转换成目的语——英语的信息顺序，让相应的信息各就各位，以适当的形式表现出来。

就本句而言，核心信息是"物理学是自然科学"，转换成英语为"Physics is a discipline of natural science"（即"物理学是自然科学中的一个学科"，英文这样表述更客观）。

"研究物质世界……"的逻辑主语是"自然科学"（a discipline of natural science），这样自然应将"研究物质世界……"转换成定语从句，修饰"自然科学"。此外，"使用的实验手段和思维方法"表示方法。根据信息之间的关系，我们得知欲译作定语从句的内容——"研究物质世界最基本的结构、最普遍的相互作用、最一般的运动规律及所使用的实验手段和思维方法"——其实表达的是"用什么方法（使用的实验手段和思维方法）来研究什么对象（研究物质世界最基本的结构、最普遍的相互作用、最一般的运动规律）"这个概念。将并列关系的信息一一罗列即可。所以，本句可译为：Physics is a discipline of natural science that uses experimental methods and thinking modes to study matter, its most basic structures, its most common forms of interactions and its most general laws of motion.

E.g. 物理学是人们对无生命自然界中物质的转变知识做出规律性总结。

将本句缩到最短，即是"物理学是总结"，这是本句的核心信息，按照英语句子层核心信息应尽量先行表达（置于句首）的做法，应译到句首，其他信息按照逻辑关系设法附着在核心信息之上。本句可译为：Physics presents a summary of the laws governing the changes which take place in inanimate matter in the natural world. 英语是形合语言，表达时信息之间的关系须尽可能明示。在本译文中，"规律"（laws）和"转变知识"（changes）之间添加"governing"（支配），这样逻辑才通畅。"无生命自然界中物质的转变知识"中"的"前作前置定语的信息可译作定语从句。

E.g. 然而如同其他很多自然科学理论一样，这些定律不能被证明，其正确性只能靠着反复的实验和观测来检验。

翻译本句时，译者要注意到，从原文信息转换成英文信息时可解读出"not...unless"这个英文结构。同时，要坚持"能直译要直译，能顺译要顺译"的翻译原则，正确罗列信息顺序。本句可译为:Like many other theories of natural science, however, these laws cannot be proven correct unless they are repeatedly tested through observations and experiments.

【参考译文】

Physics

Physics is a discipline of natural science that uses experimental methods and thinking modes to study matter, its most basic structures, its most common forms of interactions and its most general laws of motion. Physics presents a summary of the laws governing the changes which take place in inanimate matter in the natural world. Today, physics has become one of the most basic disciplines of the natural sciences. Physical theories are normally expressed in mathematical form. Physical rules which are validated by a number of strictly controlled experiments are termed "laws of physics". Like many other theories of natural science, however, these laws cannot be proven correct unless they are repeatedly tested through observations and experiments.

Physics, as a natural science, mainly studies the movement of matter (in space and time) and all interrelated concepts, including energy and force. More broadly speaking, physics is the study and analysis of nature whose goal is to understand the behavior of the universe.

Physics is one of the oldest disciplines. During the past two thousand years, physics, philosophy, chemistry, and so on, have often been confused and thus, classified together. It was not until after the scientific revolution in the 16th century that physics became a modern science.

In the field of physics, the object of study is the basic components that make up the universe: matter, energy, space, time and their interactions. Basic laws and rules are analyzed to help understand this system completely. Physics grew out of classical natural philosophy, to which it is very similar, and did not develop into an empirical science until the nineteenth century when it was separated from philosophy.

【原文2】

急性单核细胞白血病(M5)是急性髓性白血病中较常见的类型,临床表现具有髓外浸润、高白细胞计数、完全缓解率低、无病存活时间短、预后差、死亡率高,常规化疗的总体疗效有限等特点。免疫治疗是目前最有希望彻底清除白血病微小残留病灶、延长治疗后缓解期、预防复发的疗法,其中肿瘤疫苗已在部分白血病患者中获得肯定疗效。近年来,已有数个被自身CTL所识别的肿瘤抗原基因被发现,许多由这些肿瘤抗原基因编码的HLA-Ⅰ类分子限制性CTL表位也被相继证实。在这些肿瘤抗原基因中,MLAA抗原(MLAA-22,MLAA-34)基因已被证实在急性单核细胞白血病中有高表达,而在正常组织中未见表达。MLAA-22

(GENEBANK 登录号：AAQ93061.1)为我室首次报道，它与急性单核细胞白血病关系密切。

尽管对急性单核细胞白血病的治疗已取得一些临床进展，但对于晚期患者的治疗和预防复发及转移的疗效仍不理想。鉴于 AML 极差的预后，在化疗或干细胞移植之后，患者十分需要一种新疗法来消除体内残留的白血病细胞以减少复发的危险。靶向作用于白血病相关抗原是一种能改善 AML 治疗结果、防止复发的免疫治疗方法。白血病相关抗原已显示在白血病患者可诱发特异性 T 细胞免疫反应，因而成为特异免疫治疗的潜在靶标。免疫治疗目前虽主要作为临床治疗辅助手段，但被认为是有希望的治疗手段。由于中国 AML 患者中 HLA－A＊0201比例较高，因此研究限制性的 MLAA－22 HLA－A＊0201抗原表位以诱导针对 TPH－1 细胞的特异性 CTL 具有十分重要的意义。

上段文字是笔者曾经翻译过的一篇医学专业文章中的 2 个段落信息，其中有很多专业术语，如"髓性白血病""髓外浸润""病灶""肿瘤抗原"。作为非医学专业人士，译者翻译时要更加细心，应用医学专业的术语和原理，用英语完整再现原文信息，符合医学英语的表达规范。

翻译操作步骤：

1）词汇层

单核细胞白血病 monocytic leukemia；髓性白血病 myeloid leukemia；髓外浸润 extramedullary infiltration；化疗 chemotherapy；病灶 residual disease；肿瘤疫苗 tumor vaccine；肿瘤抗原基因 tumor antigen gene；预后 prognosis

2）句子层

E. g. 急性单核细胞白血病(M5)是急性髓性白血病中较常见的类型，临床表现具有髓外浸润、高白细胞计数、完全缓解率低、无病存活时间短、预后差、死亡率高，常规化疗的总体疗效有限等特点。

这个句子包含 2 个意思，翻译时需要断为 2 句。"临床表现具有……特点"中有较多的并列信息，翻译时须注意确保信息呈并列形式；还要将汉语表达法转换成英语的表达法，如"临床特点包括……"。所以，这个句子可译为：Acute monocytic leukemia (M5) is a common type of acute myeloid leukemia. Its clinical features include extramedullary infiltration, high white blood cell count, low complete remission rate, short disease-free survival time, poor prognosis, high mortality rate, limit effect of conventional chemotherapy, and et al.

E. g. 近年来，已有数个被自身 CTL 所识别的肿瘤抗原基因被发现，许多由这些肿瘤抗原基因编码的 HLA－Ⅰ类分子限制性 CTL 表位也被相继证实。

专业文章翻译看似比较难，实则不然。首先，"难"主要表现在术语和原理上，译者须确保词汇层用词规范，原理无错误；其次，专业文章表述一般不会有第二个意思；最后，在确保术语和原理无误后，透彻理解信息之间的关系，学会用目的语明示信息之间的关系，即可动手翻译了。

翻译"许多由这些肿瘤抗原基因编码的 HLA－Ⅰ类分子限制性 CTL 表位"前，译者一定要抓住核心意思，透彻理解信息之间关系。本句核心信息是"CTL 表位"，主要有 2 个修饰语：

"HLA-I类分子限制性"和"由这些肿瘤抗原基因编码的",转换成英语修饰语,一前一后修饰核心信息,即可动手翻译了。本句可译为:Recently, several tumor antigen genes recognized by CTL itself have been found, and lots of HLA-I restricted CTL epitopes coded by tumor antigen genes have been certified one after another.

E.g. 由于中国AML患者中HLA-A*0201比例较高,因此研究限制性的MLAA-22 HLA-A*0201抗原表位以诱导针对TPH-1细胞的特异性CTL具有十分重要的意义。

本句的翻译困难在"因此研究限制性的MLAA-22 HLA-A*0201抗原表位以诱导针对TPH-1细胞的特异性CTL具有十分重要的意义"。首先,译者须透彻理解信息,抓住核心信息,可知此处主要结构为"研究……以诱导……特异性具有十分重要的意义"。其次,搭建英语句式。本句的核心信息"研究……具有十分重要的意义",一般须用it作形式主语,"研究……"作真正的主语搭建英语句子架子。本句可译为:For a high expression rate of HLA-A*0201 in Chinese AML patients, it has a very important significance to research the restricted antigen epitope of MLAA-22 HLA-A*0201 CTL epitope for the induction of specificity CTL on TPH-1 cells.

【参考译文】

Acute monocytic leukemia (M5) is a common type of acute myeloid leukemia. Its clinical features include extramedullary infiltration, high white blood cell count, low complete remission rate, short disease-free survival time, poor prognosis, high mortality rate, limit effect of conventional chemotherapy, and et al. Currently immunotherapy is the most hopeful treatment to remove leukemia minimal residual disease completely, prolonged remission period and prevent recurrence. Among immunotherapy, tumor vaccine has presented positive effect in some leukemia patients. Recently, several tumor antigen genes recognized by CTL itself have been found, and lots of HLA-I restricted CTL epitopes coded by tumor antigen genes have been certified one after another. In these tumor antigen genes, MLAA (MLAA-22, MLAA-34) genes have been proved high expression in Acute monocytic leukemia, while none expression in normal organ. MLAA-22 (Gene bank number: AAQ93061.1) was first reported by our department, which had a close relationship with acute monocytic leukemia.

Although some treatments for acute monocytic leukemia have made some clinical progress, the curative effect and the prevention of recurrence and metastasis in terminal cancer patients are still not ideal. As the poor prognosis of AML, patients badly need a new treatment to eliminate residual leukemia cells to reduce the risk of recurrence after chemotherapy or stem cell transplantation. Targeting leukemia associated antigen is an immunotherapy method to improve the AML treatment results and prevent recurrence. Leukemia associated antigen has showed an effective induction of specific T cell immune response in leukemia patients. Therefore, it has been a potential target in specific immunotherapy. Immunotherapy, as a major complimentary clinical approach, has been considered a promising treatment method. For a high expression rate of HLA - A * 0201 in Chinese AML patients, it has a very important significance to research the restricted antigen epitope of MLAA - 22 HLA - A * 0201 CTL epitope for the induction of specificity CTL on TPH - 1 cells.

练 习 题

一、英译汉练习

Network topology

The physical layout of a network is usually less important than the topology that connects network nodes. Most diagrams that describe a physical network are therefore topological, rather than geographic. The symbols on these diagrams usually denote network links and network nodes.

Network links

The transmission media (often referred to in the literature as the physical media) used to link devices to form a computer network include electrical cable (Ethernet, HomePNA, power line communication, G. hn), optical fiber (fiber-optic communication), and radio waves (wireless networking). In the OSI model, these are defined at layers 1 and 2—the physical layer and the data link layer.

A widely adopted family of transmission media used in local area network (LAN) technology is collectively known as Ethernet. The media and protocol standards that enable communication between networked devices over Ethernet are defined by IEEE 802. 3. Ethernet transmits data over both copper and fiber cables. Wireless LAN standards (e. g. those defined by IEEE 802. 11) use radio waves, or other infrared signals as a transmission medium. Power line communication uses a building's power cabling to transmit data.

(作者不详,维基百科)

二、汉译英练习

计算机系统是按人的要求接收和存储信息,自动进行数据处理和计算,并输出结果信息的机器系统。计算机是脑力的延伸和扩充,是近代科学的重大成就之一。

计算机系统由硬件(子)系统和软件(子)系统组成。前者是借助电、磁、光、机械等原理构成的各种物理部件的有机组合,是系统赖以工作的实体。后者是各种程序和文件,用于指挥全系统按指定的要求进行工作。

自1946年第一台电子计算机问世以来,计算机技术在元件器件、硬件系统结构、软件系统、应用等方面均有惊人进步,现代计算机系统小到微型计算机和个人计算机,大到巨型计算机及其网络,形态、特性多种多样,已广泛用于科学计算、事务处理和过程控制,日益深入社会各个领域,对社会的进步产生深刻影响。

(作者不详,360百科词条名:计算机系统)

第九章　工作留学语篇的翻译

一、书信的翻译

1. 书信的特点

书信由笺文及封文两部分构成。笺文即写在信笺上的文字,即寄信人对收信人的招呼、问候、祝颂等。笺文是书信内容的主体,书信的繁简、俗雅及其他方面的风格特征,几乎都由内容主体决定。

书信是正式的交流方式,一般情况下,写信人要流露出真情实感,清晰地叙述或议论等,语言质朴,格式完整。英文书信种类较多,一般包含以下内容。

(1) 信封(envelope)

英语的信封和中文的一样,主要由三部分组成,即发信人地址、收信人地址和邮票。英文发信人地址和收信人地址书写位置与汉语恰恰相反,信息顺序由小到大(见图9.1),而汉语由大到小。

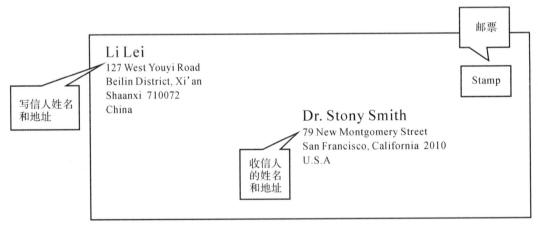

图 9.1　信封

(2) 信头(heading)

信头即发信人的地址和日期(一般写在信纸的右上角)。(不一定都有)

(3) 信内地址(inside address)

信内地址即收信人的姓名和地址(写信日期下隔一行靠右侧书写)。(不一定都有)

(4) 称呼(salutation)

称呼即写对收信人的尊称。

(5) 正文(body)

正文即信件内的主要内容。

(6)信尾客套语(complimentary close)

(7)信尾签名(signature)

2.书信翻译实例

【原文1】

5 November, 2005

A Letter of Invitation

Dear Mr. Zhang,

  We would like to invite you to visit our factory and give you an overview of our facilities and production methods from November 15 to November 20. This would also be an opportunity for you to visit our Head Office in Los Angeles to meet our design team and Marketing and Sales Directors to discuss common areas of interest.

  As you would be our guest, we would of course meet all your expenses. We can also put a company car and driver at your disposal during your stay here.

  I do hope your schedule will allow you to accept our invitation.

  I look forward to meeting you here.

Yours sincerely,
Angela Goddard
Communication Manager

  所有翻译操作都是在英汉语言强烈的差异意识下完成的,因为翻译是目的语写作(甚至是重写),只有在差异意识下完成词层(准确措辞)、句子层(句子结构的搭建)、段落层(段落中信息的推进和段落话题的突显)和篇章层(篇章结构合理安排)的转换,译文才会字正句顺,言之有理。

  汉语的写信日期位于信末签名下,这是汉语和英语书信的不同之一。

  翻译操作步骤:

1)词汇层

  overview 综述;概观;common areas of interest 共同感兴趣的话题;meet expense 支付费用;at one's disposal 由其支配,由某人做主;Yours sincerely 谨启;communication manager 公关部经理

2)句子层

  E. g. We would like to invite you to visit our factory and give you an overview of our facilities and production methods from November 15 to November 20.

  这个句子比较易于理解。翻译时,译者要注意口吻和译文的阅读效果。这是一封邀请函,属于正式文体,字里行间要透出邀请人的诚意和敬意,所以"We would like to invite you to…"不宜按照字面译为"我们愿意邀请你……"。"give you an overview of…"也不宜翻译成"给你一个……的概述",否则会显得语言没有力量感。因为汉语是动态语言,动词使用频

繁。本句可译为:我们诚邀您于 11 月 15 日到 11 月 20 日期间参观我们的工厂,届时会向您大致介绍我们厂的设备和生产方法。

E. g. This would also be an opportunity for you to visit our Head Office in Los Angeles to meet our design team and Marketing and Sales Directors to discuss common areas of interest.

书面英语物称多(主语为物),汉语人称多(主语为人)。如果按照字面翻译,这句话的汉语意思是"对您来说……这将是一个机会",但这样读来不够通顺。译者最好迎合汉语人称多用的特点重述原文信息,可将本句译为:您将有机会访问我们洛杉矶总部,与我们的设计团队和市场营销总监会面,讨论我们共同感兴趣的话题。

【参考译文】

邀 请 函

尊敬的张先生:

我们诚邀您于 11 月 15 日到 11 月 20 日期间参观我们的工厂,届时会向您大致介绍我们厂的设备和生产方法。您将有机会访问我们洛杉矶总部,与我们的设计团队和市场营销总监会面,讨论我们共同感兴趣的话题。

您是我们的客人,我们当然会为您支付全部的费用。在您来访期间,我们会准备一辆公司轿车并配备专职司机供您使用、差遣。

我真心希望您日程宽松,这样您就可以接受我们的邀请了。

我盼望着与您在此相见!

谨启

公关经理 安吉拉·戈达德
2005 年 11 月 5 日

【原文 2】

Samuel Johnson's letter to Lord Chesterfield

To the Right Honorable the Earl of Chesterfield

7th February, 1755

My Lord,

I have been lately informed, by the proprietor of *The World* that two papers, in which my Dictionary is recommended to the public, were written by your lordship. To be so distinguished is an honor which, being very little accustomed to favors from the great, I know not well how to receive, or in what terms to acknowledge.

When, upon some slight encouragement, I first visited your lordship, I was overpowered, like the rest of mankind, by the enchantment of your address, and could not forbear to wish that I might boast myself "Le vainqueur du vainqueur de la terre"—that I might obtain that regard for which I saw the world contending; but I found my attendance so little encouraged, that neither pride nor modesty would suffer me to continue it. When I had once addressed your Lordship in public, I had exhausted all the art of pleasing which a retired and uncourtly scholar can possess. I had done all that I could; and no man is well pleased to have his all neglected, be it ever so little.

Seven years, my lord, have now passed, since I waited in your outward rooms, or was repulsed from your door; during which time I have been pushing on my work through difficulties, of which it is useless to complain, and have brought it, at last, to the verge of publication, without one act of assistance, one word of encouragement, or one smile of favor. Such treatment I did not expect, for I never had a patron before. The shepherd in Virgil grew at last acquainted with Love, and found him a native of the rocks.

Is not a patron my lord, one who looks with unconcern on a man struggling for life in the water, and, when he has reached ground, encumbers him with help? The notice which you have been pleased to take of my labors, had it been early, had been kind; but it has been delayed till I am indifferent, and cannot enjoy it; till I am solitary, and cannot impart it; till I am known, and do not want it. I hope it is no very cynical asperity not to confess obligations where no benefit has been received, or to be unwilling that the public should consider me as owing that to a patron, which providence has enabled me to do for myself.

Having carried on my work thus far with so little obligation to any favorer of learning, I shall not be disappointed though I should conclude it, if less be possible, with less; for I have been long wakened from that dream of hope, in which I once boasted myself with so much exultation.

My Lord,

Your lordship's most humble, most obedient servant,

SAM. JOHNSON.

这封信是塞缪尔·约翰逊于1755年2月7日写给切斯特菲尔德伯爵菲力普·多默·斯坦霍普(Philip Dormer Stanhope)名传千秋的著名信函,不仅思想深刻,而且文笔优美,语句典雅。

翻译操作步骤：

1)词汇层

lord(此处指)伯爵；earl(英)伯爵；proprietor(企业等的)业主,老板；lordship 阁下；贵族身份(或权威)；Le vainqueur du vainqueur de la terre 吾乃天下征服者之征服者也；regard 敬重；contend for 争夺；uncourtly 无礼的；patron 赞助人；solitary 孤独的；cynical 愤世嫉俗的；asperity(性格)粗暴；humble(级别或地位)低下的；obedient 顺从的

2)句子层

E. g. I have been lately informed, by the proprietor of *The World* that two papers, in which my Dictionary is recommended to the public, were written by your lordship.

本句属于英语主从复合句,措辞较正式,句式较复杂,但易于理解,翻译起来不难。书面英语多用被动语态,而汉语多用主动语态,所以译者翻译时要语态转换适当,这样译文读起来顺畅。然后,对于英语长句,译者须厘清信息之间关系,按照汉语"话题＋评价"模式再现原文信

息。辜正坤先生将本句译为:近日从《世界报》馆主得知,该报刊载了两篇文章,对拙编词典颇多举荐滥美之词,这些文章据悉均出自阁下您的手笔。

E. g. When, upon some slight encouragement, I first visited your lordship, I was overpowered, like the rest of mankind, by the enchantment of your address, and could not forbear to wish that I might boast myself "Le vainqueur du vainqueur de la terre"—that I might obtain that regard for which I saw the world contending.

本句翻译较难。根据上下文,"upon some slight encouragement"中的"encouragement"不宜直译为"鼓励",因为没有这一动作的发出者。

英语是形合语言,是"化零为整"的语言,信息之间的关系须通过词法、语法或句法明示,信息环环相扣,表述似一气呵成。汉语是意合语言,是"化整为零"的语言,信息之间的关系隐藏在字里行间,语言表述似竹子生长,一节一节相连。辜正坤先生将此句译为:回想当年,也不知哪来的勇气,我竟第一次拜访了大人阁下。我像所有的人一样,深为大人的言谈丰采所倾倒,不禁玄想他年能口出大言"吾乃天下征服者之征服者也"。虽知此殊荣是举世学人所欲得,仍希望有朝一日能侥幸获取。这个译文将原英语1个句子断为汉语3个句子,分别表达。这样处理源于英汉语言的表述差异。

E. g. I hope it is no very cynical asperity not to confess obligations where no benefit has been received, or to be unwilling that the public should consider me as owing that to a patron, which providence has enabled me to do for myself.

辜正坤先生将此句译为:既然是上帝助我独立完成这桩大业,我自然不愿让公众产生错觉,似乎我曾受惠于某一赞助人。但愿上面这番话不致被认为太苛刻、太不近人情。

辜正坤先生显然深入地理解了原文信息之间的关系,大胆地做了信息调整,从句末起笔翻译,有增译——"让公众产生错觉",有省译——"where no benefit has been received",译文读来圆滑顺畅,一点儿也没有翻译腔,译文与原文信息等量。这样的译文让人不由得敬佩辜正坤先生对原文入木三分的理解力和高超的汉语语言驾驭力。

【参考译文】

致切斯特菲尔德大人函

——给正直、高贵的切斯特菲尔德伯爵

伯爵大人:

近日从《世界报》馆主得知,该报刊载了两篇文章,对拙编词典颇多举荐滥美之词,这些文章据悉均出自阁下您的手笔。承蒙您如此的推崇,本应是一种荣耀,只可惜在下自来无缘得到王公大人的青睐,所以真不知道该如何来领受这份荣耀,也不知道该用些什么言辞来聊表谢意。

回想当年,也不知哪来的勇气,我竟第一次拜访了大人阁下。我像所有的人一样,深为大人的言谈丰采所倾倒,不禁玄想他年能口出大言"吾乃天下征服者之征服者也"。虽知此殊荣是举世学人所欲得,仍希望有朝一日能侥幸获取。然而我很快发现自己的趋走逢迎根本没有得到鼓励。不管是出于自尊也好,自矜也好,我反正无法再周旋下去。我本是一个与世无争、不善逢迎的书生,但那时我也曾尽平生所学的阿谀奉承的言辞,当众赞美过阁下。能做的一切我都做了。如果一个人在这方面付出的一切努力（不管是多么微不足道）受到完全的忽视，他是绝不会感到舒服的。

大人阁下，从我第一次候立于贵府门下，或者说被您拒于门外时算起，已经7年过去了。7年多来，我一直苦苦地撑持着我的编撰工作。这些苦楚，现在再来倾诉，已经没有用处。所幸我的劳作而今终于快要出版，在这之前我没有获得过一个赞助的行为，一句鼓励的话语，一抹称许的微笑。我固然不曾指望这样的礼遇，因为我从未有过一位赞助人。维吉尔笔下的牧童最后终于和爱神相识，这才发现所谓爱神只不过是岩穴土人而已。

大人阁下，有的人眼见落水者在水中拼命挣扎而无动于衷，等他安全抵岸之后，却才多余地伸出所谓援手，莫非这就叫赞助人么？大人而今忽有雅兴来关照在下的劳作，这原本是一桩美意，只可惜太迟了一点。迟到我已经意懒心灰，再无法快乐地消受；迟到我已经是孤身一人，无从与家人分享；迟到我已经名闻海内，再不需阁下附丽张扬。我既然本来就没有得到过实惠，自然无须怀感恩之心；既然是上帝助我独立完成这桩大业，我自然不愿让公众产生错觉，似乎我曾受惠于某一赞助人。但愿上面这番话不致被认为太苛刻、太不近人情。

我已经在根本没有所谓学术赞助人赞助的情况下使自己的工作完成到目前这个地步，那么，尽管我将要在更艰难无助的情况下——假如还有可能更艰难无助的话——完成全稿，我也绝不会感到沮丧。因为我已经早就从那个赞助的美梦里幡然猛醒；曾几何时，我还在那梦中得意非凡地自诩是大人。

您门下最卑微、最驯顺的仆人
塞缪尔·约翰逊
1755年2月7日
（辜正坤先生白话体译文）

二、个人简历的翻译

1. 个人简历的特点

一般情况下，个人简历是求职、求学时申请者须提供给有关单位或部门的重要材料。在个人简历中，申请者除提供姓名、籍贯、联系方式等基本信息外，还要提供自己学历、工作经历、获奖情况等重要信息。个人简历一旦审核通过将会获得面试机会，提高申请的成功概率。个人简历有以下几个特点。

（1）真实性

真实性是个人简历重要的特点。申请人须提供真实的个人所有情况，而且最好附有佐证材料，这样就增加了个人简历上信息的可信度。材料的真实性直接反映申请人的诚信品质。

（2）正面性

个人简历的正面性即在写个人简历的时候，要以正面的信息为主。"金无足赤，人无完人。"申请人提供的信息一般都是正面的，这样会获得一个正面的印象，加大把自己推销出去的可能性。非正面的信息要尽可能省略。

（3）简洁性

个人简历，顾名思义，就是"个人简洁的经历"，书写时要精简，不拖泥带水。英文的个人简历主要分为短语和句子两种形式。申请人提供的信息最好以短语的形式出现，这样信息历历在目，一目了然。

2. 个人简历的翻译实例
(1)英译汉
【原文】

Resume

Jim Johnson

Houston, Texas 77034,

(315) 525-5445

Jimjohnson@yahoo.com

Objective:

An opportunity to obtain a treasury analyst position in a finance company that can allow me to apply my knowledge of accounting and finance.

Education:

Bachelor's Degree in Finance, University of Houston (1991)

Master of Business Administration in Finance, University of Houston (1993)

Special Knowledge, Abilities, Skills:

Strong analytical skills to perform in depth financial analysis

Strong accounting, negotiation, and influencing skills

Ability in interface with senior levels of management internally and externally

Strong knowledge of financial principles and capital markets

Proficient with MS Excel, Word and PowerPoint

Excellent verbal and written communication skills

Excellent customer service skills

Professional Experience:

1. Pfizer, Inc., Houston, TX (1997—Present)

Senior Treasury Analyst

Responsibilities:

Performed analysis of all daily and non-daily financial treasury operations activities

Participated in cross-functional finance projects as necessary

Assisted in developing and performing treasury transactions according to personal goals, objectives and annual accountabilities

Worked closely with business customers to identify, prioritize and document business requirements

2. FMC Technologies, Houston, TX, (1993—1997)

Treasury Analyst

Responsibilities:

Prepared internal treasury reporting

Assisted with subsidiary capital structure management

Analyzed operating procedures for the purpose of improving or replacing with more effective substitutes

Assisted in the design, testing and implementation of new or enhanced information systems

个人简历属于实用文体文本(如书信、个人简历、通知等),尤其是以短语的形式书写的个人简历,比一般非实用文体文本易于翻译。译者准确把握原文信息之后,忠实、通顺地用译入语再现原文信息即可。

本篇属于较短的个人简历,其中 Professional Experience 部分的信息以句子的形式呈现,省略了主语"I"而已。

【参考译文】

个 人 简 历

吉姆·约翰逊
地址:得克萨斯州休斯敦市
邮编:77034
电话:(315) 525-5445
邮箱:Jimjohnson@yahoo.com

求职目标
在一家金融公司谋得财务分析师职位,将我的会计和金融知识加以应用。

学历
休斯敦大学　金融学士学位(1991年)
休斯敦大学　工商管理硕士(1993年)

专门知识、能力和技能
强大的分析能力,可执行财务深度分析
强大的会计、谈判和影响力技能
能够与内部和外部的高层管理人员沟通
熟悉金融原理和资本市场
熟练使用微软公司的 Excel、Word 和 PowerPoint
优秀的口头和书面沟通能力
优秀的客户服务能力

从业经历
1. 得州休斯敦辉瑞制药公司（1997年至今）
职位:高级财务分析师
职责:
对所有日常和非日常财务运作活动进行分析
必要时参与跨部门金融项目
根据个人目标、工作目标和年度岗位职责,协助开发和执行国库券交易
与企业客户紧密合作,确定、优先处理和记录业务需求

2.得州休斯敦美信达科技公司(1993—1997年)
职位:财务分析师
职责:
准备内部财政报告
辅助津贴结构管理
分析操作程序,以求改进或替换为更高效的操作程序
协助设计、测试和应用新的或增强版信息系统
(2)汉译英

个 人 简 历

姓名:×××

性别:女

民族:汉

籍贯:云南昆明

出生日期:1989年4月2日

教育背景

1. 2007年9月—2010年7月,云南师范大学文理学院对外汉语(汉泰)专业
2. 2010年8月—2011年7月,赴泰国实习,在泰国一小学担任中文老师

主修课程

泰语口语、听力,基础泰语,泰国历史概况,泰国社会及宗教,中国现代文学,新闻学概论,语言学概论,人际关系学,教育学和基本教学理论,公共关系学,跨文化交际,大学英语等

求职意向

外贸商务、泰语翻译、新闻工作类或行政管理类

社会实践与校园活动

1. 在校期间参加学校开办的各项活动。与泰国同学共同组织了多项表演活动,增强了自己的团队合作精神。
2. 曾在学校组织的对外汉语文化节中,接待泰国朋友学生,带领泰国朋友参观学校,参加各项交流活动,提高了自己的交际沟通能力。
3. 2010年10月到2011年7月赴泰担任泰国一小学的中文老师,不仅提高了自己的泰语会话水平,也传播了中国语言和文化。
4. 参加出演了学院以及班级组织的健美操比赛和话剧表演,陶冶了情操,提高了自己的素养。

兴趣爱好

跑步、登山、舞蹈、音乐、交际

自我评价

本人性格开朗乐观、为人诚恳、独立自主,不断进取,吃苦耐劳,拥有较强的适应能力和组织、公关能力,能很好地与人沟通,具有团队合作精神,对工作会付出全部精力和热情。有不到最后一刻绝不轻易放弃的恒心和毅力。

【参考译文】

Resume

Name: ×××

Gender: Female

Ethnicity: Han

Native place: Kunming, Yunnan Province

Date of Birth: April 2, 1989

Education

1. Yunnan Normal University, School of Arts and Sciences, September 2007—July 2010 Major: Chinese as a Foreign Language

2. Primary school, Thailand, August 2010—July 2011   Internship: Teacher of Chinese

Main Courses Taken

Thai Speaking and Listening, Basic Thai, Survey of Thai History, Historical Prevue in Thailand, Thai Society and Religion, Modern Chinese Literature, An Introduction to Journalism, An Introduction to Linguistics, Interpersonal Relations, Pedagogy and Basic Teaching Theories, Public Relations, Intercultural Communication, College English, etc.

Employment Preferences

Foreign Trade and Commerce, Thai Translation, Journalism, Business Administration (or Management)

Social & Campus Activities

1. As a university student, I participated in a variety of school activities. My team spirit increased while co-organizing many performance events together with Thai students.

2. During the Chinese cultural festival, which was organized by the school, I welcomed Thai students and showed them around the campus. I also participated in many language exchange activities and my communication skills improved accordingly.

3. I went to teach Chinese in a primary school in Thailand from October 2010 to July 2011. As a result, I not only spread knowledge of the Chinese language and culture, but also improved my Thai conversational skills.

4. I participated in aerobic dance contests and modern drama performances on both the class and school levels, thereby adding to my accomplishments while cultivating my character.

Hobbies

Jogging, mountain climbing, dancing, music, social interaction

Self-assessment

I am optimistic, sincere, independent, and enterprising as well as industrious and able to bear hardships. Furthermore, I possess a strong adaptive, organizational and PR capacity as well as very good interpersonal skills and a cooperative team spirit. In addition, I invest all my passion and energy in my work. Perseverance and willpower will triumph in the end.

三、个人陈述的翻译

1. 个人陈述的特点

对于学生来说,个人陈述是申请学习或工作时由申请人写的关于自我的一篇漫谈体文章。欧美大学录取学生、发放奖学金是通过全面综合考察申请者的条件来决定的,如果个人陈述写作得当,可以很大程度地提高申请者被录取和获得奖学金的机会,所以自我陈述也是重要的申请材料之一。

一般情况下,个人陈述包含以下内容:申请者的学术或专业兴趣及背景;欲研究的方向;未来的职业目标。

一篇成功的个人陈述具有以下特点:语言流畅;逻辑严谨;层次分明;充分显示申请人的才华并抓住审阅人的注意力。

要明确陈述申请人的长处、资格、团队精神、长短期目标、经验等信息;要紧紧抓住审阅人的注意力,甚至超越审阅人的期待,达到"非你不录"的效果。

【案例】

2017年,17岁女孩×××收到了美国常春藤盟校的录取通知书,成为华人世界的热门话题。

这8所学校分别是享誉世界的哈佛大学、耶鲁大学、普林斯顿大学、布朗大学、哥伦比亚大学、康奈尔大学、宾夕法尼亚大学及达特茅斯学院。这些大学都是美国首屈一指的大学,历史悠久,治学严谨,许多著名的科学家、政界要人、商贾巨子都毕业于此。在美国,常春藤盟校被视为顶尖名校的代名词。

有人说,该女生之所以这么受常春藤盟校青睐是因为她写的个人陈述很优秀。笔者不认同这个说法,她一定还有其他过硬的资质(如成绩、技能、证书等)。我们先欣赏2段她写的个人陈述吧。

In our house, English is not English. Not in the phonetic sense, like short a is for apple, but rather in the pronunciation—in our house, snake is snack. Words do not roll off our tongues correctly—yet I, who was pulled out of class to meet with language specialists, and my mother from Malaysia, who pronounces film as flim, understand each other perfectly.

[在我们家,英语不是英语,不是在语音意义上,而是发音上的。在我们家,"snake"(蛇)会被读成"snack"(小吃)。我们的舌头总是卷不对。我常被语言专家纠正发音,我妈妈来自马来西亚,她说"film"的时候总是发成"flim",但是我们完全能听得懂对方。]

In our house, there is no difference between cast and cash, which was why at a church retreat, people made fun of me for "cashing out demons". I did not realize the glaring difference between the two Englishes until my teacher corrected my pronunciations of hammock, ladle, and siphon. Classmates laughed because I pronounce accept as except, success as sussess. I was in the Creative Writing conservatory, and yet words failed me when I needed them most.

[在我们家,"cast"(抛掷)和"cash"(兑现、现金)没有分别,这就是为什么在离开教堂时,人们常常取笑我"cashing out demons"(兑现恶魔,本应为赶走恶魔)。我没有意识到两个英语

单词之间的差异,直到老师纠正了我的 hammock、ladle 和 siphon 的发音。同学们笑我,因为我将 accept(接受)读成 except(除外),将 success 读成 sussess。尽管我已参加了创意写作,但常常词不达意。]

从这两段英文文字可见,该女生的个人陈述具有语言流畅、逻辑严谨、层次分明等特点,语言生动有趣,真的会抓住审阅人的注意力。

2. 个人陈述翻译实例

(1)英译汉

【原文】

Personal Statement

I have completed my four year Bachelor of Technology program at the Indian Institute of Technology, Bombay. I graduated in July 1998 with a degree in Mechanical Engineering. Many of my courses and research activities in the final year were in the field of Industrial Engineering and Operations Research with a strong focus on production and operations management. I am presently working in Tata Technologies India Ltd., an information technology firm that is involved in the areas of enterprise integration and CAD/CAM. I am applying for admission and financial aid to the Ph.D. program in Operations Management at the Krannert Graduate School of Management, Purdue University. Detailed information about my academic record and my research and other experience is attached to this statement.

I was introduced to mathematics and the physical sciences while at school and it was in high school that I considered a career in this area. The desire to study the applied physical sciences and mathematics prompted me to take the Joint Entrance Examination (JEE) for admission to the Indian Institutes of Technology. I was ranked in the top 0.25% of the nearly 100,000 students who took the examination.

My undergraduate education at IIT Bombay has not only given me a certain set of skills but has also helped me understand my fields of interest and my academic strengths and weaknesses. This understanding has made me realize that though the applied physical sciences appeal to me, my strengths lie in applied mathematics and in abstractions of reality. In particular, I am interested in the managerial aspects of industrial and technological systems. This interest developed during my junior year seminar titled "Productivity Management" in which I explored the relationship between manufacturing strategy and productivity improvement. I continued further research in this area through my senior year project titled "Decision Support System for Quality Control" which sought to investigate various decision making mechanisms in the quality function and provide corresponding computer support. The project also enabled me to appreciate the interaction between manufacturing and the other functions of the firm especially information systems. The reading of certain outstanding books during the course of my research such as Skinner's *Manufacturing in the Corporate Strategy*, Deming's *Out of the Crisis* and Goldratt's *The*

Goal finally convinced me to pursue a Ph. D. in operations management and an academic career thereafter.

My past work in the area of industrial engineering and operations research was characterised by a dichotomy of approaches. The courses that I took in this area dealt with various operational and tactical issues. The basic aim was to understand a specific problem, model the problem appropriately and find an optimal or reasonably optimal solution using the techniques of operations research. This has given me a good background in issues related to methodology, modelling, and heuristic solutions. On the other hand, my research has been oriented towards strategic issues. The basic thrust of my junior year seminar and senior year project has been "integrative". Through my future research efforts I would like to understand this dichotomy better. Initially, I want to study rigorous model-based methods and do research on operational and tactical topics. After gaining a thorough grounding in these topics, I am interested in applying the same methodologies and techniques to strategic topics in operations management.

I believe that I have the qualities to be a good researcher and teacher. I am a creative person and often think in a contemplative way about various issues of practical importance. Being able to identify patterns and relationships that are not obvious to others is perhaps my greatest strength. This will prove very valuable because an integral part of being a researcher and teacher is to perceive the balance between theory and practice, analytical rigor and intuition. My communication skills are good and I like expressing ideas and concepts both in oral and written form—an ideal platform for the dissemination of knowledge in my chosen field of specialization.

The Krannert Graduate School of Management is one of the best schools of management in the world with a strong orientation towards research. The diversity of research interests in the operations management group is of particular interest to me. The eminent faculty and the individualized nature of the doctoral program will definitely bring out the best in me. I would like to reiterate that I possess the background, the ability and the motivation to make a significant contribution to Operations Management. I hope you will take a favorable decision regarding my admission to the Ph. D. program and I look forward to joining the Krannert Graduate School of Management and Purdue University.

(作者不详,liuxue86.com)

【参考译文】

个 人 陈 述

在印度理工学院就读四年后,我已获得科技学士学位。1998 年 7 月,我毕业后获得机械工程学位。在学业最后一年里,我在工业工程和运营研究领域选修了许多课程,也做了很多研究工作,主要集中在生产和运营管理方面。目前,我在塔塔技术(印度)有限公司工作。该公司是一家从事企业整合、计算机辅助设计和计算机辅助制造领域的信息技术公司。我正在申请普渡大学克兰纳特管理研究院运营管理博士项目入学资格和经济资助。有关我的学习、研究和其他经历的详细信息附在这份陈述后。

在校时,我就开始接触数学和物理学知识。上高中时,我曾考虑过在这个领域从业。学习应用物理学和数学的愿望促使我参加联合入学考试并进入印度理工学院学习。在参加考试的近10万名学生中,我位列前250名。

在印度理工学院的本科学习期间,我不仅学得一套技能,而且了解到我感兴趣的领域,以及我的学术强项和弱项。这种理解使我认识到,尽管应用物理学对我很有吸引力,但是我的强项在于应用数学和现实生活中的抽象概念。尤其是,我对工业和技术系统的管理方面很感兴趣。大三时,我曾参加题为"生产力管理"的研讨会,探索了制造策略与提高生产力之间的关系,之后对这个领域产生了更浓厚的兴趣。大四时,通过"质量控制决策支持系统"项目,我在这一领域做了深入研究。该项目旨在调查质量功能中的各种决策机制,并提供相应的计算机支持。通过这个项目,我意识到公司制造和其他业务(特别是信息系统)之间存在交互作用。在研究期间,我阅读了一些优秀著作,比如斯金纳《企业战略下的制造业》、戴明的《转危为安》和高德拉特的《目标》等,最终让我坚定攻读运营管理博士学位、毕业后做学术研究工作的信念。

过去,我在工业工程和运营研究领域工作方法迥然不同。这个领域我学习的课程涉及各种运营和战术问题,基本目标是了解一个具体问题,适当地对问题进行建模,并利用运筹学技术找到一个最优或相对最优的解决方案。就这样,我学会了与方法论、建模和启发式解决方案有关的很多知识。另一方面,我的研究侧重战略问题。大三时我参加研讨会,大四时做项目,主要是想将二者结合起来。通过未来的研究工作,我希望能更好地理解这种分歧。起初,我想学习基于模型的严格方法,并研究运营和战术问题。对这些话题有了深入的了解之后,我有兴趣运用相同的方法和技术解决运营管理中的战略问题。

我相信我有能力成为一名优秀的研究者和教师。我是一个有创造力的人,经常沉思各种有实用价值的问题。能够识别别人不容易发现的模式和关系也许是我最大的优点。这一点将非常有价值,因为研究者和教师必须在理论与实践、分析的严密性和直觉之间找到平衡点。我的交际技能强,喜欢通过口头和书面形式表达想法和概念,这是我在选择的专业领域传播知识的理想方式。

克兰纳特管理研究院是世界上最好的管理学院之一,具有很强的研究倾向。我特别感兴趣的是运营管理团队研究兴趣的多样性。优秀的教师和个性化的博士课程肯定有助于我展示出最好的自我。我想重申的是,我拥有为运营管理做出重大贡献的背景、能力和动机。我希望您能对我的博士学位申请做出一个有利于我的决定。我期待着加入克兰纳特管理研究院和普渡大学。

(2)汉译英

【原文】

个 人 陈 述

我目前就读于×××大学。在学习当中,我逐渐体会到我心中真正感兴趣的两个研究领域是人力资源管理和精算学。此番衷情,首先源于我需要更正规的高等教育达到自我提高的强烈愿望,受到不遗余力想出人头地的鞭策,受到让我接触到各种实践活动和经历的机会的吸引,而现在,申请贵校研究生项目的强烈决心正为我的心愿护航。

我申请在××大学学习主要归因于其在人力资源管理和精算学研究方面斐然的国际声誉,通过相关学习我能够掌握最先进的理论知识以此来为中国人力资源或是精算学领域的发展和完善做出贡献。同时,我对于贵校不局限于教学大纲的独特的文化知识感到很兴奋。贵校丰富的人才和实践资源将开拓我的视野,让我的世界更宽更广。

我从来不局限于纯粹的纯理论学习,一直都致力于丰富我的大学生活,通过参加各种课外活动进一步提高能力。2008年,我和其他队友一起加入了艺术团,参与了众多活动,例如帮助组织校园歌手大赛,在篮球比赛和足球比赛的开幕仪式上跳舞,帮助主持蛋糕派对和时装秀等。接下来的大二学年,大一时期积累的各方面能力使我赢得了艺术团主席的职位,那也是我第一次接触管理层面的工作。

除了上述学校里的活动之外,我还参加了一些社会实践,例如荷兰皇家壳牌集团的实习和支教。这些社会实践增强了我作为一个人的责任感。这方面很好的例子就是我在2010年支教项目的实习经历。该项目旨在帮助落后乡村的学校。通过亲身经历,我体验到贫穷乡村地区不太好的教育条件,并且更加珍惜我拥有的较好的教育资源和多彩的城市生活。同时通过这次经历,我感觉到通过帮助其他人我实现了自我价值,并感受到为需要的人群表达人文主义关怀的义务。

人生总是令人惊奇,因为每天都有奇迹发生,只要我们足够坚忍,足够积极,足够勤奋。我也相信,贵校凭着良好的声誉,悠久的历史以及人文内涵将给学生提供优秀的老师,最有利的学习环境以及最优质的教育。这些都能够磨炼我的学习和实践技能,以此帮助我应对在我所选择的领域内目前和未来的挑战。我真诚地希望您慎重考虑我的申请。

期待您的回信!谢谢!

签名:申请人×××
(作者不详,百度文库)

【参考译文】

Personal Statement

I am presently studying at the ××× university. In the course of my studies, I have gradually realized that the two areas of research I am really interested in are human resource management and actuarial science. My love for these research areas has its origins in, firstly, a strong desire for self-improvement through the attainment of the higher education I need; secondly, an inner urge to do my utmost to excel; and thirdly, the attraction of opportunities to have new experiences and to participate in all kinds of practical activities. I eagerly hope that my dream will come true.

The reason why I am applying for admission to ××× university is its remarkable international reputation for human resource management and actuarial scientific research. Here, I will be able to master the most advanced theoretical knowledge and thereby contribute to the development and improvement of either the field of human resources, or that of actuarial science in China. At the same time, I am excited about the unique cultural knowledge, not restricted to the syllabus, which is available, at your university. The school's rich endowment of human and practical resources will expand my horizons and thus widen my world.

I have never limited my studies to purely theoretical issues. By taking part in various extra curricular activities, I have been constantly working to enrich my college life and improve my abilities. In 2008, I joined an art troupe, together with other teammates, and participated in many activities, such as helping organize campus singing contests and opening ceremony dancing for football and basketball games. I also hosted a cake party and a fashion show. I was elected chairman of the art troupe in my sophomore year, mainly owing to the various skills I had acquired during my freshman year. That was my first exposure to management level work.

In addition to the above-mentioned school activities, I also took part in some social work, such as that of intern volunteer teacher for the Royal Dutch Shell Corporation. This practical experience has enhanced my sense of responsibility. A good example is my internship experience as a teacher with a voluntary teaching program in 2010, which aimed at helping backward rural schools. When I myself witnessed the grim conditions of education in the poor rural areas, I began to more dearly cherish the superior education resources and colorful life of the city. At the same time, by helping others, I experienced a feeling of self-worth, and a sense of obligation to show a humane concern for the needy.

Life is always full of surprises because miracles happen every day, so long as we are sufficiently positive, diligent, and persevering. I am also fully convinced that your school, by virtue of its good reputation, time-honored history and cultural endowments, will provide students with excellent teachers, a most favorable learning environment, and a high quality education. These will hone my learning and practical skills so that I will be able to address the present and future challenges in my chosen field. I sincerely hope that you will carefully consider my application.

Looking forward to hearing from you! Thank you!

Signature:×××(the applicant)

练 习 题

一、英译汉练习

Joey
Mobile　　　　×××××××××××
Email　　　　××××××@gmail.com
Address　　　Room ×××, ×× Rd
　　　　　　×××× District, ××× City
Postcode　　　××××××

CAREER OBJECTIVE

Seeking a marketing development position that requires strong communication and relationship building skills. Interests include marketing planner and brand related position.

PERSONAL PROFILE

Enthusiastic person with comprehensive knowledge in business and multi-cultural experiences. Highly creative, recognized as a customer oriented and solution-focused individual. Areas of strength include:

- Capability to achieve success in negotiation
- Solid English communication and people skills
- Fast learner and always ready to learn new things
- Creative problem-solving abilities

WORK EXPERIENCES AND PRACTICES

1. Business Developer　　Decoraimport Asia Ltd.　　Shanghai—Ningbo, China
　　May 2007—Present
- Explore market potential based on external environment analysis
- Approach potential client, local and international, via various marketing tool and maintain the existing business relationship
- Administrate and operate accounts in Zhejiang and Guangdong Provinces, including service/solution design, liaising contractors, leading business negotiation, issuing contract
- Improve the efficiency and efficacy of the business process via information flow enhancement

2. International Marketing Executive　　Rainbow Outdoor Articles Co., Ltd
　　Ningbo, China　　Oct. 2005—Apr. 2007
- Process the joint venture with American partner to enter U.S. market of garden furniture
- Build brand equity and introduce new product through different channel, i.e. seasonal trade exhibitions and media
- Lead and monitor the contract issuing process and provide relative support

3. Market Researcher & Project Assistant　　Kadence (UK) Ltd.
　　London, UK　　Oct. 2004—Mar. 2005
- Conducted domestic and international market research via computer aided telephone interview
- Compiled information, input data, dealt with customer's complaint and arranged appointment
- Cooperated with team members to make sure the project meet the deadline
- Provided essential consult service

4. Propaganda Committee Member, School Newspaper Editor　　Wuhan University
　　Wuhan, China　　Sept. 1998—Jun. 2002

Headed a team of six students to previewed articles, edit and visual image of school newspaper, as well as budget controlled for the publication. Successfully organized members to take part in the 1st Wuhan Comic Festival and displayed five works on the exhibition on 19th April 2000. Awarded "Excellent student leader of Wuhan University" in 2000—2001 academic year.

EDUCATION AND QUALIFICATIONS

1. The University of Greenwich London，UK
   MA in International Business Oct. 2003—Jun. 2005
2. Wuhan University Wuhan，China
   LLB degree in Law Sept. 1998—Dec. 2002

OTHER INFORMATION

Language Skills：Mandarin（Mother tongue），English（Fluent）
Computer Skills：MS Office，Internet Package
Interests：swimming，sketching and painting，photograph

（Joey，豆丁网）

二、汉译英练习

推 荐 信

  四川大学经济学院财政专业2006级本科生××是本人××课班上的学生。该生在学习的过程中积极主动，认真踏实，并在本课程取得了良好成绩，在专业名列前茅。

  在教授该课程时，我比较注重对学生运用基本理论和基础知识分析和思考问题的能力及实际计算和操作能力的培养。该生在学习期间表现比较突出，不仅上课认真听讲，能提出很有独创性的问题，而且针对我提出的案例分析题，他/她勇于上台发言，能清楚地阐述自己的观点。他/她思维活跃，思考问题全面客观，很能深入问题的本质，具有较强的分析问题的能力；专业基础扎实，能灵活运用所学的基本理论和基础知识。

  该生综合表现突出，予以推荐，希望审核通过。

推荐人：×××
（作者不详，百度文库）

附 录

附录1　练习题参考译文

第一章

一、英译汉练习

上大学时,巴拉克·奥巴马反对南非种族隔离政府,参加了抗议活动。那时,他注意到,"人们开始倾听我的意见。"年轻的奥巴马意识到,语言有产生"变革"的力量:"恰当的言辞可以让一切发生改变——无论是南非贫民窟孩子的生活状况,还是我自己在世界上微不足道的地位。"

人们夸赞奥巴马的口才,称赞他的演讲语言具有劝导、激励或提升听众思想境界的作用。他欣赏语言的魔力,热爱阅读,这不但赋予他异于寻常的能力,能够设身处地地思考种族和宗教这样的复杂问题,将想法传递给数以百万计的美国人,而且有助于他逐渐认识自我,理解世界。

《我父亲的梦想》(这无疑是一个未来总统写的最能引起回忆、最富有抒情诗调、最直言不讳的自传)是奥巴马写的第一本书。在该书中,他表明,终其一生,他读书是为了获取别人的见解和信息。通过读书,他突破自我认识,最近还看破了权力和名声。他回忆起,在青少年时代,他读詹姆斯·鲍德温、拉尔夫·埃里森、兰斯顿·休斯、理查德·赖特和杜波伊斯等人的著作是为了认同种族身份。后来,在苦行僧般的大学阶段,他沉浸在像尼采和圣奥古斯丁等大思想家的作品里,在知识和精神层面寻找他真正的信仰。

二、汉译英练习

May 5, 2018 marks the 200th anniversary of the birth of Karl Marx. Although he may be considered to be the most familiar German to Chinese people, most of us usually associate Marx with abstract political ideas and philosophical thoughts, because when it comes to Marx, the image of a serious philosopher is what, more often than not, first comes to mind. The German film, *Karl Marx in His Youth*, released in 2017, presents a more authentic Marx to the audience.

The film tells of the formation of young Marx's revolutionary ideas from 1843 to 1848 and the birth of *the Communist Manifesto*. During this short but turbulent period, Karl

Marx and Friedrich Engels completely changed the course of human history.

第二章

一、英译汉练习

周一,中国总理李克强在纽约参加了一个高层峰会,承诺对难民提供 1 亿美元的额外人道主义援助。

联合国这个具有历史意义的峰会致力于解决难民和移民的大规模流动问题。在峰会上,李总理说难民危机对政治、社会和安全构成了威胁,为恐怖分子提供了可乘之机。

李总理表示,中国还将"认真考虑提供中国—联合国和平与发展基金,为发展中国家努力解决这一问题提供发展基金。"

去年 9 月,在联合国世界各国领导人年会期间,中国宣布建立一个为期 10 年、总金额达 10 亿美元的基金,以支持联合国的工作。今年 5 月,中国与联合国签署了一项为期 10 年、每年支付 2 000 万美元的协议,为和平、安全和发展提供资金支持。这是履行该承诺采取的第一步。

分析人员认为,在峰会场外区域,人们期望李克强总理与美国总统巴拉克·奥巴马会面,解决经济问题,甚至将朝核这样棘手的问题提到议事日程上来。

周一,中国社会科学院美国研究所副所长倪峰告诉《环球时报》:"就朝核问题,李总理不能给奥巴马任何承诺。与李总理交谈时,美国应该现实点。"

中国人民大学国际关系学院副院长金灿荣表示,美国指责中国没有对朝鲜实施严厉的制裁,但是中国表示,美国应该就核问题与朝鲜开始谈判,而不是发动军事演习、部署末端高空区域防御(萨德)系统来激怒朝鲜。

二、汉译英练习

After the *Dandong 1* was identified as the *Chinese cruiser Zhiyuan*, the two-year underwater investigation ended and the archaeological excavations began. Reporters of *the Huaxi Metropolitan Daily* learned that the archaeological team officially launched the underwater excavation on October 4, the first excavating operation to take place after the original confirmation of the ship's identity. This marked the beginning of a new stage in the archaeological work.

More cultural relics were retrieved from the water, including a seal, engraved with the four Chinese characters—Yun Zhong Bai He (which means white cranes in the cloud in English). Experts believe that this seal might have been one of Deng Shichang's personal belongings. (Deng was a patriotic general of the Qing Dynasty's Beiyang Navy.)

Earlier, a lot of other articles for daily use were salvaged (retrieved), including blue and white bowls decorated with pictures of *the Seven Sages of the Bamboo Forest*, and some keys, locks, and silver ingots as well as a Hong Kong dollar coin of the time.

第三章

一、请将下列英语句子翻译成汉语，注意粗体字的正确译法。

1. 如果你将盒子竖起来，就可以少**占**些空间。
2. 那颗炸弹一旦爆炸，会把每个人都**炸死**的！
3. 她信誓**旦旦**地说一定要把此事**告**到法庭。
4. **采取**任何你认为最好的措施。
5. 每隔四小时**喝**十滴（药）。

二、请将下列汉语句子翻译成英语，注意粗体字的正确译法。

1. She can **play** basketball as well as tennis.
2. He **banged on** the door until she let him in.
3. This wooden thing is for **beating** the eggs.
4. You must **play** a spade if you have one.
5. Their clothes were all **bunched up** after being in suitcases for so long.
6. They **play** bridge for recreation.

三、英译汉练习

约翰·厄普代克是 20 世纪最伟大的一位作家，76 岁时肺癌夺去了他的生命。这位白发苍苍的老人获得"伟大"的桂冠实属不易。他在宾夕法尼亚州的一个小镇长大，头脑聪明，说话结巴。后来，他就读于哈佛大学，担任校园幽默杂志《妙文》的负责人，而不是传奇文学杂志《倡导者》的负责人。他还涉足漫画制作，在《纽约客》上首次发表的作品是一组谐趣诗。

然而实际上，他是一位小说家，是小说和短篇故事使他怀有持久的，甚至一生的浪漫情怀。然而，似乎厄普代克到他第二部小说《兔子，跑吧》出版时才清楚地明白这一点。这是"兔子五部曲"中的第一部小说，记录了厄普代克的大英雄——兔子埃斯屈朗的生活。埃斯屈朗并非是作者自己虚构的一个人物，而是一个俗人，一个粗俗的、精力充沛的中产阶级推销员，作者通过剖析这个人物，在小说中刻画了他这一代美国人面临的精神和文化危机。

厄普代克小说明显的特点是他光彩夺目、异常生动的写作风格。他的天赋——恰当安排细节，在小说中捕捉最微弱的光的变化或人物情绪的变化，是无与伦比的。这固然不是最值得称赞的天赋。当他的同代人在实践海明威和卡弗顽固的现实主义或元小说家复杂的想法时，厄普代克却几乎独自提高自己的口才和智慧。具有讽刺意味的是，有时候这样做对他不利，让人觉得他是一个无足轻重的人物。

（注："兔子五部曲"包括《兔子，跑吧》《兔子归来》《兔子富了》《兔子歇了》《怀念兔子》。）

四、汉译英练习

On October 4, at Sotheby's auction house in Hong Kong, Ma Yun's first oil painting, *the Land of Peach Blossoms*, was sold for $33 million, a high price, after frenzied (intense) bidding—more than 40 bids. At one point during the auction, someone bid up the price from 3.6 million straight to 5 million while another, soon after, raised it from 9 million to 18 million.

This painting, on which Mr. Ma worked with Chinese artist Zeng Fanzhi, was produced in order to raise funds for the Taohuayuan Ecological Protection Foundation. Mr. Ma said that he was deeply honored to do a canvas painting with Mr. Zeng for the first time. It is reported that the profits from the auctioning of this painting will go to Taohuayuan Ecological Protection Foundation.

Zeng Fanzhi is considered to be one of the more representative and internationally influential of modern Chinese artists.

第四章

一、英译汉句子练习

1. 如果你经常使用因特网,那么你的上网活动很可能遍及整个网络。
2. 长期以来,医生用鸦片制剂缓解重病者或重伤者的疼痛。
3. 在工程设计中,安全因素和经济节约不容忽视。
4. 周日,一位航天高级工程师声称,中国计划发射第二艘载人航天宇宙飞船神州六号,标志中国的载人航天已进入有真人参与的空间科学试验新阶段。
5. 显然,低温可降低细菌的活动速度。
6. 因具有许多有用的性能,钢在工业上得到广泛应用。
7. 读者可以通过电话交谈。在电话中,信息从以声速传输的压缩空气分子模式转换到沿着铜导线以近似光速传播的电子脉冲模式。
8. 所有选民(特别是民主党选民)态度发生变化,候选人相信若想赢得民主党领导权,就必须支持同性婚姻。
9. 在2007年至2011年期间(即在奥巴马就任总统的最初几年),共和党人的态度曾发生改变。
10. 五年前,迈克尔·普雷斯曼曾发誓:服装在线零售商——艾芙兰永远不开设实体店。
11. 鉴于全国范围内普遍出现商店关门潮(迄今为止,今年已有7 000多家商店关闭),业主和购物中心也愿意和小众品牌公司就月租期或年租期签订灵活的协议。
12. 与2017年的产量相比,该地区苹果产量增长了2倍。
13. 在商业活动中,价格是决定有线和无线技术选择方案的重要因素。
14. 正如我们上面所提到的,煤炭的生产和使用伴有严重的环境(污染)问题。
15. 人们往往喜欢美化过去,总是想象着在以往的日子里,亲人和朋友们围坐在温暖的壁炉前玩游戏、讲故事其乐融融的场景,但是我认为亲人和朋友之间缺乏沟通,电视不应成为罪魁祸首。

二、汉译英句子练习

1. As one of the Chinese Four Great Inventions, papermaking is considered to be a major Chinese contribution to world civilization.

2. It is predicted that by 2050 one out of three Chinese will be over 60 years old.

3. When it comes to Chinese sports, we cannot avoid mentioning table tennis.

4. Located in Hangzhou, the provincial capital of Zhejiang Province, the West Lake covers an area of over 6 square kilometers.

5. From then on he spent 17 years touring China and visiting many Chinese cities.

6. This paper discusses four aspects of grammatical cohesion: reference, substitution, omission and conjunction.

7. For natives of Xi'an, the Youyi Road is of unusual significance.

8. Many roads in Xi'an are lined with towering trees on both sides.

9. Xi'an, called Chang'an or Haojing in ancient times, is the capital of Shaanxi Province.

10. You can also find a super-beautiful beltway around a mountain in Xi'an even when you do not go to Tibet.

11. Within only ten years, Qin vanquished the Han, Zhao, Wei, Chu, Yan and Qi one after another, and united the whole of China in 221 BC.

12. When teaching this course, I focus on developing students' ability to use basic theory and basic knowledge to analyze and think about problems, as well as on their ability to calculate and perform operations.

13. If the supplier of the pharmaceutical production enterprise changes, the enterprise shall, for the record, report the change to the food and drug administration at the municipal or provincial level within 15 working days after the change.

三、英译汉练习

美国依然是新移民的天堂吗？

最近，美国颁布严酷法律，成千上万的移民如同爱丽丝跟随白兔（掉入一口深井）一样，来到美国后却陷入了混乱而强大的法律网中不能自拔。美国政府要求移民归化局执行这些法律规定。这些联邦法令不符合正当程序标准，违背了保护美国公民的司法体制中固有的基本公正性。显然，这样做是对移民执行了双重标准。

例如，关于埃利安·冈萨雷斯遣返时间存在争议。六岁的小男孩冈萨雷斯杀死了自己的母亲和其他几个人，企图逃离古巴，在佛罗里达州沿海海域被救起。正当冈萨雷斯遣返问题争议到不可开交时，中国一位小女孩出现在复审听证会上。这个女孩逃离了中国，试图进入美国,警方抓获了她。她不懂英语,感到异常恐惧,眼泪不住地从脸颊流下,却因双臂被绑在腰间而无法擦拭。她一定曾处于惊恐之中,因为她逃离了自己的家园,结果却被关在异国他乡的监狱里,双手戴着锁链,被带到陌生人前受审,而她一句话也听不懂。她现在面临被驱逐的困境。

此外,再看看同样面临要被驱逐出境困境的两个母亲那引人注目的故事吧。第一个是一个年轻的德国女人,她曾被人收养,带到佐治亚州。现在,身为两个孩子母亲的她最近申请公民身份时,官方却下令要将她驱逐出境,仅仅是因为在她十几岁时,为了一个喜欢的男孩扯了另一个女孩的头发,尽管她当时受到控告已认罪。

第二位也是一位年轻的母亲,在被丈夫残忍殴打之后报了警,现在却面临与孩子分离并遭驱逐出境的危险。警方非但没有保护她,还逮捕了她,因为当她丈夫骑在她身上不停打她时,她咬了她丈夫。令人难以置信的是,两位母亲都将被驱逐出境,而她们的孩子由于均在美国出生却可以待在美国。

拉扯头发或咬人事件怎能成为被驱逐出境的理由呢?同样重要的是,对那些为自己和家人努力获得自由、安全感和成功的人而言,美国怎么已变成了一个拆散家庭、拒绝走正当程序的国家呢?

四、汉译英练习

It is quite normal for college students who have lived in an "ivory tower" for a long time to have only limited contact with society. They do not know what to do after graduation and are unclear as to what future choices to make.

However, it becomes really problematic when you say, "I hope to get to know myself first."

Imagine that from today on, you get up each day and set goals for yourself and spend more time than ever before reflecting on and trying to know yourself. A year from now, will you have a clearer understanding of yourself?

The answer is no, because knowing oneself cannot be done by daydreaming, but requires that one leave "comfort zones", like dorms and schools, and learn by trial and error, constantly rejecting ideas while adjusting and optimizing for the next attempt.

第五章

一、英译汉练习

穆里尔·赫斯洛普是一位骨骼粗大的年轻胖女子,来自纽约一个问题家庭。她的父亲比尔·赫斯洛普是一个失意的政客。他总是将自己的失败归咎于家人,经常公开训斥孩子们,说他们一无所用。穆里尔的母亲贝蒂·赫斯洛普是一位不快乐的家庭主妇,常常默默淹没在一大堆脏衣服和要洗的脏碗碟中,而穆里尔的兄弟姐妹却整天坐在沙发上看电视。

穆里尔经常与中学同学塔妮娅、妮可和其他女孩混在一起。塔妮娅和玩伴中其他女孩都是身材苗条、皮肤黝黑、有自恋癖的年轻女子。穆里尔却又胖又丑，失业在家，不懂穿着打扮，因此她们把穆里尔的陪伴视作对自己的侮辱。穆里尔喜欢听20世纪70年代的歌，与那些派对狂相比，她不够疯狂。悲伤时，穆里尔经常会回到卧室，将自己封闭起来，听ABBA乐队的歌。

当塔妮娅婚礼上的花束刚好落进穆里尔的手里时，穆里尔几乎不敢相信自己的好运。她还没有来得及想象下一个是自己结婚的快乐情景，塔妮娅和其他女子就强迫她将花束交给另一个女孩，因为她们认为穆里尔将来即使出嫁，也是世界上最后一个嫁出去的女人。更为糟糕的是，穆里尔不适合在婚礼上穿的豹皮裙子太过抢眼，以至于被她偷裙子的那家店的保安认了出来。婚宴期间，警察拘捕了穆里尔，开警车送她回家，让她拿出购买这条裙子的收据，穆里尔当然拿不出来。她的父亲比尔向办案的两名警察行贿了一箱啤酒，警察就把她放了……

二、汉译英练习

That Zhou Ziyang is an emotional person can be proven (confirmed) by his love of weeping. One time after watching a film, *the Old Beast*, with the producers for the first time, Zhou Ziyang hid himself in a room alone and wept heartily. Another time, as he was waiting to accept Taipei Golden Horse Awards, he suddenly had mixed feelings of joy and sorrow and burst into tears.

As a young director who had not received professional training, he spent a decade producing his first film, *the Old Beast*, which was well received at the time of its appearance and won three awards at the 11th FIRST Youth Film Festival in 2016. What's more, at the ceremony of the 54th Golden Horse Awards, this film also won awards for Best Original Screenplay, and Best Leading Actor as well as the FIPRESCI Prize respectively.

第六章

一、英译汉练习

叙利亚紧张局势加剧　雷克斯·蒂勒森在莫斯科面临艰巨任务

美国国务卿访问俄罗斯，承诺推动建立更紧密的联系。

当雷克斯·蒂勒森乘坐的飞机降落时，一张巨大的红地毯在莫斯科机场停机坪上徐徐展开。雷克斯·蒂勒森呼吁俄罗斯停止支持叙利亚巴沙尔·阿萨德政权，俄罗斯不太可能像欢迎蒂勒森来访一样接受这个提议。

最初似乎为了突出白宫渴望改善与俄罗斯的关系，美国国务卿决定不参加北约峰会而访问莫斯科，但是情况在唐纳德·特朗普上周命令发射巡航导弹打击叙利亚空军基地之后发生了改变，克里姆林宫谴责美国这一做法。

俄罗斯政客曾经谈论与美国改善关系，俄罗斯国家电视台曾鼓吹特朗普是"真正的男子汉",然而这样的日子已经过去了。

随着蒂勒森周三在莫斯科开始会谈,出现的问题与其说是他是否可以在叙利亚问题上与莫斯科达成一致意见,不如说是他是否可以开启任何形式的对话。在2月德国主办的20国集团峰会上,他第一次见到俄罗斯外长谢尔盖·拉夫罗夫,双方就记者是否出席会议存在明显分歧。与拉夫罗夫和美国前国务卿约翰·克里会谈时气氛相比,他们之间的互动显得冷淡。

周二,普京的发言人德米特里·帕斯科夫说,与蒂勒森会谈暂时并不在弗拉基米尔·普京的日程中。美国大使馆表示,没有可能举行会谈的任何信息。

俄罗斯的分析人士表示,只有当与拉夫罗夫会谈显得相对友好且富有成效时,普京才可能会见蒂勒森。俄罗斯政治分析家阿列克谢·马卡尔金表示:"如果他们会谈中一直持相反意见,只是谈论美国提出的最后要求而俄罗斯拒绝接受,那么(与普京)会谈是毫无意义的"。

在蒂勒森访问前,形势不容乐观。上周,叙利亚发生化学袭击,造成70多人死亡。周二,蒂勒森表示俄罗斯"没有坚守"摧毁阿萨德化学武器2013年做出的这一承诺。他补充道,华盛顿没有看到身为叙利亚领导人的阿萨德采取的"进一步行动"。与之前对阿萨德的批评相比,此次言辞更为严厉。

作为回应,普京加倍支持阿萨德政权,将西方对叙利亚当局发动了化学袭击的指责比作2003年美国入侵伊拉克之前做出伊拉克拥有大规模杀伤性武器的错误断言。他呼吁联合国调查此次袭击事件,同时表示某些邪恶势力"正计划再次找借口指责叙利亚当局使用化学武器"……

二、汉译英练习

During his visit to the United States, Chinese President Xi Jinping exchanged in-depth views on Afghan issues with American President Barack Obama. Regarding those issues, both men decided to maintain communication and cooperation, to promote trilateral dialogue, and to support peaceful reconstruction and economic development in Afghanistan as well as an "Afghan-led, Afghan-owned" reconciliation process.

A few days ago, the opening ceremony for "the Fourth US-China sponsored Afghan Diplomat Training Class" was held in the United States. China's Foreign Minister Wang Yi said that, as a successful example of China-US cooperation in third world countries, this training program for Afghan diplomats had enhanced mutual understanding among the three sides—China, the United States, and Afghanistan, and that it reflected a joint effort in the reestablishment of peace in Afghanistan with the support of the international community. China and the United States also co-chaired high-level meetings in New York on Afghanistan's reconstruction and on regional cooperation, promising to continue to provide strong international support to the Afghan government and to regional economic cooperation.

第七章

一、英译汉练习

瑞典首访之旅(续)

"看见那位过马路的盲人了吗?汽车都停下来让他过马路。"

我们去斯德哥尔摩观光。斯蒂芬是我们的一位东道主,陪着我们。我们刚刚去过了国王岛,接下来去乘渡船。突然,斯蒂芬对我说:"看见那位过马路的盲人了吗?汽车都停下来让他过马路。""但是,司机怎么知道那位盲人在过马路呢?那位盲人又是如何示意司机他要过马路的呢?"我问。"十字路口的灯柱上有一个按钮,盲人按下这个按钮就可以把信号传给司机。"他回答说。这个小装置是公众关爱残疾人的表现,我深受感动。如果政府关心人民,城市管理将非常人性化。

在市政厅会面

按照安排,林雪平市女市长伊娃将与代表团见面。长春市副市长将与她举行友好会谈,讨论这两个城市之间建立友好城市的可能性。一大清早,我们去了市政厅。

当我们接近市政厅时,我们看到了中国和瑞典两国国旗在空中飘扬。市长和她的助理在门口等候我们。她和我们一一握手后,带我们进了市政厅。她说着一口流利的英语,借助图片和图表,向我们介绍这座城市。不知为什么,我遇到的每个瑞典人英语说得都很好。有人告诉我,英语是必修课,每个孩子在校都要学英语。也就是说,孩子们一上学就开始学习英语,一直到他们高中毕业。

"他们在对壁画做什么?"

一些人要将林雪平教堂内一副古老的壁画运到马尔默市。"但是他们怎样才能做到不损坏这幅画呢?"我对此很好奇。"我们去看一看!"有人提议。进入教堂后,我们看到一群人正忙着从墙上取画。这是一幅讲述基督教故事的旧画。有些设备我不知道是干什么用的,还有两台电脑。在一台电脑屏幕上可见,这幅画的一部分已经扫描成图片了。另一台电脑上显示的是位于马尔默的目的地。两群人分别在林雪平和马尔默通过电脑讨论,交换想法。他们通过互联网传输图片。

都很好客,但方式不同

有好几次,我们受邀就餐,东道主既有市长也有我们参观的工厂和公司的高管。这些是工作午餐,而不是我们国内招待客人的那种正餐。客人和主人各拿一个盘子就餐,饭后没有剩饭剩菜。受邀参加的都是与项目有关的人。没人劝酒,没有噪音。东道主负责人对客人简短致辞,客人也发表讲话,以示感谢。我们为彼此的健康干杯,然后边吃饭边小声交谈,空气中弥漫着善意和友好的气氛。

"这是因为法律。"

一天晚上,我们驱车前往马尔默市。在十字路口,司机斯蒂芬遇红灯停下了车。我看到另一条大街上没有汽车,附近也没有警车巡逻,因此我问史蒂芬:"为什么你不继续开车呢?周围没有别的车,天色也晚了。"但是他什么也没说,一直等绿灯亮起才开走。后来他对我说:"这是因为法律。"来瑞典前,从杂志上我读过这样的故事,我以为一定夸大其词了。但是现在,我真的相信瑞典人会无条件遵守法律。

二、汉译英练习

Mount Tai, called Mount Dai, also Mount Daizong in ancient times, is located in central Shandong Province. It is one of China's five sacred mountains (namely, Mount Tai, Mount Hua, Mount Song, and 2 Mounts of Heng, one in Hunan Province, and the other in Shanxi Province). "Dongyue" (East Sacred Mountain), is so-named because of its location in the eastern part of China. With a total area of 426 square kilometers and highest peak (Yuhuangding) rising 1532.8 meters above sea level, Mount Tai, owing to its imposing form, boundless grandeur, and numerous scenic spots and historical sites, enjoys the laudatory title of "Wu Yue Du Zun" (the most revered/esteemed of China's five sacred mountains). Confucius said in his poem, "Ascending Mount Tai, one gets the feeling that the world below is suddenly very small"; and Du Fu, a great poet of the Tang Dynasty, wrote the following line in one of his poems, "Only when you stand on the top of the Mount Tai, can you see others as small." Mount Tai has now become a symbol of greatness and majesty in people's minds.

第八章

一、英译汉练习

网络拓扑

网络物理布局的重要性通常低于连接网络节点的拓扑结构。用于描述物理网络的大多数图表均为拓扑图,而并非地理位置图。拓扑图上的符号通常用于代表网络链接和网络节点。

网络链接

用于链接设备构成计算机网络的传输介质(在文献中通常称为物理介质)包括电缆(以太网、家庭网络、电力线通信以及电源线、电话线和同轴电缆的一套协议规范等)、光纤(光纤通信)和无线电波(无线网络)。在OSI模型中,此类传输介质处于第1层和第2层——即物理层和数据链路层。

局域网(LAN)技术广泛采用的传输介质统称为以太网。利用IEEE 802.3明文界定的介质和协议标准,可实现以太网中的网络设备相互通信。以太网通过铜缆和光纤光缆传输数据。无线局域网标准(如IEEE 802.11明文定义的标准)使用无线电波或其他红外信号作为传输介质。电力线通信使用建筑物中的电力电缆传输数据。

二、汉译英练习

A computer system is a machine system that receives and stores information at the request of an operator, automatically performs data processing and calculating, and outputs resultant information. A computer, as the extension and expansion of brain power, is one of the great achievements of modern science.

The computer system consists of a hardware system (subsystem) and a software system (subsystem). The former, which is the entity on which the system works, is an organic combination of various physical components based on the principles of electricity, magnetism, light and machinery; the latter is a variety of programs and files used to direct the whole system to work according to specified requirements.

Since the time the first electronic computer came out in 1946, computer technology has made remarkable progress in the areas of components and devices, hardware system structure, software systems, applications and so on. Modern computer systems, ranging from microcomputers and personal computers to giant computers and their networks—with their various forms and characteristics—have been widely used in scientific computing, transaction processing and process control. With each passing day, modern computer systems are penetrating ever more deeply into all areas of society and are thus having a profound impact on society's progress.

第九章

一、英译汉练习

乔伊

电话：××××××××××
电子邮箱：×××××××@gmail.com
地址：××市××区××路××××室
邮编：××××××

求职目标
寻求市场开发职位，沟通及关系构建能力强。意向职位包括营销策划以及品牌相关职位。

个人简介
本人待人接物热情，具有丰富的商业知识和多元文化经历，创造力强，以客户为中心，注重提供问题解决方案，能力得到认可。我的优势包括：
- 能够确保谈判取得成功
- 拥有扎实的英语沟通和人际交往能力
- 学习速度快，乐于学习新事物
- 能够想方设法解决问题

工作经历和实践活动
1. 业务开发人员　　　　　　　　　Decoraimport（亚洲）有限公司
   中国上海市—宁波市　　　　　　2007年5月—至今
   - 根据外部环境分析探索市场发展潜力；
   - 利用各种营销工具，接洽本地和国际潜在客户，维护现有业务关系；
   - 管理和经营浙江省和广东省的账目。业务包括服务/解决方案设计、联系承包商、主导业务谈判、签发合同；
   - 通过改善信息流，提高业务流程效率和效力。
2. 国际市场营销专员　　　　　　　彩虹户外用品有限公司

中国宁波市   2005年10月—2007年4月
- 通过与美国合作伙伴建立合资企业,进入美国庭院家具市场;
- 通过不同渠道(如季节性贸易展和媒体宣传),建立品牌资产并推出新产品;
- 领导和监督合同签发过程,提供相关支持。

3. 市场研究员 & 项目助理   卡登斯(英国)有限公司
   英国伦敦市   2004年10月—2005年3月
- 通过计算机辅助电话采访,实施国内和国际市场研究;
- 编辑信息、输入数据、处理客户投诉和安排预约等事项;
- 与团队成员合作,确保项目按时完成。

4. 宣传委员会成员,校报编辑   武汉大学
   中国武汉市   1998年9月—2002年6月

领导由六名学生组成的团队,负责预审校报文章、编辑校报和设计视觉形象、控制校报出版预算。成功组织团队成员参加2000年4月19日召开的第一届武汉动漫节,并展出五幅作品。在2000—2001学年,获得"武汉大学优秀学生干部"称号。

教育经历和资质

1. 格林威治大学   英国伦敦市
   国际商务硕士   2003年10月—2005年6月
2. 武汉大学   中国武汉市
   法学学士   1998年9月—2002年12月

其他信息

语言能力:汉语(母语)、英语(流利)
计算机能力:熟练使用微软公司的办公软件和各种互联网软件
兴趣爱好:游泳、素描、油画和摄影

二、汉译英练习

Letter of Recommendation

××, an undergraduate (the class of 2006), majoring in Finance at the School of Economics, Sichuan University, is a student in my ××× class. ×× is a positive, conscientious, pragmatic and proactive learner, who gets good grades and ranks among the top students in his/her major field.

When teaching this course, I focus on cultivating students' ability to analyze and think about problems by using basic theories and knowledge and applying their actual computing and operating skills. This student performed notably well in my course in that s/he not only listened attentively in class and raised ingenious questions, but also had the courage to take the floor and formulate her/his ideas on the questions I raised for case analysis. Possessing an active mind, s/he usually thinks in a comprehensive and objective manner and is able to go deeply into the nature of issues owing to her/his strong analytical skills. Moreover, s/he also has a solid professional foundation and shows flexibility when applying basic theories and knowledge (to practical work).

This student has outstanding general qualities. Accordingly, I hereby recommend him/her in the hope of your approval.

Recommended by ×××

附录 2 翻译补充练习

一、英译汉练习

1.

EU rebukes Hungary as refugees, riot police clash

Croatia overwhelmed by migrants as EU to hold summit over crisis

Two Croatian police officers watch migrants as they wait for a train at a railway station, near the official border between Serbia and Croatia, close to the eastern Croatian town of Tovarnik, on Thursday. Photo: AFP

The EU's migration chief rebuked Hungary on Thursday for its tough handling of a flood of refugees, as asylum seekers thwarted by a new Hungarian border fence and repelled by riot police poured into Croatia, spreading the strain. Croatian police said more than 5,000 migrants had arrived from Serbia since Hungary sealed its southern EU border with Serbia on Tuesday. Hungarian security forces fired tear gas and water cannons to disperse rock-throwing refugees on Wednesday. The head of Germany's Office for Migration and Refugees resigned for personal reasons after being criticized for being slow in processing applications from a record number of asylum seekers. German police said the number of refugees arriving in Germany more than doubled on Wednesday to 7,266.

Deep differences over how to cope with the influx of people mostly fleeing war and poverty in Syria, Iraq, Afghanistan and Pakistan have triggered a chain of beggar-thy-neighbor actions among European countries, sparking a crisis in the 28-nation EU.

EU commissioner for migration Dimitris Avromopoulos told a joint news conference with Hungary's foreign and interior ministers that most of those arriving in Europe were Syrians "in need of our help". "There is no wall you would not climb, no sea you would not cross if you are fleeing violence and terror," he declared, saying barriers of the kind Hungary has erected were temporary solutions that only diverted refugees and migrants, increasing tensions.

Hungarian Foreign Minister Peter Szijjarto hit back at criticism from UN and European officials, saying that siding with rioting migrants, who pelted police with rocks in clashes that injured 20 police, was encouraging violence.

Religious differences

Hungarian Prime Minister Victor Orban, who has blamed Germany for stoking the wave of migrants entering his country after Chancellor Angela Merkel rolled out the welcome mat for Syrian refugees, said Muslims would end up outnumbering Christians in Europe if the policy continued.

"I am speaking about God. I am speaking about culture and the everyday principles of life, such as sexual habits, freedom of expression, equality between men and women and all those kinds of values which I call Christianity. If we let the Muslims into the continent to compete with us, they will outnumber us. It's mathematics. And we don't like it," Orban said in an interview published in several European newspapers, including *The Times*.

Neighboring Slovakia has also invoked religious differences as a reason for rejecting mandatory quotas to share out refugees among EU nations, as the European Commission has proposed. The EU executive says the right to asylum is indivisible and cannot be linked to religious or ethnic considerations.

EU interior ministers are due to hold another special meeting on Tuesday to try to overcome differences on handling the migration crisis, which has prompted several EU countries led by Germany to reintroduce temporary border controls.

Mixed response

Amid chaotic scenes at its border with Serbia, Croatia said on Thursday it could not cope with a flood of migrants seeking a new route into the EU. More than 7,300 people entered Croatia from Serbia in the 24 hours after Wednesday's clashes between Hungarian riot police and stone-throwing refugees.

Slovenian Prime Minister Miro Cerar said his country would stick to the Schengen rules, which require it to register and fingerprint migrants and asylum seekers on arrival. Many refugees have refused to be registered and destroyed their identity papers in their quest to reach Germany.

Romanian President Klaus Iohannis said on Thursday that the country did not consider mandatory quotas a solution to EU's migrant crisis. Romania said previously it can take in a maximum 1,785 of migrants. But under a relocation scheme from the EU, Romania would have to take in more people.

Bulgaria said it was sending more soldiers to strengthen controls along its border with Turkey and avoid a refugee influx. About 600 migrants tried to cross the border in the last 25 hours but returned voluntarily after seeing it was well guarded, a Bulgarian Interior Ministry official said.

(作者不详,中国日报网)

2.

High-speed rail in China

High-speed rail (HSR) in China refers to any railway in China with commercial train service at the speed of 200 km/h (124 mph) or higher. By that measure, China has the world's longest HSR network with over 16,000 km (9,900 mi) of track in service as of December 2014 (19,369.8 km if mixed railway with freight services included) which is more than the rest of the world's high-speed rail tracks combined. China's high speed rail system also includes the world's longest line, the 2,298 km (1,428 mi) Beijing – Guangzhou High-Speed Railway.

Since high-speed rail service in China was introduced on April 18, 2007, daily ridership has grown from 237,000 in 2007 to 2.49 million in 2014, making the Chinese HSR network the most heavily used in the world. Cumulative ridership had reached 2.9 billion by October 2014.

The nationwide HSR network consists mainly of conventional track railways including upgraded mixed passenger and freight lines, newly built passenger designated lines (PDLs) and intercity lines. There is also the Shanghai Maglev, the world's first high-speed commercial magnetic levitation (maglev) line, which is operated by the Shanghai municipality government. Nearly all high-sped rail lines and rolling stock are operated by the China Railway Corporation, the state enterprise formerly known as the Railway Ministry.

Over the past decade, the country has undergone an HSR building boom with generous funding from the Chinese government's economic stimulus program. The pace of high-speed rail expansion slowed for a period in 2011 after the removal of Chinese Railways Minister Liu Zhijun for corruption and a fatal high-speed railway accident near Wenzhou, but has since rebounded. Concerns about HSR safety, high ticket prices, low ridership, financial sustainability of high-speed rail projects and environmental impact have drawn greater scrutiny from the Chinese press.

China's early high-speed trains were imported or built under technology transfer agreements with foreign train-makers including Alstom, Siemens, Bombardier and Kawasaki Heavy Industries. Chinese engineers then re-designed internal train components and built indigenous trains that can reach operational speeds of up to 380 km/h (240 mph).

(作者不详,维基百科)

3.

The ways in which air-conditioners work to "clean" the air can inadvertently cause health problems, too. One such way is with the use of an electrostatic precipitator, which removes dust and smoke particles from the air. What precipitators also do, however, is emit large quantities of positive air ions into the ventilation system. A growing number of studies show that overexposure to positive air ions can result in headaches, fatigue and feelings of irritation.

Large air-conditioning systems add water to the air they circulate by means of humidifiers. In older systems, the water used for this process is kept in special reservoirs, the bottoms of which provide breeding grounds for bacteria and fungi which can find their way into the ventilation system. The risk to human health from this situation has been highlighted by the fact that the immune systems of approximately half of workers in air-conditioned office buildings have developed antibodies to fight off the organisms found at the bottom of system reservoirs. Chemical disinfectants, called "biocides", that are added to reservoirs to make them germ-free, are dangerous in their own right in sufficient quantities, as they often contain compounds such as pentachlorophenol, which is strongly linked to abdominal cancers.

Finally, it should be pointed out that the artificial climatic environment created by air-conditioners can also adversely affect us. In a natural environment, whether indoor or outdoor, there are small variations in temperature and humidity. Indeed, the human body has long been accustomed to these normal changes. In an air-conditioned living or work environment, however, body temperatures remain well under 37℃, our normal temperature. This leads to a weakened immune system and thus greater susceptibility to diseases such as colds and flu.

(Robi Stauber,《英语学习》)

4.

Japan, U.S. urged to act prudently in revising *Mutual Defense Guidelines*

BEIJING, Oct. 9 (Xinhua)—China urged Japan and the United States to act prudently in revising their *Mutual Defense Guidelines* on Thursday, advising they play a constructive role in maintaining regional peace and stability.

Foreign Ministry spokesman Hong Lei made the comment after media reports suggested Japan and the U.S. targeted China's Diaoyu Islands in an interim report on the revision of the guidelines. He reiterated the Diaoyu Islands and its affiliated islands are part of China's inherent territory. "Foreign pressure will not shake China's determination to safeguard national sovereignty and territorial integrity." The Japan—U.S. alliance is a bilateral arrangement made under special historical conditions. It should not go beyond its bilateral scope or undermine third parties'interests, including China's, Hong said.

China will closely follow the revision of the Japan—U. S. defense cooperation guidelines, he said.

China-Japan relations have soured since the Japanese government's "purchase" of the Diaoyu Islands in September 2012.

(Mo Hong'e,新华网)

5.

Xi's visit helps clarify unique relationship

Editor's Note:

Chinese President Xi Jinping will pay his first state visit to the US next week. Where does the bilateral relationship stand? What's the significance of Xi's visit? Two renowned US experts shared their insights.

Elizabeth Economy, C. V. Starr senior fellow and director for Asia studies at the Council on Foreign Relations

Right now the US—China relationship is a little bit difficult. Traditionally we had a very stable relationship with some frictions managed reasonably well. I think both sides were committed to maintaining the relationship and trying to grow it.

But we have several significant challenges before us and no clear path forward to address them, such as cyber security. We are also looking at the progress of China's economic reforms. From Chinese perspective, China is concerned about the US position in the South China Sea, the role in US—Japan alliance, the Trans-Pacific Partnership and what kind of room the US will make for China in the region. There are a number of issues that both sides try to grapple with.

There are two different strategies. One is that we really need to have transparent and open dialogue about these issues. Both sides need to clearly state what the challenges are and try to find a way forward on each one of these frictions. At the same time, we need to look for new areas of cooperation. One of the strengths of last meeting between Xi and Obama at the APEC summit last year was that we were able to come forward with three very concrete agreements between the two countries. There is a range of global challenges that our two countries can cooperate to address.

During his visit, Xi has a number of opportunities to reach out to the American people and express his vision for China and the US—China relationship. He'll have several days of meetings and opportunities to engage, not only with US policymakers, but also with the broad public. I hope he will be able to explain his vision for China, the bilateral relationship and for China in the world. There are a lot of uncertainties in the US about the Chinese leadership and where they are taking the country. That will be one major accomplishment.

The other area that we may be able to make further steps forward would be the *Bilateral Investment Treaty*. Over next year, if we can make real progress on this particular issue, that can do a lot to support the relationship.

James Steinberg, former Deputy Secretary of State and currently dean of social science, international affairs and law at the Maxwell School of Citizenship and Public Affairs, Syracuse University

For Americans, Xi is a significant leader who we hope to build a good relationship with and we are encouraged by his upcoming visit to the US to continue the dialogues between our two countries. There will be candor, an openness from both sides with willingness to try to understand each other and to find common solutions to problems.

The US – China relationship is a unique one. Trying to put it in a box or relate it to past historical relations misses the richness and complexity of the relationship we have today.

There are many positive signs of the bilateral relationship. We have many areas to cooperate on issues such as climate change, global public health or dealing with nuclear proliferation, and the US and China work together very well—contributing not only to the wellbeing of our two countries, but also the world.

With challenges and differences, the two sides do have responsibilities to manage them in a way that won't unnecessarily provoke conflicts and to find ways to reassure each other that we actually want each country to be successful and prosperous and the region to be peaceful.

As China becomes more successful, the question is what kind of role it seeks to play. China does have a responsibility as a rising power, to provide reassurances not just to the US, but all its neighbors and others, that it intends to use its success in a positive way. So Xi's visit is an opportunity to address those questions, help others understand what China's goals and intentions are and how we should understand those actions we have seen.

Economic interdependence is a critical feature of our relationship. But I believe strongly that's not enough. Economic interdependence alone doesn't guarantee peace and tranquility. You have to work on the full range of issues.

The UN is also a great opportunity for multilateral exchange. The US and China have great responsibilities as members of the UN Security Council to provide global leadership and promote peace and prosperity.

（作者不详，新华网）

6.

Yuan exchange rate stable: official

The yuans exchange rate has become stable, an official with the State Administration of Foreign Exchange (SAFE) said during a press conference on Thursday.

China is unlikely to see large-scale capital inflows or outflows at the moment, said Wang Yungui, director of the Comprehensive Department at the SAFE, during the administrations regular third-quarter press conference. Wang also noted that the yuan would depreciate against the US dollar if the US Federal Reserve announces an interest rate hike in the near future, but this would be a normal phenomenon and wouldn't trigger abnormal capital flows.

The yuan has seen some exchange rate fluctuations in recent weeks. On August 11, it depreciated by about 2 percent against the US dollar, the biggest one-day slide in nearly two decades. The 2 percent change followed the announcement by the People's Bank of China (PBC), the Central Bank, on August 11 that it would adjust the system for fixing the yuans central parity rate.

The new mechanism takes market supply and demand into consideration, as well as price movements in major currencies, the PBC said.

Xi Junyang, a professor with the Department of Finance at the Shanghai University of Finance and Economics, told the *Global Times* on Thursday that the yuan had been too reliant upon the US dollar under the old system. When the US dollar became stronger, the yuan also appreciated against non-dollar currencies. This has had a negative effect on China's exports to those countries, Xi said.

Xi noted that the PBC's move shows China is taking a further step toward a market-oriented exchange rate system. He also noted that the new central parity system reduces the exchange rate gap between offshore yuan and domestically held currency, thus deterring speculative capital flows.

The yuan's depreciation caused some concern about the possibility of large-scale capital outflows, but experts have noted that such flows depend more on the outlook for the yuan's future trend.

If people see the August depreciation as a prelude to more rounds of depreciation, capital outflows would take place. If they consider the depreciation as a single event, then there won't be large-scale capital outflows, Xi said. He also pointed out that based on the current situation, the likelihood of large-scale fluctuations in the exchange rate is small.

Wang also said that the depreciation pressure on the yuan has been eased following the launch of the new central parity system, making large capital outflows less likely. According to Wang, SAFE has taken some measures to curb capital outflows recently and will intensify a crackdown on outflows conducted through illegal money dealers. But he stressed that SAFE hasn't launched any new policies to restrict people's foreign currency purchasing rights, and the authorities will be able to meet the genuine and legal demand for foreign exchange by firms and individuals.

Bai Ming, a research fellow with the Chinese Academy of International Trade and Economic Cooperation, told the *Global Times* on Thursday that it is hard to tell whether the yuan's recent depreciation can help to boost China's exports to other countries. The yuan's depreciation would cause exports to rise only under certain conditions, such as improved competitiveness of Chinese products, more support from government policies, and an increase in demand in international markets, he said.

According to a statement from the Ministry of Commerce on Wednesday, the yuan's depreciation was not aimed at boosting exports. Statistics from the General Administration of Customs on September 8 showed that China's exports slumped 6.1 percent year-on-year to about 1.204 trillion yuan ($189 billion) in August.

(李言,《环球时报》)

7.

The Search for Life

The ancient spaceship, *Life Finder*, is on its way back to Earth after an amazing seven hundred years exploring the Galaxy, looking for alien life.

Travelling at close to the speed of light, the ship has searched the Milky Way, analyzing more than ten billion planets for signs of intelligent life. During the mission, whole generations of human astronauts have lived and died on board. As they come to the last few weeks of their round trip, I spoke to the ship's robot commander, Big Nose Two.

—So, Big Nose Two, has the mission been a success?

—700 years, 10 billion planets examined, and nothing. No, I wouldn't call that success, exactly.

—Were there no signs of intelligent life?

—No. Not even stupid life. Not even a scrap of seaweed. Not even a single one-celled speck of bacteria. There's nothing out there but lumps of rock and clouds of gas. The galaxy is the deadest place I've ever been. I believe the Earth is the only planet in the whole galaxy with any life on it. I can't wait to get back home.

But all is not lost. Aren't you passing through the Big Ugly Chicken Cluster soon? That contains a thousand planets the same size and temperature as Earth.

—We will be entering the Big Ugly Chicken Constellation in 24 hours' time. It will take us a week to analyze all those planets.

—So, this time next week you might have some exciting news for us!

—I doubt it.

—But one of these thousand planets might be the one where you find alien life.

—Perhaps. But if I were you, I wouldn't get too excited. As you humans say, don't hold your breath.

—Good luck in the Big Ugly Chicken Constellation. We will talk to you next week.

(Norman Buchwald,《英语学习》)

8.

Trust

Last night I was driving from Harrisburg to Lewisburg, Pa., a distance of about eighty miles. It was late. I was late and if anyone asked me how fast I was driving, I'd have to plead the *Fifth Amendment* to avoid self-incrimination. Several times I got stuck behind a slow-moving truck on a narrow road with a solid white line on my left, and I was clinching my fists with impatience.

At one point along an open highway, I came to a crossroads with a traffic light. I was alone on the road by now, but as I approached the light, it turned red and I braked to a halt. I looked left, right and behind me. Nothing. Not a car, no suggestion of headlights, but there I sat, waiting for the light to change, the only human being for at least a mile in any direction.

I started wondering why I refused to run the light. I was not afraid of being arrested, because there was obviously no cop around, and there certainty would have been no danger in going through it.

Much later that night, after I'd met with a group in Lewisburg and had climbed into bed near midnight, the question of why I'd stopped for that light came back to me. I think I stopped because it's part of a contract we all have with each other. It's not only the law, but it's an agreement we have, and we trust each other to honor it: we don't go through red lights. Like most of us, I'm more apt to be restrained from doing something bad by the social convention that disapproves of it than by any law against it…

（Andy Rooney, 豆丁网）

9.

Baihe, one of China's largest online dating and matchmaking websites, is no stranger to legal disputes.

In a recent lawsuit, a woman claimed that she met a man via the website who told her he was single and was the chairman of a listed company, but only after she developed a relationship with him and was pregnant did she discover that he was actually married and had faked all of his career information.

After she alerted the police, the man was arrested for fraud. She also took the website to court, saying it failed to verify member information. But with so many matchmaking websites on the rise in China, making sure that members are single is important for both the websites and their clients.

So, what do you think? Do matchmaking websites have an obligation to verify their members' personal information?

（21st,《21世纪英文报》,第 1004 期）

10.

An Ohio teenager opened fire on five classmates, killing three students and injuring two others. In Seattle, the 9-year-old boy brought a gun to school and seriously injured a classmate when it was accidentally discharged in his backpack.

Children are injured and murdered every day, but school violence carries a symbolic potency because we like to think of schools as safe havens from the harshness of adult life. It's horrifying to think that the institutions could be a place of injury or even death.

（作者不详，豆丁网）

11.

Education for life (Excepts)

When one travels around the world, one notices to what an extraordinary degree human nature is the same, whether in India, America or Australia. This is especially true in colleges and universities. We are turning out, as if through a mold, a type of human being whose chief interest is to find security, to become somebody important, or to have a good time with as little thought as possible.

Conventional education makes independent thinking extremely difficult. Conformity leads to mediocrity. To be different from the group or to resist environment is not easy and is often risky as long as we worship success. The urge to be successful, which is the pursuit of reward whether in the material or in the so-called spiritual sphere, the search for inward or outward security, the desire for comfort—this whole process smothers discontent, puts an end to spontaneity and breeds fear; and blocks the intelligent understanding of life. With increasing age, dullness of mind and heart sets in.

In seeking comfort, we generally find a quiet corner in life where there is a minimum of conflict, and then we are afraid to step out of that seclusion. This fear of life, this fear of struggle and of new experience, kills in us the spirit of adventure; our whole upbringing and education have made us afraid to be different from our neighbor, afraid to think contrary to the established pattern of society, falsely respectful of authority and traditions.

(J. Krishnamurti, *Education for life*)

12.

John G. Blair was born in New York City and raised in the Northeastern USA. He studied at Brown University in Providence, Rhode Island and earned a Ph.D. in English and American Literature in 1962.

After teaching most of the 1960s at Oakland University, Michigan, he transferred his career to French-speaking Europe, first as a Fulbright Exchange Professor of American Literature at Strasbourg University, and then permanently at the University of Geneva in Switzerland as Professor of American Literature & Civilization until his retirement in 2000. Now he is teaching at Beijing Foreign Studies University as a foreign expert. He concentrates on graduate courses in American Culture Studies and a new course entitled Western Civilization with Chinese Comparisons.

Over the years he has published many articles on American literature and American culture and three scholarly monographs: *The Poetic Art of W. H. Auden*; *The Confidence Man in Modern Fiction*; *Modular America*; *Cross Cultural Perspectives on the Emergence of an American Way*. The manuscript for this last publication won the Ralph Henry Gabriel Prize of the American Studies Association for Interdisciplinary American Studies.

(John G. Blair,《英语学习》)

13.

Ellen Woods is a beautiful blonde majoring in Fashion Merchandising at University of California at Los Angeles (UCLA). Because of her lovely personality and excellence in studies, she is elected the president of her sorority called Delta Nu and voted homecoming queen of the year. What's more, she has a very smart and handsome boyfriend named Warner Huntington, a famous senator's son. One night, Warner invites her to an expensive restaurant for a special dinner, an indication that he is to propose to her. Ellen's friends are very happy for her and help her to choose the right dress and perfume for the special occasion. What Ellen does not expect is that instead of proposing to her, Warner tells her that he decides to break up with her and get serious about his future since he's going to Harvard Law School to be a lawyer and future senator like his father.

After the blow, Ellen changes into a different person who no longer cares about making up and eats a lot of junk food. Her friends' comfort and advice have little effect on her. One day Ellen happens to see a picture on a celebrity magazine. It's Warner's brother with his plain looking girlfriend as first-year students at Harvard Law School. Ellen hits upon a good idea that Warner will come back to her if she can enter the same law school and show him her talent. Thus she begins to inquire about the procedure and prepare her LSAT (Law School Admission Test) exam. After a period of intensive hard work, she passes the exam and is admitted into Harvard Law School.

Arriving at Harvard, Ellen immediately catches the eye of the students there. But they talk about her in a sarcastic way since law school means hard work and high I. Q., not skin-deep beauty...

(宋云峰,《英语学习》,2003 年 5 月)

14.

I arrived at Incheon International Airport one early morning. Although it was in April, I did not feel cold at all. The well-decorated and furnished airport gave me a fresh feeling. Everything was clean, neat and in order.

Surprisingly I saw some airport signboards were printed in Chinese as well as English and Hangul—the Korean language. My Korean friend explained to me, "Those are not Chinese in fact, but Chinese characters (Hanja) used by Hangul." The Korean language has a long history linked with Chinese. Before Hangul was developed by one Korean King in the 15th century, the Korean language had been written in Chinese characters (Hanja). Like Japanese, Koreans have borrowed nearly 70% of their vocabulary from Chinese. But Chinese and Hangul are different languages after all, therefore, the Chinese characters (Hanja) are mainly restricted to be used in maps, and occasionally in newspapers and people's written names. It reminded me that the Visa application form is also printed in Chinese characters. In order to prove what he said, my Korean friend showed me his business card, where his name is printed in Chinese as well as Hangul characters.

On this particular occasion, the local government tried to use more Chinese characters in the road signs and maps for the coming FIFA World Cup football matches, in order to attract more Chinese visitors and boost the tourism. Nowadays there are increasing numbers of road signs in Seoul written in English, Japanese and Chinese to help foreign visitors.

(潘晓,《英语学习》,2002 年)

15.

English students need more than language skills

Let's be honest, with 6.99 million college graduates in China swarming into a dim job market, it's going to be tough. Figures from the Beijing Municipal Education Commission indicate that the employment rate of graduates in Beijing is now 33.6 percent, much less than the 89.7 percent 10 years ago. English majors, who are looking for jobs based on their language skills, face pressure from all sides.

In order to help students get the big picture of this year's job market, the staff of 21*st Century* talked to 10 HR managers from leading companies to offer students inside information on what employers want. In addition, faculty members and experts provide an analysis of the prospects for English majors.

(21st,《21 世纪报》1007 期)

16.

Writing is a skill that is indispensable for successful university work. All those who write natively in English agree on certain core conceptions that constitute Anglo-American academic writing. Since the guidelines for academic writing are not the same as those for conversational or informal English and since Chinese traditions for academic writing are not the same as those for English, it may be worthwhile spelling out some basic rules of the game.

The main aim of academic writing in English is to convince the reader that the writer has something new and worthwhile to communicate. Therefore, the reader needs to be treated with a certain respect. The vocabulary and the sentence structures should be precise and college-level, not what would be suitable for a conversation with a friend. Do not use contractions. Avoid incomplete sentences. Only a complete sentence can be assessed for convincingness because in English only a complete sentence affirms a definite meaning, thereby asserting something.

(John G. Blair,《英语学习》,2004 年)

17.

Do we need GM food?

Should people support genetically modified (GM) food? The debate has been ongoing across the world in recent years, as global climate change has led to a series of disastrous weather conditions that are reducing crop yields, and turning food supply into a global issue.

Opponents worry that GM food is not safe for human consumption and that it poses long-term health risks that can only be determined many generations later. They also point to research results that suggest some GM foods increase the chances of getting certain diseases in test subjects.

However, the increased growth and consumption of GM food has shown that some modified crops require less water and fertilizer, yield more nutrients, and are more resistant to natural disasters, diseases and pests. Supporters also point to a lack of concrete evidence that the consumption of GM food has produced any widespread health risks.

(21st,《21 世纪报》,第 1019 期)

18.

Within the first few sentences the reader needs to know what idea the writer seeks to make credible. Whereas essays in the Chinese tradition often try to save their principal insight for later, the Anglo-American tradition takes the opposite approach. By "giving away" the main point at the very outset, the English writer focuses attention less on the main point itself than on the evidence that will be offered in favor of it.

For English speakers, the conception of writing dictates a particular structure for papers. After the writer's main point is stated, the following paragraphs focus on relevant aspects of the view, each one presenting appropriate evidence to support the writers' main point. These substantive paragraphs typically begin with a transition showing how the new focus relates to what came before. After the presentation of evidence, each paragraph or section should then point out what the writer believes has been added to the argument so far (a mini-conclusion). The final paragraph restates the main point, taking into account any refinements that may have emerged in the process of the presentation.

Obviously, there is a cultural mindset implicit in this mode of writing. It presumes that both writers and readers are rational individuals who are free to exercise their own judgments. The writer claims to offer some fresh understanding to the reader, who is treated as having been relatively unenlightened in the past. In the English-language heritage, everyone is entitled to his or her own views, but these will gain adherents only insofar as credible evidence can be brought to bear in favor of them. The writer is expected to make the strongest arguments possible for what he or she believes to be the case.

(John G. Blair,《英语学习》)

19.

Clarence Saunders was an American grocer who first developed the modern retail sales model of self service. His ideas have had a massive influence on the development of the modern supermarket. Clarence Saunders worked for most of his life trying to develop a truly automated store, developing Piggly Wiggly, Keedoozle, and Foodelectric store concept.

Born in Virginia, Saunders left school at 14 to clerk in a general store. Later he worked in an Alabama coke plant and in a Tennessee sawmill before he returned to the grocery business. By 1900, when he was nineteen years old, he was earning $30 a month as a salesman for a wholesale grocer. In 1902 he moved to Memphis where he formed a grocery wholesale cooperative. Through his experiences he became convinced that many small grocers failed because of heavy credit losses and high overhead. Consequently in 1915 he organized the Saunders-Blackburn Co., a grocery wholesaler which sold for cash only and encouraged its retail customers to do the same.

After leaving Clarksville, Tennessee, on September 6, 1916, Saunders launched the self-service revolution in the USA by opening the first self-service Piggly Wiggly store, at 79 Jefferson Street in Memphis, Tennessee, with its characteristic turnstile at the entrance. Customers paid cash and selected their own goods from the shelves.

The store incorporated shopping baskets, self-service branded products, and checkouts at the front. Removing unnecessary clerks, creating elaborate aisle displays, and rearranging the store to force customers to view all of the merchandise were just some of the characteristics of the early Piggly Wiggly stores. The concept of the "Self-Serving Store" was patented by Saunders in 1917.

(作者不详,2017 年 2 月雅思考试真题)

20.

When I was in Australia in 2011, I accompanied a friend on his driving test. I was amazed to learn that in Australia, just like in the US, people hardly go to driving school. Instead, many practice on the road with a licensed driver sitting next to them. But this doesn't mean that getting a driving license is a piece of cake. This was the third time that my friend had applied to take the driving test.

The first time, after confidently driving over an intersection, the examiner asked him to pull over and said that he should have stopped the car and looked right and then left (turning his neck) to make sure there was no other car approaching.

The second time, a car rushing in front caught him by surprise and he hit the brakes too hard. "The examiner got angry and told me to get out." My friend said.

"In Australia, the test is not about your driving skills, but about following every rule," he said.

(Wang Zi,《21 世纪报》,第 988 期)

21.

Spring Festival is a time to get together and do all the little things you enjoy. As most university students are packing their bags, boarding trains or flying home, some will stay behind to spend the holiday on campus. Zhou Yunyun, 22, a senior finance major at Jilin

University, has decided that instead of traveling to Hainan Province, he will kill the time by playing computer games with his online friends. "I'm used to chatting and playing with them every day. We send each other gifts frequently. It's just fun to make friends this way," he said. Zhou found it too expensive to fly all the way home, which would have cost him about ￥6,000 for a return trip. Now he can save that money for job-hunting.

（作者不详,《中国日报》双语新闻）

22.

Most scientists believe the link between rising Arctic temperatures and the resulting disruption of the jet stream is the most convincing explanation for the increased bouts of extreme weather in the northern hemisphere. However, some sound notes of caution. "I think the link between Arctic warming and weather disruption is convincing but it is not the only possible explanation," said Klingaman. "For example, there is a phenomenon known as the Madden-Julian oscillation which controls how rainfall is distributed around the tropics on a weekly and monthly basis and it has been shown to influence the position of the jet streams. It is possible this oscillation may have been involved in some way in our changing weather patterns."

（作者不详,道客巴巴,2016 年）

23.

The climate phenomenon that is being blamed for floods, hurricanes and snowstorms also deserves credit for invigorating plants and helping to control the pollutant linked to global warming, a new study shows. Natural weather events, such as the brief Warming caused by El Nino, have a much more dramatic effect than previously believed on how much carbon dioxide is absorbed by plants and how much of the gas is expelled by the soils, said David Schimel of the National Center for Atmospheric Research. He is co-author of a study to be published in the journal *Science*.

Atmospheric carbon dioxide, or CO_2, has been increasing steadily for decades. This is thought to be caused by an expanded use of fossil fuels and by toppling of tropical forests. Scientists have linked the CO_2 rise to global warming, a phenomenon known as the greenhouse effect. Nations of the world now are drawing up plans to reduce fossil-fuel burning in hopes of reducing greenhouse gases in the atmosphere...

（作者不详,上学吧,2018 年）

24.

It almost seemed as if government officials in three of China's biggest cities, Beijing, Shanghai and Guangzhou, had reached a secret agreement to synchronize their action. After months of debate and controversy, all three cities on Dec. 30 rolled out new policies on the sensitive issue of college entrance examinations for the children of migrant workers. These much-anticipated policies are being seen as indicative of national-level reforms on equal education rights in the future.

Until now, no matter how long migrant children lived with their parents in these cities, they would almost always have to return to their rural hometown to take the exams, creating a lot of problems for young students.

All three cities now say they are opening the gates for qualified migrant children to take college entrance exams in the cities they live in. However, the stringent conditions set out in the new policy guidelines are a disappointment to many…

(21st, *Toward Fairer Education*,《21 世纪报》,第 987 期)

25.

On his first day back on campus after Spring Festival, Li Yanbin felt sick. His stomach hurt and he kept throwing up. Doctor later told him that it is his water cooler to blame. Having stood there since before the vacation began, it had become a pool of bacteria.

Water safety matters. A UN report indicates that every year 3.5 million people die due to unsafe drinking water. Urban water quality issues in China came into the spotlight again recently after Shandong-based factories dumped industrial wastewater underground.

According to the Ministry of Land and Resources, 55 percent of groundwater is rated "bad" or "very bad" and poses a severe health hazard to the public.

Groundwater is a major source of water for urban areas. But it faces numerous pollution risks. Zhao Zhangyuan, a researcher at the Chinese Research Academy of Environmental Sciences (CRAES), said that many landfill sites don't have sufficient measures in place to prevent toxins from seeping into groundwater, reported *Guangming Daily* last week.

(Wang Zi, *It's a world of water*,《21 世纪报》,第 994 期)

26.

China sent its first medical aid team to Algeria in 1963. Since then, more than 170,000 medical personnel have been placed in 48 African countries treating more than 200 million patients, according to *China Daily*. During his visit to the Republic of Congo, Chinese President Xi Jinping thanked Chinese volunteers for the outstanding services they have provided to local residents and the honor they have earned for their country.

Yu Zhongjie has been on a training program for six months. The chief physician of the orthopedics department at Changzhou No. 2 People's Hospital will soon be dispatched to Zanzibar Tanzania's semi-autonomous region, on a two-year medical aid program that was launched in 1963. "The ones in training are all elite doctors from across Jiangsu province," said Yu, explaining that the Chinese government attaches great importance to medical aid for Africa.

Every day, Yu and his 20 teammates are instructed on disease prevention, language, indoor exercise, local taboos, religious etiquette and many other topics to make sure they keep up their health and image.

According to Yu Guoding, from Daishan People's Hospital in Zhejiang province, the image of Chinese doctors can be explained by a popular saying in the Central African Republic, "If there is a disease Chinese doctors cannot cure, it can't be cured."

(Wang Zi, *Medical aid marks 50th anniversary*,《英文报刊精华集萃》(第四辑),2015 年)

27.

Every time we make a phone call, log on to a WiFi network or browse the Internet, we leave a digital trail of data that can be tracked. The revelations that the US'National Security Agency (NSA) is accessing millions of US customer phone records and looking into the digital data stored by Internet companies show how aggressively personal data is being collected and analyzed.

Yahoo, along with other tech giants like Apple, Microsoft and Facebook published data requests from the government, which show that over the last six months it received more than 12,000 requests based on the *Foreign Intelligence Surveillance Act* (FISA), in addition to requests from other US law enforcement agencies.

What the telecommunication service providers hand over to the NSA is called metadata—excerpts of information generated as people use technology. Rather than personal or content-specific details, the data collected contains transactional information about the user, the device and activities taking place...

(21st, *What you should know about mass surveillance*,《21世纪报》,第1010期)

28.

There are around 6,000 languages in the world today. At least there were until January of 2001. Then Carlos Westez died. Westez was the last speaker of the native American language Catawba. With him passed away the language itself.

The death of Westez was mourned not just by professional linguists, but more generally by advocates of cultural diversity. Writing in *the Independent* of London, Peter Popham warned that "when a language dies" we lose "the possibility of a unique way of perceiving and describing the world." What particularly worries people like Popham is that many other languages are likely to follow the fate of Catawba. Aore is a language native to one of the islands of the Pacific state of Vanuatu. When the island's single inhabitant dies, so will the language. Ironically, the status of Gafat, an Ethiopian language spoken by fewer than 30 people, has been made more precarious thanks to the efforts of linguists attempting to preserve it. A language researcher took two speakers out of their native land, whereupon they caught cold and died...

(作者不详,*Time*)

二、汉译英练习

1.

潇湘晨报消息:10月2日11时30分左右,湖南省高警局怀化支队接到报警称一名11岁男孩在安江服务区走失了,请求高速交警帮忙寻找。

打电话求助的是来自广东深圳的霍先生,一家人带孩子去贵州旅游,途经怀化高速安江服务区休息时,11岁的儿子嫌车上太闷,独自下车玩,而他们在休息一会儿后以为孩子还在睡觉就继续出发,走出70千米到达下一个服务区时才发现孩子不见了。于是他们赶忙打了12122报警电话,当时已经从土桥收费站掉头前去寻找儿子。12点左右,民警在安江服务区找到了小男孩,并通知了小男孩的父母。

(袁廷轩、粟金欣、龙思瑶,《潇湘晨报》)

2.

奥林匹克运动会,是国际奥林匹克委员会主办的世界规模最大的综合性运动会,每四年一届,会期不超过16日,分为夏季奥运会、夏季残奥会、冬季奥运会、冬季残奥会、夏季青年奥运会和冬季青年奥运会。奥运会是各个国家用运动交流各国文化,以及切磋体育技能,其目的是为了鼓励人民的运动精神。奥林匹克运动会发源于两千多年前的古希腊,因举办地在奥林匹亚而得名。古代奥林匹克运动会停办了大约1500年之后,1896年举办了首届现代奥运会。

(作者不详,百度百科)

3.

端午节龙舟赛、元宵节舞龙及二月二龙头节是大东亚龙文化区重要的民间活动。龙舟就是船上画着龙的形状或做成龙的形状的船。赛龙舟是中国民间传统水上体育娱乐项目,多是在喜庆节日举行,是多人集体划桨竞赛。赛龙舟最早兴起于汉代。赛龙舟不仅是一种体育娱乐活动,更体现出我国传统的悠久历史文化继承性和人们的集体主义精神。

(宓澜,百度知道)

4.

唐诗泛指创作于唐代(618年—907年)的诗,也可以引申指以唐朝风格创作的诗。唐代被视为中国历来诗歌水平最高的黄金时期,因此有唐诗之说,与宋词并举。大部分唐诗都收录在《全唐诗》中,自唐朝开始,有关唐诗的选本不断涌现,而流传最广的当属蘅塘退士选编的《唐诗三百首》。唐诗是汉民族最珍贵的文化遗产,是汉文化宝库中的一颗明珠,同时也对周边民族和国家的文化发展产生了很大影响。按照时间,唐诗的创作分四个阶段初唐、盛唐、中唐、晚唐。

(作者不详,搜狗百科)

5.

唐代的诗人特别多。李白、杜甫、白居易、王维是世界闻名的伟大诗人,除他们之外,还有其他许多的诗人。就像满天的星斗一般。这些诗人,知名的就还有二千三百多人。他们的作品,保存在《全唐诗》中的也还有四万二千八百六十三首。当然,《全唐诗》并非"全",也有很多辞藻华丽、脍炙人口的诗篇,在那隐士之间流过,或者不予正面对待的消失在历史的长廊之中了。

(作者不详,搜狗百科)

6.

唐诗的题材非常广泛:有的反映当时社会的阶级状况和阶级矛盾,揭露封建社会的黑暗;有的歌颂正义战争,抒发爱国思想;有的描绘祖国河山的秀丽多娇;此外,还有抒写个人抱负和遭遇的,有表达儿女爱慕之情的,有诉说朋友交情、人生悲欢的。总之从自然现象、政治动态、劳动生活、社会风习,直到个人感受,都逃不过诗人敏锐的目光,成为他们写作的题材。在创作方法上,既有现实主义的流派,也有浪漫主义的流派,而许多伟大的作品,则又是这两种创作方法相结合的典范,形成了我国古典诗歌的优秀传统。

(作者不详,搜狗百科)

7.

10月5日报道 美媒称,日前,在一次破产拍卖中,纽约军事学院一所有126年历史的寄宿学校,其毕业生包括共和党总统竞选人唐纳德·特朗普——以近1600万美元的价格,被中国投资者控制下的一家非营利性组织所买下。投资者对学院负责人说,他们将使学院作为一所中学保持开办。

美国《纽约时报》10月1日报道称,自然保护研究中心成功中标位于哈得孙河附近的这片风景秀丽的区域。区域内有一座座建筑、兵营和大片土地。该中心成立于2011年,为的是收购纽约州的一个酒店。那次交易的标的物为一处"镀金时代"的地产,由铁路大亨哈里曼建成。

(王昕晨,《参考消息网》)

8.

李克强"大数据词典":共享、开放、安全

政府大数据建设,首先要实现所有部门的数据"共享"。

2014年3月5日,李克强在第十二届全国人民代表大会第二次会议上做政府工作报告时说,要设立新兴产业创业创新平台,在新一代移动通信、集成电路、大数据、先进制造、新能源、新材料等方面赶超先进,引领未来产业发展。

这是"大数据"首次进入政府工作报告,也表明其作为一种新兴产业,将得到国家层面的大力支持。

4个月后李克强在山东浪潮考察时的一番话更是表明,利用大数据绝不仅仅是企业的事,也是政府部门的事。当时,他把相关部门负责人叫到身边"现场办公",要求他们要以云计算、大数据理念,与企业信息技术平台有机对接,建立统一综合信用信息平台,实现"大数据"共享。

昨天召开的国务院常务会议上,他向有关部门明确要求:政府大数据建设,首先要实现所有部门的数据"共享"。

"目前,政府各部门已经建成了十几个数据平台,但问题是,这些平台相互不连通,只是一个一个的'信息孤岛'。"李克强针对政府大数据现状说,"本来,信息的连接是最容易的,商业网站之间都是连接的,但我们各部门的数据就不行,我的网就是我的网,别的部门要用,就是进不来!"

除了共享,李克强对于政府大数据建设谈到的第二个关键词是"开放"。他说:"有一些引导社会经济发展的数据,不涉及国家秘密的,都应该向公众开放,以方便大家使用。"

"数据,已经渗透到当今每一个行业和业务职能领域,"全球知名咨询公司麦肯锡指出,大数据是"创新、竞争和生产率的新边疆。"

不过,如果没有信息的开放,大数据将是无源之水。李克强总理深谙此道。他说,特别是一些与信用相关的数据平台,如果信息不共享、不开放,就会阻碍社会信用体系的建立。"我之前和企业家座谈,很多外贸企业负责人说,做出口贸易,挣钱再少至少收入可预期,回款正常,而在国内做生意,有时候搞不清楚,款拿不到,货物运送过程中还可能出现滞留。"

从另一方面讲,相关数据的开放,也会倒逼政府数据发布的真实性和规范性。

"现在一些地方、部门发布的数据,有时候会相互'打架',老百姓都搞不清楚究竟哪些数据是真实的。"李克强说,"这怎么提高社会治理能力,怎么建设现代政府呢?"

要完善产业标准体系,依法依规打击数据滥用、侵犯隐私等行为,让各类市场主体公平分享大数据带来的技术、制度和创新活力。

大数据广泛应用后,个人隐私怎么保护:搜索引擎知道我想搜什么,购物网站知道我想买什么,餐厅商店知道我偏好什么,这样的场景逐渐成为现实,个人信息会不会被滥用、个人隐私会不会被侵犯?

在8月19日的常务会议上,李克强强调的第三个关键词就是"安全"。他说,互联网等行业已经在不断创新、发展大数据产业。"因此,政府既要'扶持',为大数据产业创造一个健康发展的环境,又要'引导''规范',保障信息安全。"

(杨芳,人民网,2015年)

9.

近来,为进入海外大学读书而参加雅思考试(IELTS)的学生人数不断增加,雅思考试的组织者们也相应增加了考试次数来满足需求。去年5月和7月间的雅思考试中,上海考生达到了10 000人,今年这个数字增加到了17 000左右,比去年同期增长了约70%。不断增长的就业竞争压力是许多大学毕业生选择到海外继续读书的主要原因。

(作者不详,无忧考网)

10.

在美国的普林斯顿大学,一个男孩深深地爱上了一个女孩,但是,他一直不知道该如何向她表白,因为他怕被拒绝。一天,他终于想到了一个接近女孩的好办法。于是,他鼓起勇气,向正在校园里读书的女孩走去。

他对女孩说:"你好,我在这张字条上写了一句关于你的话。如果你觉得我写的是事实的话,那就麻烦你送我一张你的照片好吗?"

女孩立即想到,这又是一个找借口追求自己的男孩。

[(英)诺曼·列布雷奇,《逻辑的力量》,《读者》,2006年第13期]

11.

中国是图书产量最多的国家之一,但国人的阅读量却相对偏低。近几十年来,书籍供应量大大增加,但人们对书籍的兴趣却未同步增长。调查显示,国人年平均读书量仅为4.39本,与发达国家有很大差距。比如,美国人年均读书7本,法国人8.4本。调查数据还显示,只有1.3%的国人认为自己的阅读量多,53.1%的国人则认为自己的阅读量很少。

(作者不详,学小易网)

12.

酒后驾驶

2008年世界卫生组织的事故调查显示,大约50%~60%的交通事故与酒后驾驶有关,酒后驾驶已经被列为车祸致死的主要原因。在中国,每年由于酒后驾车引发的交通事故达数万起;而造成死亡的事故中50%以上都与酒后驾车有关。酒后驾车的危害触目惊心,已经成为交通事故的第一大"杀手"。

(作者不详,360百科)

13.

美国共和党总统初选参选人特朗普10月4号接受电视访问,谈到中东问题,表示利比亚前领导人卡扎菲,以及伊拉克前总统萨达姆继续掌权的话,中东会更稳定。他又表示,支持俄罗斯空袭叙利亚的极端组织"伊斯兰国"据点。

现时正以32%的支持率、领先其他共和党总统初选对手的特朗普,4号接受美国全国广播公司访问,谈到中东、叙利亚,以至美国国内的枪械管制问题。

特朗普直言,萨达姆和卡扎菲被推翻后,伊拉克和利比亚都陷入一片混乱,更表示如果二人现时继续掌权,中东会更稳定。特朗普又指,叙利亚将会出现和伊拉克及利比亚一样的情况。

(千帆,凤凰卫视,2015年)

14.

四 大 发 明

中国四大发明一般是指造纸术、指南针、火药、活字印刷术。此说法最早由英国汉学家李约瑟提出并为后来许多中国的历史学家所继承,普遍认为这四种发明对中国古代的政治、经济、文化的发展产生了巨大的推动作用,且这些发明经由各种途径传至西方,对世界文明发展史也产生了很大的影响。

(作者不详,百度百科)

15.

印刷术是中国古代四大发明之一。在隋朝,出现了雕版印刷,宋朝毕昇对其进行了改进。中国的雕版印刷和活字印刷是中国印刷术发展的两个阶段,它赐予了人类发展一份珍贵的礼物。它在印刷的便捷性和灵活性上有重大突破,节约了时间和劳动力。中国印刷术推进了知识的广泛传播和文化交流。以前,文化传播靠手写材料。然而手写会耗费很多时间,并容易出错,阻碍了文化的发展。

(作者不详,百度百科)

16.

1989年春节,我第一次和刚结婚的老公回他的老家江西省永新县芦溪乡千古洲村,那是我人生第一次真正地来到乡下过春节。作为村子里第一个北京媳妇,村里人好奇地打量着我,而我也好奇地观察着他们。

之后回去过多少次,没有仔细计算过,大多是回去过节。对于生长生活在北京的我来讲,根本没有家乡的概念,总是被老公称为"没有家乡的人"。

(郭大民,《家乡究竟是什么?》)

17.

毕昇(生卒年未详),北宋布衣。湖北英山县人。宋初为书肆刻工。宋庆历年间(1041—1048),他根据实践经验,发明胶泥活字印刷技术。这一技术未及推广,毕昇就去世了。他的字印为沈括家人收藏,其事迹见《梦溪笔谈》卷十八。活字印刷术具有一字多用、重复使用、印刷多且快、省时省力、节约材料等优点,比雕版印刷术有了质的飞跃,对后世印刷术乃至世界文明的进步,有着巨大而深远的影响。

(罗学贵,《荆楚奇人奇事录》)

18.

似乎越来越多的美国家长想让学校在他们的孩子不到5岁时就教授孩子外语。教这些孩子另一门语言最流行的方法就是被称为"浸入式"教学的方法。在浸入式课堂上的孩子只能听到这种新语言。孩子们在玩游戏、唱歌、彼此交谈时都使用这种语言。一些专家说浸入式课程是幼儿学习外语最有效的方法。但当孩子在如此小的年龄学习另一门语言时,可能会遇到问题。没有多少小学在孩子长大后还继续教授外语。

19.

今天,中国幼儿园里的大多数孩子都是独生子女。他们机灵、好学、想象力丰富、精力充沛,但往往以自我为中心,不守纪律,而且比较脆弱。一般来说,刚进幼儿园的4至6岁的孩子都是以自我为中心的,但9至10岁的孩子则表现出自制力强、不怕挫折的优点。因此我们的教育强调集体主义、互助友爱,鼓励孩子们自己照顾自己,并且教育他们与人分享的好处。

(作者不详,考试资料网)

20.

我是在填报志愿时才意识到高考是件大事。

那天晚上,父亲戴着眼镜,拿过填报志愿的指南,坐在沙发上默默地看了很久。家里很安静,可以听到隔壁邻居家传来的电视广告声。我们父子俩已经很久没有这么长时间地相对了。那时候父亲40多岁,这是我第一次长时间注视他戴着老花镜的样子。

不久前,他刚刚发现自己的眼睛花了,而我已经到了高考的年龄。

因为戴着老花镜,强壮的父亲露了一丝老态。他一页一页地翻着院校指南,专注阅读的神情,似乎在决定一件性命攸关的事情,在调动他全部的生活经验和智慧,为他的儿子图谋未来。

(贾樟柯,《高考落榜,其实是给了你一把钥匙》)

21.

孟加拉国警方说,一名日本公民10月3日在孟加拉国北部遭多名蒙面男子枪杀。这是不到一周内第二名外国人在这个南亚国家遇害。

"伊斯兰国"宣称制造这两起袭击事件,威胁制造更多杀戮,报复对这一极端组织的空袭。多国使领馆对孟加拉国治安状况表示担忧,对本国公民发布安全警告。孟加拉国内政部长说:"三名头戴面罩、骑着摩托车的男子使用手枪制造这起杀人事件。"

这是不到一周内在孟加拉国发生的第二起外国人被枪杀事件。9月28日,50岁的意大利援助人员在达卡使馆区附近锻炼时遭骑摩托车的男子枪击,背后中弹,经抢救无效身亡。

(石中玉,新华网,2015年)

22.

自特朗普上任以来的首次朝美会谈计划被取消,因为美国国务院已确定拒绝向朝鲜的外交特使崔善熙核发赴美签证。

据《华尔街日报》报道,崔善熙原定于3月1日至2日在纽约与美国官员举行会谈。这是特朗普就任美国总统以来朝美官员首次传出接触计划,也是自2011年以来首次传出朝鲜高级特使要访问美国。

由于崔善熙未能拿到赴美签证,此次会谈计划已经取消。目前尚不清楚是什么原因导致了美国的拒签。但外界猜测,朝鲜日前的导弹试射以及金正男在马来西亚被杀,或许对拒签决定起到了一定作用。

(隗俊,新浪网)

23.

吴运铎,1917年出生于湖北省武汉市,早年曾在安源煤矿当矿工。1938年参加新四军,被派到新四军司令部修械所工作。1939年加入中国共产党。

1941年皖南事变后,吴运铎随部队转移到淮南抗日根据地,被任命为新四军二师军工部副部长、子弹厂厂长。吴运铎带着8名技工,赤手空拳地来到高邮县金沟区平安乡的小朱庄,在借住的两间草房里成立了建厂基地,相继制成生产子弹的所有工具、机床,建成年产60万发的子弹厂。很快设计出迫击炮弹图样,试制出第一颗炮弹。

1942年的一天黄昏,新四军二师军工部要求修复一批废迫击炮弹。吴运铎亲自动手为废炮弹除锈、填药、安装弹尾、尾管、引信……

(刘波,《拼将残躯酬壮志——吴运铎》,新华日报)

24.

习近平访美期间发表演讲,用了近两分钟时间谈及反腐,表示"大力查处腐败案件,没有什么权力斗争"。作为最高领导人,习近平此次有关反腐与权力斗争的表述,是首次对各界最为直接的公开回应。

在这次美国之行的首站西雅图,习近平发表了一场备受关注的演讲,其中反腐是这次演讲的核心关键词之一。习近平在演讲中用了近两分钟的时间来谈反腐,这在他以往的各种出访演讲中极其少见。谈及反腐败时,习近平语气坚定,当说完说到《纸牌屋》后,他停顿了一下,在座的听众随即鼓掌,习近平看了看台下,微笑示意,并发出笑声。

(熊正良,求是网)

25.

10月4日下午,受台风"彩虹"影响,广东佛山顺德、广州番禺、汕尾海丰遭遇龙卷风。据记者从当地政府了解到,截至今天上午10点,共造成6人死亡,215人受伤。其中番禺死亡3人,伤134人;顺德死亡3人,伤81人,其中顺德重伤6人。

此外,龙卷风还导致广州、佛山大面积停电,其中海珠、番禺大片街道社区停水停电、交通灯失灵、停车场拥堵。

(魏星,央视网,2015年)

26.

昨晚,厦门一位网友向澎湃新闻记者发来一段手机视频,声称画面上的老人已经在鹭江道的轮渡码头等待了好几个小时。手机镜头前,这位老人情绪激动,几度哽咽,后更掩面而泣,令人动容。

这位叫邢玉华的老人来自北京,现已76岁,今年家人决定到鼓浪屿旅游,起初她不愿意,怕太拥挤,后来她觉得"偶尔到外面看一看也好",便听从了家人的建议。未曾想,这次旅程成了一场"噩梦"。

10月3日下午5点,当邢玉华一家兴冲冲地从机场赶到鹭江道轮渡码头才知道,这里已经改成了厦门市民专用通道,售票窗口的工作人员告诉她"没票了"。

(韩雨亭,澎湃新闻)

27.

人生是一场"舍得",有选择就有割舍。被尊称为"中国核潜艇之父"的黄旭华,他的割舍远远超出人们的想象。

从1938年离家求学,到1957年去广东出差时回家,对这19年的离别,母亲没有怨言,只是叮嘱他:"你小时候四处都在打仗,回不了家。现在社会安定了,交通方便了,母亲老了,希望你常回来看看。"

黄旭华满口答应,怎料这一别竟是30年。"我既然从事了这样一份工作,就只能淡化跟家人的联系。他们总会问我在做什么,我怎么回答呢?"于是,对母亲来说,他成了一个遥远的信箱号码。

(张智美子,《黄旭华的割舍:是母亲的信箱,是妻子的"客家人"》,《人民日报》)

28.

我常想:人生意义就在我们怎样看人生。

有人说,人生是梦,是很短的梦。有人说,人生不过是肥皂泡。其实,这都是悲观的说法。而我要说就算是做梦,也要做一个热闹的、轰轰烈烈的好梦,不要做悲观的梦。

既然辛辛苦苦上台,就要好好唱戏,唱个像样子的戏,不要跑龙套。我们的一举一动、一言一行都可以有永不磨灭的影响。

民国元年,有一个英国人到我们学堂讲话,讲的内容很荒谬,但他的O字的发音,同普通人不一样,是尖声的。这也影响到我的O字的发音,许多我的学生又受到我的影响……

(胡适,《人生的意义就在我们怎样看人生》)

29.

在恋爱中,我们内心最深的情感需求就是感到恋爱,因此,很多人在恋爱中都喜欢做这两件事:证明他爱我,证明他不爱我。

因为安全感的普遍缺失,大部分喜欢去证明后者。"他都没说过爱我,那肯定没那么爱我。""她那么独立,都不需要我陪,是不是我根本没那么重要?"

你需要很多证据去证明他爱你,但只需要一个证据就可以证明他不爱你。所以很多情侣分手时常常抱怨:"我为你付出那么多,却没感觉到你有多爱我。"

但事实是:有时他并不是不爱你,而是不会表达爱,或是你并没有接收到他爱的语言。

(渲少,《"我爱你"有5种表达方式》,《东方女性》,2018年第3期)

30.

2018年3月22日,张弥曼接过由联合国教科文组织授予的2018年度"世界杰出女科学家"奖。颁奖仪式上,她身着一袭中式长裙款款上台,全程脱稿,用流利的英语致辞,其间,法语、汉语、俄语和瑞典语转换自如,优雅的气质和幽默的语言令中国的网友们备感"惊艳"。大家热情地称她为"网红女科学家""中国科研玫瑰""真正的国民女神"。

身为中国科学院资深院士、瑞典皇家科学院外籍院士,国际古脊椎动物领域最高奖"罗美尔—辛普森终身成就奖"获得者,荣誉、声望对这位世界知名的古生物学家来说早已不是什么新鲜事。而相比获奖、当"网红",对张弥曼来说,眼下最重要的事依然是做科研。

(符遥,《82岁科学家获"世界杰出女科学家"奖,
被称"国民女神"》,《中国新闻周刊》刊总第848期)

31.

1986年,我担任上海戏剧学院院长。我们学院有一位老教师,是从美国耶鲁大学戏剧系留学回来的,据说回来时与钱学森先生坐的是同一艘轮船,因此资历足够。但是,直到我担任院长,他还没有评上副教授。

这好像太怠慢他了,旁人一听都会为他叫屈。我亲自查了他的专业档案,发现他几十年来既没有上过课,也没有写过书,更没有排过戏,只留下一些凌乱的英文笔记,装订成册。我翻了一下,那些英文笔记也只是一些片断抄录,没有任何自己的观点……

(余秋雨,《评审职称往事》)

32.

美国一家媒体曾对服务生小费做过一项调查,结果发现,服务生替客人点菜时,一边聆听一边点头,或者一边轻声重复一下,得到小费的概率要比其他只顾埋头记菜名的服务生高出70%。

英国一家媒体的调查也得出类似的结论。英国餐厅里有一种传统,客人用完餐后,服务生会送一粒薄荷糖,送一粒糖的服务生得到的小费要比没送的高3%,送两粒糖的要高出14%,而如果先送了一粒糖后,再反身回来送上一粒糖的,那小费会比没送的高出25%。

这两项媒体调查非常有意思。道理其实很简单,你尊重别人,别人自然会尊重你。换言之,你与客人"互动"得越多,关系就会越融洽,得到小费就会越多。

这只是小费。如果这是人生,那么回馈会更多。

(流沙,《"互动"的价值》)

33.

鲨鱼是海洋中的强者,几乎没有什么海洋动物能够伤害到它们。鲨鱼的凶悍,不仅在于高居食物链的顶端,通吃海中众生,更在于它们那戏耍已到手猎物的本性。比如,当海豹、海狮和信天翁等不幸成为它们的猎物时,鲨鱼却不急于开吃,而是将猎物在水面上抛来抛去,戏耍一番,使得猎物在毙命前饱受煎熬。

鲨鱼虽然强悍,但它也有致命的天敌,那就是盲鳗。盲鳗弱小,论实力本不是鲨鱼的对手,鲨鱼的一颗牙齿都要比它重几十倍,但盲鳗自有它的温柔撒手锏。

(鲍海英,《致命的温柔》)

34.

上世纪六十年代,正值国家经济困难时期,我和妹妹远离父母住校读高中和初中。星期天,住校生只能吃两顿饭,而且两顿饭都吃不饱。

漫长的冬日我饥饿难耐,于是写信向母亲诉苦。几天后,我意外地收到了一个小包裹,原来是母亲寄来的,打开一看,里面装有两袋炒面并附有一纸书信。

我忙不迭地展开信纸:"儿,现在国家有困难,我们每个人都要担待点儿。熬过这一阵就会好起来的,你要有毅力啊。给你寄去你爸劳保发的两袋炒面,你和妹妹分着吃。母亲手书。"……

(董蔚建,《便条保存50年》)

35.

1875年8月4日,安徒生在一个商人朋友家里喝完早茶,觉得不舒服,在床上躺下,然后就去世了,享年70岁。

在去世前不久,他的身体就已经非常不好,有一位音乐家说,我要给你专门谱写一首葬礼进行曲。安徒生就说,我写了一辈子童话,给我送殡的人,多数会是小孩子。你写的这个进行曲,它的节拍最好能够配合小孩子那种细小的脚步。

看到这个细节,我很震撼。一个人一辈子能做成一件事,一定是因为他精神世界的每一个角落都是这件事,甚至包括葬礼的细节。一个人一辈子,如果真的做成了一件事,也一定体现为:在他的葬礼上,人们也不能忘了这件事。

(罗振宇,《如何成为一个能成事的人》)

36.

2007年本科毕业后,我来到美国芝加哥,开始了留学生活。由于大学生活过得浑浑噩噩,我发誓出国读研一定要提早规划,提前行动。憋着一股劲的我,把目标牢牢锁定在找暑期实习上。

找实习需要一份过硬的简历,于是积攒经历成了当务之急。当时听说有位金融系的教授在做一个研究项目,如饥似渴的我看到了机会。于是我堵在他上课的教室门口,一下课就冲上去做自我介绍,说我很想帮他做研究。估计他被我的诚意打动,居然真的答应让我做他的助理实习员……

(程虹,《像穿珍珠一样找工作》)

37.

老鼠具有极强的适应能力,从来不需要人类的保护。当它的天性与人类的利益发生冲突时,还曾受到人类的强力打压。熊猫具有极高的观赏价值与研究价值,早就被列为国宝,受到了人类无微不至的呵护。

商业文化中,常把那些最前线、最底层、最赤裸裸面对盈亏的机构或个人比喻为老鼠,借比的是老鼠的嗅觉、警觉性与行动力。而熊猫在商业文化中的价值,似乎就只有"物以稀为贵"了。

如果你学的就是怎样直截了当地赚钱,所有侧翼知识也都围绕着这一点展开,那你就是在学着当老鼠;如果你学的是高精尖且暂时未有市场价值的高科技,或者阳春白雪、佶屈聱牙的艺术,你就是在学着当熊猫。

(明德伦,《当老鼠,还是当熊猫》)

38.

在非洲纳米比亚北部的大草原中,生活着许多高角羚,它们体形中等,足蹄短而结实,善于奔跑和跳跃。高角羚奔跑的最高时速可达95公里,而且耐力相当好,常常令不少捕食者一无所获,悻悻而归。

在人们看来,当高角羚遭遇危险时,只要竭尽全力奔跑就行了,可是,以英国科学家艾伦·威尔逊为首的研究者们经过长期观察,发现事实并非如此。

艾伦·威尔逊和合作者们给一些高角羚和经常偷袭它们的猎豹戴上了装有全球定位系统(GPS)和加速度计的项圈,在观测了数千次追猎过程之后,得到了它们奔跑过程中每一步的速度、加速度和轨迹信息,结果发现,高角羚逃跑时很少跑出能力之内的最高时速,而是通常保持在最高时速的80%左右。这是为什么呢?

(江东旭,《不全速奔跑的高角羚》)

39.

坍缩将在深夜1时24分17秒时发生。对坍缩的观测将在国家天文台最大的观测厅进行,这个观测厅接收在同步轨道上运行的太空望远镜发回的图像,并把它投射到一面面积有一个篮球场大小的巨型屏幕上。

现在,屏幕上还是空白。到场的人并不多,但都是理论物理学、天体物理学和宇宙学的权威,对即将到来的这一时刻,他们是这个世界上少数真正能理解其含义的人。此时他们静静地坐着,等着那一时刻。只有天文台的台长在焦躁地来回踱着步。巨型屏幕出了故障,而负责维修的工程师到现在还没来。

(刘慈欣,《坍缩》)

40.

还有半年大学毕业时,我做了一个重要的决定:先不工作,用一年时间做公益。

做这个决定出于两个原因:一是我在大学里就一直参与公益活动,这种实践对我的心智健全和人格完整帮助很大,我愿意去经受更多;二是我们服务的对象,是一个即将消失在历史中的边缘老年群体,我们是在和时间抢人。

比起做决定所经历的一番挣扎,更困难的是怎样说服家里人同意。他们无法理解为什么辛辛苦苦供我读了十几年书终于毕业,我却不立即去工作赚钱,而是跑去做这种事……

(慕冬,《我从未后悔公益间隔年的选择》)

41.

认识他之后,我才知道,自己就是传说中"有趣的灵魂"。

吃午饭的时候,我认真思考晚饭吃什么;坐地铁时,我打量每一个人,偷听他们聊天。而他,每天吃同一家饭馆的肉夹馍,因为他认为翻订餐软件纯属浪费时间;地铁上不管有多挤,他都会读书。他说,其实很难读进去,但这让这件事更有了挑战性。

认识他之后,我也才知道,自己有多懒。我不只是事业心不够,连玩都不够努力。为了约我出去吃饭,他前一天加班到深夜,搞定所有工作。为了跟他吃饭,我把已经拖延的稿子又拖了拖……

(ONE·一个,《所谓爱情,就是废柴的我,爱上了打鸡血的你》)

42.

汉唐时期,中国传统文化传入日本。唐鉴真东渡,中国的佛教文化以及雕塑等传到日本,大量日本遣唐使到中国研习中国的文化,如此日本的文字、建筑深受中国文化的影响。中国传统文化在明清之际,传播到了欧洲一些国家。中国的四大发明先后传入西方后,对于促进西方资本主义社会的形成和发展,起到了重要作用。中国传统文化对法国的影响最大,法国成为当时欧洲"中国文化热"的中心。法国18世纪的启蒙思想家对中国文化的推崇程度,让我们都感到震惊……

(《中国的文化》,搜狗百科)

43.

你可能认识这样的人——他们非常聪明,精神生活无比丰富,特别喜欢学习,有很多爱好,对各种事情都了解,在各个学科都有涉猎。他们都是有意思的人,你喜欢和他们聊天,你总能跟他们学到你不知道的东西。

但是这些人,没有取得什么重大成就,他们年轻时充满自信,年龄大了却有一种失落感,觉得浪费了自己的才华,这些人可能陷入了"达·芬奇诅咒"。

《达·芬奇诅咒》是前几年出版的一本书,作者叫莱昂纳多·洛斯彭纳托。

达·芬奇是画家,还是一位建筑师,他擅长人体解剖,在科学上有很多成就,还搞了很多技术上的发明创造,是个全才。而"达·芬奇诅咒"的意思则是,一个人也像达·芬奇一样对什么东西都感兴趣,也像个全才,结果却一事无成……

(万维刚,《达·芬奇诅咒》)

44.

最近听一位民办教育专家讲到,经济是解决今天的问题,科技是解决明天的问题,教育是解决未来的问题。作为科幻作家,我听了很受触动,因为在解决未来的问题这一点上,科幻跟教育异曲同工。

说到教育,亚洲尤其是东亚教育,因为过于注重应试能力和强调死记硬背,时而受到批评。近来也有变化。中国城市里的学校开始注重培养学生的好奇心和想象力。这方面的一个表现是科幻进入学校,课文中也有了科幻小说。但是,想象力在中国教育中的分布不平衡,这或许是中国社会主要矛盾变化的一个反映……

(韩松,《两堂科幻课:想象力的城乡差异》)

45.

黄河,中国北部大河,全长约 5 464 千米,流域面积约 752 443 平方公里。世界第五大长河,中国第二长河。

黄河中上游以山地为主,下游以平原、丘陵为主。由于河流中段流经中国黄土高原地区,因此夹带了大量的泥沙,所以它也被称为世界上含沙量最多的河流。但是在中国历史上,黄河下游的改道给人类文明带来了巨大的影响。

黄河是中华文明主要的发源地,中国人称其为"母亲河"。每年都会产生 16 亿吨泥沙,其中有 12 亿吨流入大海,剩下 4 亿吨长年留在黄河下游,形成冲积平原,有利于种植。

("黄河",百度百科)

附录3 翻译补充练习参考译文

一、英译汉练习

1.

难民与防暴警察发生冲突 欧盟谴责匈牙利

移民令克罗地亚人满为患 欧盟将举办移民危机峰会

周四,两名克罗地亚警察注视着在火车站等待火车的难民。该火车站位于塞尔维亚和克罗地亚官方边境附近,靠近克罗地亚东部小镇托瓦尼克。照片来自法新社。

周四,欧盟移民局局长指责匈牙利处理大批难民手段粗暴。匈牙利在边境设置新围墙,防暴警察驱赶寻求庇护的难民,难民涌入克罗地亚,紧张局势继续蔓延。克罗地亚警察说,自周二匈牙利关闭其南边与塞尔维亚的欧盟边境以来,5 000 多名塞尔维亚移民聚集在这里。周三,匈牙利安全部队使用催泪瓦斯和高压水枪驱散投掷石块的难民。数量空前的难民申请庇护,因处理进度缓慢,德国联邦移民与难民局局长因此受到批评,后来该局长因个人原因辞职。德国警方称,周三抵达德国的难民数量增加了一倍多,达到 7 266 人。

就如何应对从叙利亚、伊拉克、阿富汗和巴基斯坦逃离战争和贫困而大量涌入的难民问题存在巨大分歧,已造成欧盟国家一连串以邻为壑的行为,给 28 国组成的欧盟带来了危机。

在匈牙利外交和内政部长联合举行的新闻发布会上,欧盟移民事务专员季米特里斯·阿夫拉莫普洛表示,抵达欧洲的大部分难民是"需要我们帮助"的叙利亚人。他宣称:"如果是因为暴力和恐惧而逃离家园,就没有翻越不了的墙,也没有横渡不了的大海。"他说,匈牙利建立隔离墙这样的临时解决方案,只能逼迫难民和移民去别处逃难,导致紧张局势上升。

匈牙利外交部部长彼得·西亚尔回击了联合国和欧洲官员的批评。他说,暴动难民在冲突中向警察投掷了石块,砸伤 20 名警察,所以支持这些暴动难民就是煽动暴力。

宗教差异

德国总理安格拉·默克尔欢迎叙利亚难民进入德国,匈牙利总理维克多·欧尔班指责德国引发大批移民进入匈牙利。他说,如果继续执行这个政策,在数目上欧洲穆斯林最终将超过基督徒。

在一次采访中,欧尔班说:"我在谈与上帝有关之事。我指的是文化和日常生活原则,如性习惯、言论自由、男女平等以及我称之为基督教的那些价值观。如果我们允许穆斯林进入欧洲大陆和我们竞争,他们的数量将超过我们。这是简单的数学运算题。这种情况我们不喜欢。"他的这些言论刊登在欧洲数家新闻报纸上,包括《泰晤士报》。

欧盟委员会提议在欧盟国家按照强制配额分配难民,邻国斯洛伐克也以宗教差异为由拒绝接受。欧盟行政官说庇护权是不可分割的,不能因宗教或种族原因予以剥夺。

周二,欧盟内政部长将再次举行特别会议,设法解决处理移民危机时存在的差异问题,促使以德国为首的几个欧盟国家再次实施边境临时管制。

各方反应

对于与塞尔维亚边境存在的混乱场面,周四克罗地亚表示无法应付寻求新路线进入欧盟的数目巨大的移民。周三,匈牙利防暴警察和投掷石块的难民发生冲突,之后 24 小时内超过 7 300 人从塞尔维亚进入克罗地亚。

斯洛文尼亚总理米罗·采拉尔说,斯洛文尼亚将坚持遵守申根条例规定,要求移民和寻求庇护者抵达时登记信息并录指纹。许多难民拒绝登记,损毁了他们的身份证明文件,要求去德国。

周四,罗马尼亚总统克劳斯·约翰尼斯表示,该国认为强制性配额不能解决欧盟移民危机。之前,罗马尼亚表示最多可以接收 1 785 名移民,但是按照欧盟的重新安置方案,罗马尼亚将不得不接收更多的移民。

保加利亚表示该国正派遣更多士兵,加强与土耳其边境控制,避免难民涌入。保加利亚内政部官员说,在过去的 25 小时,大约 600 名移民试图穿越边境,但看到边境把守严密,就自愿返回了。

2.

中国高铁

在中国,高速铁路(高铁)是指能提供商业列车服务、时速 200 千米(124 英里/小时)或以上的任何铁路。按照这个衡量标准计算,截至 2014 年 12 月,中国拥有世界上最长的高铁网络,服务里程超过 16 000 千米(9 900 英里)(如果加上货运线路,长达 19 369.8 千米)。这比世界上其他国家高铁运营里程总和还要长。中国高铁运输系统中有一条世界上最长的线路——京广高速铁路线,长达 2 298 千米(1 428 英里)。

自 2007 年 4 月 18 日中国高铁运营以来,每日客流量已从 2007 年的 23.7 万人增长到 2014 年的 249 万人,中国高铁成为世界上使用最为频繁的铁路网络。截至 2014 年 10 月,累计客流量达到 29 亿人次。

中国的高铁网络主要包括升级为客货共运线路的传统铁路、新建的客运指定线路和城际线。还有,上海磁悬浮列车是世界上第一个商用磁悬浮高速线路,由上海市政府经营。中国铁路总公司(国企)经营几乎所有的高速铁路线和全部车辆,其前身是中国铁道部。

在过去的十年中,中国经历了一个高铁建设热潮,这得益于中国政府的经济刺激方案提供了充足的资金。2011 年,中国铁道部原部长刘志军因贪腐和温州附近发生的一次致命的高铁事故遭免职,高铁发展速度放缓了一段时间,但此后又高速发展起来。高铁的安全性、票价高、上座率低、高铁项目财务的可持续性以及对环境的影响,这些民众的担忧已经引起中国媒体更密切的关注。

中国早期的高速火车要么是进口的,要么是按照外国列车制造商技术转让协议建造的。这些制造商包括阿尔斯通、西门子、庞巴迪和川崎重工。然后,中国工程师重新设计列车内部组件,建造时速可达 380 千米(240 英里)的本土列车。

3.

空调"净化"空气的方式无意中也会导致健康问题。比如,静电除尘器在除掉空气中的灰尘和烟雾颗粒的同时,还将大量的正离子空气排入通风系统。越来越多的研究表明,吸入过量正离子空气会导致头痛、疲劳和易怒情绪。

大型空调系统通过空气加湿器将水添加到流通空气中。在旧式空调系统中,系统用水储存在一个特制水箱中,水箱底部成了滋生细菌和真菌的温床,从此处细菌和真菌可进入通风系统。这种情况下的健康风险需要特别注意,因为在装有空调系统的写字楼里,大约一半人员的免疫系统已经产生了抗体,可以抵御水箱底部发现的细菌和真菌。人们将称为"杀虫剂"的化学消毒剂添加到水箱中杀菌,如果足量本身是危险的,因为他们往往含有如五氯苯酚的化合物,与腹部患癌密切相关。

最后,应该指出,空调创造的人工气候环境也对我们身体有害。在自然环境中,无论是室内还是室外,空气的温度和湿度变化不大。事实上,人体早已习惯这些正常变化。然而,在一个装有空调的生活或工作环境中,人的体温远低于正常的温度(37℃),这导致免疫系统变弱,因此人更容易患上如感冒和流感这样的疾病。

4.

日美修改《共同防御大纲》 中国敦促两国谨慎行事

10 月 9 日,北京(新华社)。周四,中国敦促日美谨慎修改《共同防御大纲》,建议两国在保持地区和平和稳定方面发挥建设性作用。

有媒体报道暗示,就防卫大纲修订的一份临时报告指出,日美这样做主要针对中国钓鱼岛。因此,中国外交部发言人洪磊做出上述评论。他重申,钓鱼岛及其附属岛屿是中国的固有领土。"外国压力不会动摇中国维护国家主权和领土完整的决心。"洪磊说,日美联盟是在特殊历史条件下签订的双边协议,不应超越双边范畴或损害包括中国在内的第三方利益。

他说,中国将密切关注日美修订防卫合作大纲。

自2012年9月日本政府"购买"钓鱼岛以来,中日关系已恶化。

5.

习主席此访有助于阐明独特的关系

编者按:

下周,中国国家主席习近平将首次对美国进行国事访问。两国双边关系立足点是什么?习主席此访有什么重要意义?美国两位著名专家给我们分享了他们的见解。

伊丽莎白·伊科诺米,C.V.斯塔尔高级研究员,对外关系委员会亚洲研究主管

当前美中关系有点困难。传统上,我们两国之间尽管有一些摩擦,但是能处理得妥当,所以两国关系非常稳定。我认为,美中双方都致力于维护、发展两国关系。

但是,摆在我们面前有几个重大挑战,未来也没有什么好办法可以解决,比如网络安全问题。我们也在关注中国经济改革取得的进步。从中国角度来看,中国担心美国在南海的立场、美日联盟的作用、跨太平洋伙伴关系以及美国在该地区对中国留出生存空间的大小。有很多问题需要双方努力解决。

有两种不同的策略。一是我们真的需要通过透明、公开的对话讨论这些问题。双方都需要清楚陈述所面临的挑战是什么,并努力找到解决每一个摩擦的方法。与此同时,我们需要探索新的合作领域。去年,习近平主席与奥巴马总统在亚太经合组织峰会上会晤,双方签署了两国之间三个非常具体的协议。有一系列全球性挑战性问题等待美中两国合作解决。

访问期间,习近平主席将有很多机会接触美国民众,表达他对中国及美中关系的愿景。好几天时间里,他不仅有机会会见美国政策制定者,而且有机会会见广大民众。我希望他能够解释他对中国、双边关系和中国之世界角色的愿景。美国认为,中国领导阶层和中国的发展方向有很多不确定因素。如果习主席能对此加以解释,这将可算作他此访取得的一个主要成就。

二是制订双边投资协定,我们在这方面可加强合作。明年过后,如果我们能在这方面取得实质性进展,会对维系中美关系提供很大帮助。

詹姆斯·斯坦伯格,美国前副国务卿,现任雪城大学公民与公共事务麦斯威尔学院社会科学、国际事务与法律系系主任

对美国人来说,习近平是一位重要领导人,我们希望与他建立良好关系。他即将访美,继续两国之间的对话,令我们倍受鼓舞。美中双方将坦诚、公开开展对话,愿意了解对方并找到共同解决问题的办法。

美中关系很独特。如果试图把美中关系封存起来避而不谈,或将(现在的)两国关系与历史上的(两国)关系联系起来,我们将不会理解今天两国关系的丰富性和复杂性。

美中双边关系有许多积极迹象。我们可以在许多领域开展合作,如气候变化、全球公共卫生和应对核扩散问题。而且,美中两国合作得很好,不仅造福两国,而且也造福世界。

尽管存在挑战和差异,但双方的确都有责任加以应对,从而不会引起不必要的冲突。双方也有义务找到让彼此放心的做法。实际上,我们希望所有国家都能取得成功,繁荣昌盛,希望本地区和平安定。

随着中国不断取得成功,问题是中国试图扮演什么样的角色。作为一个崛起中的大国,中

国确实有责任让美国、邻国和其他国家放心自己将以积极方式利用所取得的成果。所以,习近平主席将有机会在此次访问中回答这些问题,帮助他人了解中国的发展目标和发展意图,以及当前中国行为的正确解读方式。

经济相互依赖是我们两国关系的一个重要特征,但我坚信这是不够的。光有经济相互依赖并不能保证和平与安定。我们必须共同应对一系列问题。

联合国为我们提供了多边交流的机会。作为联合国安理会成员国,美国和中国有很大责任引领全球发展,促进和平与繁荣。

6.

官方消息:人民币汇率稳定

周四,在一场新闻发布会上,国家外汇管理局的一位官员说,人民币汇率保持稳定。

在国家外汇管理局召开的第三季度例行新闻发布会上,综合司司长王允贵说,目前中国不太可能出现大规模的资本流入或流出。他还指出,如果美联储不久宣布加息,人民币兑换美元时将贬值,但这是正常现象,不会引发资金的异常流动。

最近几周,人民币汇率已经出现波动。8月11日,人民币兑换美元贬值约2%,这是近20年来一天内的最大跌幅。同日,中国中央银行——中国人民银行(PBC)宣布,将调整系统以修复汇率中间价,当天人民币兑美元变化幅度达2%。

中国人民银行表示,新机制不但考虑到了外汇供求情况,还考虑到了主要货币汇率变动情形。

周四,上海财经大学金融系教授奚君羊告诉《环球时报》,人民币太依赖旧体系下的美元了。奚教授说,美元升值时,人民币兑换其他国家非美元货币时就会升值,这对中国向这些国家出口有负面影响。

奚教授指出,中国人民银行推出的改革措施表明中国正向市场导向的汇率制度迈进了一步。他还指出,新的中心汇率制度缩小了离岸人民币和国内货币汇率的差距,从而可阻止投机性资本流动。

人民币贬值引起人们对大规模资本外流可能性的担忧,但是专家指出,资金是否外流要看人民币的发展趋势。

奚教授说,如果人们认为8月份人民币贬值后会出现多轮贬值,资本就会外流;如果人们认为8月份人民币的贬值仅仅是单一事件,就不会出现资本大规模外流。他还指出,从当前的形势来看,汇率大规模波动的可能性很小。

王允贵还说,新的中心汇率制度实施后,人民币贬值的压力已经得到缓解,大量资本外流的可能性就会变小。他表示,国家外汇管理局最近采取了一些措施以限制资本外流,将加大打击力度,阻止通过非法货币商造成的资本外流。但他强调,国家外汇管理局还没有推出任何限制公众购买外币的新政策,有关机构能够满足公司和个人对外汇真实、合法的需求。

周四,中国商务部国际贸易经济合作研究院研究员白明告诉《环球时报》,很难判断最近人民币的贬值是否有助于促进中国对外出口业务。他说,仅在特定条件下,人民币的贬值会使出口量增多,比如中国产品竞争力增强、政府政策倾斜力度加大或者国际市场需求增加。

据商务部周三发表的一份声明可知,人民币的贬值并不是为了增加出口。9月8日的海关总署统计数据显示,8月份中国出口同比下滑6.1%,下降至约1.204万亿元人民币(合

1 890亿美元)。

7.

寻 找 生 命

古老的宇宙飞船"生命探测号",在探索宇宙星系、寻找外星生命700年后,即将返回地球。

这艘飞船的飞行速度接近光速,已搜遍银河系,分析了100多亿颗行星,寻找智慧生命。在执行任务期间,一代又一代的人类宇航员在飞船上生活、死去。就在他们结束往返旅程的最后几周时,我与飞船上的机器人指挥官——大鼻子2号展开了一番对话。

——那么,大鼻子2号,任务取得成功了吗?

——我们用了700年搜索了100亿颗行星,但是没有找到外星生命。不,准确地说,我不会称之为成功。

——没有智慧生命的任何迹象吗?

——没有,连愚蠢的生命都没有,甚至连一小片海藻都没找到,甚至连一个单细胞的细菌都没找到。除了块块岩石和朵朵云团外,那里什么也没有。星系是我去过的最死气沉沉的地方。我相信地球是整个星系中唯一有生命的行星。我迫不及待地想回家。

但是,还有一线希望。你不是很快要穿过大丑鸡云团吗?那里有一千颗大小和温度与地球相同的行星。

——24小时后,我们将进入大丑鸡星座。我们要用一星期时间分析那里所有的行星。

——那么,下周这个时候,你可能会给我们带来一些令人兴奋的消息!

——不一定。

——但是,你有可能在其中的一个行星上找到外星生命呀!

——也许吧。但是,如果我是你的话,我不会太兴奋的。就像你们人类说的,别憋着呼吸。

——祝你在大丑鸡星座有好运。我们下周再谈。

8.

信 任

昨晚,我驱车从宾夕法尼亚州的哈里斯堡赶赴刘易斯堡,其间约有八十英里的路程。天色已晚,我动身也晚了。要是有人问我车开得有多快,我会根据《美国宪法修正案》第五条而不予回答,以免自证其罪。在狭窄的公路上,有好几次,我的车被缓慢行驶的货车挡在后面,而左侧是一条严禁超越的白色实线,急得我把拳头握得紧紧的。

在一条开阔的公路某处,我行至一个有交通指示灯的十字路口,当时公路上就我一人。我的车刚驶近路口,红灯就亮了,我赶紧刹住车。我环顾四周,什么也没看到,没有一辆汽车,连车灯的影子也没有。尽管如此,我还是一直端坐着,等待交通指示灯变色。至少在周围一英里范围内,就我一个人。

我开始琢磨起自己不肯闯红灯的原因来。我并不是害怕被警察拘留,因为周围根本没有警察,即使闯红灯也不会有什么危险。

当晚我在刘易斯堡会见了一群人,到爬上床时已是半夜时分了,为什么不肯闯红灯这个问题又一次出现在我的脑海中。我认为,我之所以不闯红灯,是因为这是人们遵守的契约的一部分。这既是法律规定,也是我们签署的协议。我们相信大家都会遵守该协议内容:不闯红灯。

和大多数人一样,我之所以不做坏事,主要是因为社会惯例不赞成这么做,而不是因为法律不允许这么做。

9.

百合网是中国最大的在线约会和相亲网站,但法律纠纷不断。

在最近的一次诉讼中,一位女士声称,通过该网站,她结识了一位男士,他声称自己单身,是一家上市公司的董事会主席。但是当他们发生关系她怀孕后,她才发现他实际上已婚,伪造了他职业生涯的所有信息。

她报了警,警方以欺诈罪拘捕了他。她还将网站告上法庭,称该网站未能验证会员信息。在中国,众多相亲网站不断出现,确保会员是单身的确对网站和客户都很重要。

所以,你怎么看这个问题?你认为相亲网站有义务验证注册会员的个人信息吗?

10.

俄亥俄州的一名少年向五位同学开枪,造成三人死亡,两人受伤。西雅图一名九岁男孩带枪上学,结果枪支在背包中意外走火,造成一名同学受重伤。

每天都有儿童受伤或者遭到谋杀,但是校园暴力却有象征性的影响,因为我们都认为学校是安全的港湾,那里远离成人世界中的残酷景象。因此,一想到学校可能是一个带来伤害甚至致人死亡的地方,人们就会不寒而栗。

11.

终生教育(节选)

周游世界时,我们会惊讶地发现,无论是在印度、美国抑或是澳大利亚,人性是何其相似。在大学里尤其如此。在这里,仿佛用一个模子做出的一样,我们都变成了这样的一类人:主要兴趣是找到安全感,变成大人物,或无忧无虑地过快乐日子。

传统教育使独立思考变得异常困难。因循守旧带来的是平庸。只要我们崇尚成功,那么要做到与众不同或抵御环境因素侵扰就困难多多,危险重重。渴望成功,即获取物质上或所谓的精神领域的回报,寻求内心或外在的安全感,渴望过上舒适生活等,整个过程抑制了人的不满情绪,扼杀了人的自发性,让人心生恐惧,因而人们无法真正领悟生命的意义。随着年龄的增加,心智越发变得迟钝了。

追求舒适生活时,一般我们会在生活中找一个尽可能没有冲突的安静角落待着,害怕走出那个隐蔽的地方。这种对生活、对奋斗、对新体验的恐惧感,致使我们的冒险精神遗失殆尽;我们的成长历程和所接受的教育使我们害怕自己与邻居不同,不敢怀有与社会现有模式相悖的想法,导致我们错误地尊重权威、恪守传统。

12.

约翰·G.布莱尔在纽约出生,在美国东北部长大。他曾就读于美国罗德岛州普罗维登斯的布朗大学,1962年获得英美文学博士学位。

20世纪60年代的大部分时间里,他在密歇根州的奥克兰大学从教,之后去了欧洲讲法语的地区。他先在斯特拉斯堡大学做富布赖特美国文学专业的交换教授,然后一直在瑞士日内瓦大学教授美国文学与文明课,直到2000年退休。现在,作为一名外国专家,他在北京外国语大学教书,主要教授美国文化研究和中西方文明比较(新课程)等面向研究生开设的课程。

多年来,他发表了许多关于美国文学和美国文化方面的文章,出版了三本学术专著:《W.

H. 奥登的诗歌艺术》《现代小说中的邪盗魅影》《模块化美国：美国道路出现的跨文化视角》。最后一部专著因涉及美国跨学科研究而获得了美国研究协会颁发的拉尔夫·亨利·加布里埃尔奖。

13.
埃伦·伍兹是一位美丽的金发女郎，在加州大学洛杉矶分校读时装销售专业。她性格可爱，学习优异，当选"德尔塔·努"女生联谊会主席和返校节女王。她的男友华纳·亨廷顿，聪明过人，英俊潇洒，是一位著名参议员的儿子。一天晚上，华纳邀请她去高档餐馆参加特殊晚宴，有迹象表明他将向她求婚。埃伦的朋友为她感到异常高兴，帮她选适合这种场合穿的衣服和喷的香水。然而，出乎埃伦意料的是，华纳非但没有向她求婚，而且决定跟她分手，正视未来，因为他打算去哈佛大学法学院读书，将来当律师，或像他父亲一样当参议员。

受此打击后，埃伦变了，变得不修边幅，吃很多垃圾食品。她朋友安慰她，给她提建议，但对她没有丝毫作用。一天，她看到名人杂志上的一张照片，照片上是华纳的哥哥和他相貌平平的女友，他俩都是哈佛大学法学院一年级学生。埃伦突然想到，如果她也能考入哈佛大学法学院并展示自己的才华，华纳就会回到她的身边。于是，她开始咨询报考程序，准备法学院入学考试。经过一段时间的紧张学习，她通过了考试，被哈佛大学法学院录取。

来到哈佛，她立即吸引了同学的瞩目，但是他们谈论她时不乏带有讽刺意味，因为来法学院学习意味着勤奋和高智商，而不是表面的美丽……

14.
一个清晨，我到达韩国仁川国际机场。虽然是4月，但我一点都不觉得冷。机场装修精良，设施齐全，给我一种新鲜的感觉。一切都显得干净、整洁、有序。

令我感到惊讶的是，我看见机场的一些指示牌上的信息同时用中文、英文和韩语书写。我的韩国朋友向我解释说："那些字其实不是中文，而是韩语中的汉字。"韩语与汉语有悠久的历史联系。15世纪时，韩国一位国王创造了韩语。之前，韩国人用汉字（韩语汉字）书写信息。和日语一样，韩语中有近70%的中文词汇。但是，中文和韩语语言毕竟不同，因此汉字（韩语汉字）主要局限于地图上，偶尔会出现在报纸上和人名中。这让我想起，签证申请表上的信息也是用汉字书写的。为了证明他所说的话，我的韩国朋友给我看了他的名片，他的名字是同时用中文和韩语汉字写的。

世界杯足球比赛即将到来，在这个特殊的时刻，当地政府尽量在路标和地图上使用更多汉字，以吸引更多中国游客去韩国旅游，促进韩国旅游业发展。现在，为方便外国游客，首尔越来越多的路标同时用英语、日语和中文书写。

15.

英语专业学生不仅仅需要语言技能

在中国，699万大学毕业生涌向一个暗淡的就业市场，说实话，就业将会变得艰难。北京市教育委员会的数据显示，北京毕业生的就业率现在是33.6%，远低于10年前的89.7%。利用语言技能求职的英语专业学生面临来自各方面的压力。

为帮助学生了解今年就业市场的大趋势，《21世纪报》记者与来自一流企业的10位人力资源部经理座谈，为学生提供雇主需要什么样的人才的内部信息。此外，教师和专家为英语专业学生分析职业前景。

16.

写作是确保大学学习取得成功必不可少的一项技能。英语母语作者认同英美学术写作的某些核心概念。学术写作准则与传统英语或非正式英语不尽相同,汉语和英语学术写作传统也不同,故此弄清楚写作"游戏"的一些基本规则是非常值得的。

英语学术写作旨在让读者相信作者可以提供一些值得交流的新信息。因此,作者需要尊重读者。词汇和句子结构应该是大学难度,且准确无误,应同与朋友对话的语言风格不同。不要使用缩写表达法,不写不完整的句子。只有完整的句子才有说服力,因为在英语中只有完整的句子才能表达确定的含义,从而传达出作者的观点。

17.

我们需要转基因食品吗?

我们应该支持食用转基因食品吗?近年来,在世界各地,这一争论一直在持续。全球气候变化导致了一系列灾难性天气状况,农作物产量减少,食品供应变成了一个全球性问题。

反对者担心,人类食用转基因食品不安全,会带来长期的健康风险,而风险在多代人后才能发现。他们还指出,研究结果表明,一些转基因食品增加了测试对象患某些疾病的风险。

然而,转基因作物种植面积的扩大和转基因食品消费量的增多表明,一些改良的作物在生长过程中需要的水和肥料更少,产出的养分更多,对自然灾害、疾病和害虫的抵抗力更强。支持者还指出,食用转基因食品给健康带来很大的风险这一说法缺乏确凿的证据。

18.

通过阅读前面几个句子,读者需要明白作者试图表达的可信的观点是什么。按照中文写作习惯,作者通常在文章后半部分才表明自己的主要见解,英美写作习惯却恰恰相反。英语作家在文章一开始往往就给出主要论点,这样他们就可以将注意力更多地放到提供的支撑论据上,来阐述论点了。

对以英语为母语的人而言,写作意味着按照论文的特定结构进行。作者陈述了主要观点后,在下面的段落中呈现主要观点的相关方面,每一个方面应提供适当的论据来支撑作者的主要观点。通常,这些独立存在的段落以一个过渡词/句开头,表明新的段落与前文的关系。在每个段落(或部分)中提供论据后,作者应该指出到目前为止论证到了什么地步(小结一下)。在最后一段,作者需考虑论述过程中出现的各种润饰情形,重申主要观点。

显然,写作模式中隐含一种文化心理倾向。我们通常假定作者和读者都是理性的、有自主判断力的个体。作者提供的是读者过去相对不了解的新鲜思想。根据英语语言传统,每个人都有权发表自己的观点,但是只有提供可信的证据,观点才会获得认同。我们往往期望作者能提出最有力的观点,以呈现作者对所涉及事件的看法。

19.

美国杂货商克拉伦斯·桑德斯最先建立了现代自助式零售模式,其思想对现代超市的发展影响巨大。在一生的大部分时间里,他致力于开办真正意义上的自动化店铺,创立了自助式购物商店皮格利威格利(Piggly Wiggly)、可多族(Keedoozle)、富德莱(Foodelectric)等的商店理念。

桑德斯出生于弗吉尼亚州,14岁时便离开学校去一家杂货店当店员。后来,他先后去阿拉巴马州一家可乐厂和田纳西州一个伐木厂工作,之后又重新回到杂货销售行业。1900年,

19岁的他为一位杂货批发商推销商品,每月薪水30美元。1902年,他搬到孟菲斯,成立了一个杂货批发合作社。他的经历让他坚信,很多小杂货店倒闭了,源于这些店借贷严重失信、开销大。因此,他于1915年成立了桑德斯-布莱克本杂货批发有限公司,只用现金交易货品,鼓励其零售客户也这样做。

1916年9月6日,桑德斯离开田纳西州克拉克斯维尔市,在孟菲斯市杰佛逊大街79号开设了第一家皮格利威格利自助购物商店,开启了美国自助服务革命。该店的特点是:店门口有旋转式栅门,顾客付现金自主挑选货架上的商品。

该店提供购物篮,顾客自助挑选品牌产品,在出口处结账。早期的皮格利威格利连锁店的部分特点是:遣散不必要的员工,搭建精心设计的通道货架展示货品,改变店内布局,以便顾客可看到所有的商品。1917年,桑德斯为"自助式服务商店"概念申请了专利。

20.
2011年,我在澳大利亚。有一天,我陪一个朋友去参加驾驶考试。在澳大利亚,就像在美国一样,人们几乎不去驾驶学校学习驾驶。这一点令我感到惊讶。许多人在路上练车,旁边坐着一位有驾照的司机指导他们。但是这并不意味着获得驾照是小菜一碟。这已经是我的朋友第三次报名参加驾驶考试了。

第一次参加考试时,在他信心满满地将车开过一个十字路口后,考官让他将车靠边停下,说我的朋友本应该先停车,左右看看,以确保没有其他车靠近。

第二次参加考试时,前方一辆车冲过来,把我的朋友吓了一跳。他猛地踩下刹车,但用力过猛。"考官很生气,让我从车里滚出来。"我的朋友说。

他说:"在澳大利亚,驾驶考试考查的不是你的驾驶技能,而是要遵守每一条驾驶规则。"

21.
春节,人们与亲朋团聚,做自己喜欢做的小事。当大多数大学生整理行囊,登上火车或坐飞机回家时,一些学生却留下来在学校过春节。22岁的周云云是吉林大学金融专业大四学生,决定不回海南过年了,他打算与网友一起打电脑游戏消磨时光。他说:"每天,我习惯和网友聊天、打游戏。我们经常互送礼物,这样交朋友真有趣!"若全程坐飞机回家,来回路程将花费大约六千元,周云云觉得太贵了。现在,他可节省下这笔钱找工作时用。

22.
大多数科学家认为这种说法最让人信服:北极圈温度升高导致喷流遭到破坏,造成北半球出现极端天气越来越频繁。然而,有些人表示(做出这种论断时)要谨慎。克林格曼说:"我认为北极变暖与气候破坏之间存在联系这种说法的确让人信服,但是这并非唯一可能的解释。""例如,有一种叫作季内震荡的现象,每周、每月左右着热带地区雨量的分布情况。有证据表明,这种现象影响喷流的方位。这种现象可能与正在发生变化的天气模式之间存在某种联系。"

23.
一项新的研究显示,引发洪水、飓风和暴风雪的气候现象也有好的一面。这种气候现象不但有助于植物生长,而且也有助于控制与全球变暖有关的污染物。美国国家大气研究中心大卫·舒密尔说,与之前人们认为的影响相比,像厄尔尼诺这种短暂造成天气变暖的自然天气现象对植物吸收二氧化碳的量和土壤排出气体的量影响更大。舒密尔是发表在《科学》杂志上一项研究的作者之一。

几十年来,大气中的二氧化碳(CO_2)一直在持续增多。人们通常认为,这是由于化石燃料的广泛使用和对热带森林的滥砍滥伐造成的。科学家们认为是二氧化碳的增多造成全球变暖,人们把这个现象称为"温室效应"。世界各国正在制定计划以减少化石燃料燃烧,希望减少大气中的温室气体。

24.

北京、上海和广州——中国这三大城市的政府官员似乎已经达成了一项秘密协议,以同步采取行动。经过数月的辩论和争论,12月30日,这三个城市针对外来务工人员子女参加高考这个敏感话题出台了新的政策。人们认为,这些万众期待的政策表明我国开始针对未来教育平等权利进行改革。

到目前为止,不管外来务工人员子女及其父母在这些城市居住时间有多久,他们几乎都要回到农村老家参加考试,这给这些年轻学生带来了很多问题。

现在,这三个城市都表示,他们正在为合乎条件的外来务工人员子女打开大门,允许他们在所居住城市参加高考。然而,新政策指南中规定的严格条件让许多人感到失望……

25.

春节后回到校园的第一天,李彦斌感到很不舒服。他胃疼,不停地呕吐。医生后来告诉他,问题出在他的饮水机上。自假期开始前,他的饮水机就一直放在那里,已经变成了一个细菌池。

用水安全很重要。联合国的一份报告显示,每年有350万人因饮用不安全水而死亡。最近,山东的工厂将工业废水排放至地下后,中国城市的水质问题再次成为人们关注的焦点。

国土资源部的数据显示,55%的地下水被评为"较差"或"极差"的水质,严重危害公众的健康。

地下水是城市地区的主要水源,但面临着许多污染风险。据《光明日报》上周报道,中国环境科学研究院研究员赵章元说,许多垃圾填埋场没有采取足够的措施防止毒素渗入地下水。

26.

1963年,我国将第一支医疗队派往阿尔及利亚。《中国日报》报道,自那时起,超过17万名医务人员被派往非洲48个国家,至今已治疗了2亿多名患者。在访问刚果共和国期间,我国国家主席习近平对志愿者为当地居民提供优质的医疗服务表示感谢,感谢他们为我国赢得了荣誉。

于忠杰已经接受了六个月的培训。这位常州市第二人民医院整形外科主任医师将很快被派往坦桑尼亚的半自治地区,援助期为两年。这是一个1963年启动的医疗援助项目。他说:"参加培训的人都是来自江苏的精英医生。"他解释道,我国政府非常重视对非洲的医疗援助。

每天,于大夫和他的20名队友接受疾病预防、语言交流、室内锻炼、当地禁忌、宗教礼仪和许多其他方面的指导,以确保他们保持健康和形象。

来自浙江省岱山人民医院的余国定表示,我国医生的形象可以用中非共和国的一句话来解释:"如果有一种疾病,中国医生都无法治愈,就真的无法治愈了。"……

27.

每次我们打电话、登录无线网络或者浏览互联网时,都会留下可供追踪数据的数字足迹。据爆料,美国国家安全局(NSA)正在访问美国人民数以百万计的电话记录,并浏览互联网公司存储的数字数据,这表明该局正肆无忌惮地收集和分析个人数据。

雅虎,连同苹果、微软和脸书等其他科技巨头,公布了美国政府的数据请求。结果显示,在过去6个月里,根据《外国情报监控法案》(FISA),雅虎共收到1.2万多份数据请求,这还不包括美国其他执法机构的数据请求。

人们把电信服务提供商向美国国安局提交的信息称作元数据,即使用科技时产生的信息摘录。收集的数据包含用户、设备和正在进行的活动的交互信息,不包括个人或内容具体的细节信息……

28.

今天,世界上大约有6 000种语言,至少到2001年1月卡洛斯·韦斯特死前是这样的。韦斯特是最后一位会讲美洲本土语——卡陶巴语的人。他死了,这种语言也消亡了。

职业语言学家对韦斯特的死亡感到哀痛,文化多样性的倡导者们更是如此。彼得·波帕姆在伦敦《独立报》上撰稿提醒人们,当"一种语言消亡"时,人类也失去了"用一种独特方式感知和描写世界的可能性"。尤其让波帕姆这样的人担忧的是,许多其他语言可能会和卡陶巴语一样逐渐消亡。奥雷语(Aore)是瓦努阿图(太平洋岛国)一个岛上的本土语言。当岛上唯一的居民死亡后,这种语言也会随之消亡。具有讽刺意味的是埃塞俄比亚的盖珐特语(Gafat)所面临的状况:会讲这种语言的不到30人,语言学家试图保护这种语言反而令其变得更加岌岌可危。为了保护这种语言,一位语言研究人员将两个说这种语言的人从当地带走,可是他们因此而感冒了,最后死了……

二、汉译英练习

1.

Xiaoxiang Morning News: Around 11:30 the office of the Huaihua Branch of the Hunan Highway Traffic Police received a report requesting help in searching for an 11-year-old boy who had gone missing at the Anjiang Expressway Service Station.

The caller requesting help was Mr. Huo, from Shenzhen, Guangdong Province. While passing through Guizhou Province, he and his family had stopped to take a short rest at the Anjiang Expressway Service Station. Meanwhile the 11-year-old, left alone, had got out of the stuffy car to play. Returning from their break and believing the boy to be asleep in the car, the family drove on for 70 kilometers. Only when they reached the next service station did they discover that their son was missing. Thereupon, they dialed 12122 to report a missing child to the police. They then turned the car around and drove back to look for their son. Around 12 o'clock the local police found the little boy at the Anjiang Expressway Service Station, and informed his parents.

2.

The Olympic Games, organized by the International Olympic Committee, are the world's most comprehensive sporting event. These games, which are held for not more than 16 days every four years, comprise/are divided into the following categories: the Summer Olympic Games, the Summer Paralympic Games, the Winter Olympic Games, the Winter Paralympic Games, the Summer Youth Olympic Games and the Winter Youth Olympic Games. The Olympic Games offer an opportunity for cultural exchanges between different countries as well for participants to learn athletic skills from one another, the purpose being to encourage a sporting spirit among the peoples of the world. The Olympic Games originated in ancient Greece two thousand years ago and are named after Olympia, the site, where they were first held. The first modern Olympic Games were held in 1896, 1500 years after the ancient Olympic Games were discontinued.

3.

Boat races on Dragon Boat Festival Day, dragon dances on Lantern Festival Day and celebrations on Dragon Heads-Raising Day are important folk activities in the big dragon culture areas of East Asia. Dragon boats, just as the name indicates, are boats which are shaped like a dragon and painted with dragon patterns on the hulls. Dragon boat racing, a traditional Chinese folk water sport and recreational event at which paddling teams compete, is usually held on festive occasions Dragon boat racing, which came into being during the Han Dynasty, is not only a sporting and recreational activity, but also an expression of the people's collective spirit and a reflection of the long traditional cultural heritage in Chinese history.

4.

"Tang poetry" generally refers to the poems written during the Tang Dynasty (618 – 907 AD); however, this designation has also been extended to refer to poems written in the same style as the Tang poems. The Tang Dynasty is regarded as the golden age of poetry in Chinese history when poetic standards were at their highest with the result that both Tang poetry and Song poetry are usually discussed together as being of equal importance. Most Tang poems are preserved in *the Complete Collection of Tang Poems*. From the Tang Dynasty onwards, collections of Tang poems have been updated, the most popular of them being *Three Hundred Poems of the Tang Dynasty*, a book edited by Heng Tang Tui Shi. Tang poetry, like a pearl in a treasure house is the most precious legacy of Han Chinese culture, and had a huge impact on the cultural development of surrounding ethnic groups and countries. The era of Tang poetry can be divided into four periods, namely, the early period, the prosperous period, the middle period and the late period.

5.

The number of poets active during the Tang Dynasty was particularly high. Aside from world-renowned poets like Li bai, Du Fu, Bai Juyi and Wang Wei, there were many others, who were as numerous as the stars in the sky. The number of Tang poets whose names are known today is well over 2,300. Their poems are preserved in *the Complete Collection of Tang Poems*, a book that includes 42,863 poems in total. However, this book is not "complete" in the real sense of the word, since some popular and rhetorical poems, as well as those that circulated among hermits and those that were not positively received had already disappeared into the long corridors of history.

6.

Tang poetry covers a very wide range of topics. Some poems present a picture of the social classes and class conflicts of the time, exposing the darkness of a feudal society. Some, expressing patriotic ideas, eulogize just wars. Some are tender depictions of the beauty of China's mountains and rivers. Still other poems describe the poet's personal aspirations and encounters, his admiration and affection for loved ones, his friendships, life's ups and downs, etc. In short, no possible subject, from natural phenomena, political developments, everyday working life and public morals to personal feelings and experiences escaped the keen eye of the Tang poet. When it comes to creative craftsmanship, the Tang poet's combining of elements from both the realistic and romantic schools, which is usually to be seen in the great poems, gave rise to the splendid tradition of Chinese classical poetry.

7.

On October 5, American media reported that the New York Military Academy, a historic 126-year-old boarding school, which happens to number among its alumni the present Republican presidential candidate Donald Trump, had been bought a few days ago at a bankruptcy auction by a non-profit Chinese organization (which is under the control of Chinese investors) at a price of nearly $16 million dollars. Investors told the academy director that the school would continue to remain open as a middle school.

On October 1, the *New York Times* reported that the Research Center on Natural Conservation successfully won a bid for a beautiful scenic area near the Hudson River. The area comprises various buildings and military barracks, as well as a large tract of land. The research center was established in 2011 in order to purchase a hotel in New York State. At that time, the business transaction involved the acquisition of the "Gilded Age" estate of railroad tycoon, E. H. Harriman.

8.

**Key Words from Premier Li Keqiang's
"big data dictionary": Sharing, Openness & Security**

The "sharing" of data of all departments must precede governmental construction of big data.

On March 5, 2014, Mr. Li said in the governmental work report at the second conference of the 12th National People's Congress, that entrepreneurial & innovative platforms for new industries must be set up in order to catch up with, even surpass the developed countries in terms of mobile communications of the new generation, integrated circuit, big data, advanced manufacturing, new energy, new materials and so forth, leading the industrial development of the future.

This is the first time the "big data" has appeared in the governmental work report, which indicates that as a new industry, it will gain strong support at the national level.

Four months later, Li inspected Shandong Inspur Group and made clear in his talk that the use of big data are not just a matter of businesses, but also of governmental departments. At that time, he called the heads of related departments to the "field office", asking them to establish a unified, comprehensive platform of credit information to share "big data" by means of integrating cloud computing, big data and entrepreneurial information platform.

Yesterday at a state council executive meeting, he made clear requirements to the departments concerned that the "sharing" of data of all departments must precede governmental construction of big data.

"At present, the government departments have already built a dozen or so data platforms, but the problem is that these platforms are not connected to one another, but simply "information islands". In the light of the current status, Li said, "information connection is most easy to achieve. As you can see, all commercial web sites are connected, but the data of our departments are not, because we usually think that this is only my net, which other departments should not use!"

"Openness" is the second key word Li Keqiang used when it comes to governmental construction of big data. He said, "Data that does not involve state secrets but leads social and economic development should be accessible to the public, so it is convenient to use."

"Today, the data has penetrated into every industry and its functional areas," the global consulting firm McKinsey ever stated that big data is the new frontier of innovation, competition and productivity.

However, big data will be like water with no source without the openness of information. Premier Li knows this well. He said, especially for those data platforms related to credit, if the information is not shared or open, it will hinder the establishment of social credit system. "I ever talked with some entrepreneurs. Many of them in foreign trade companies told me that revenue can be anticipated and capital return is normal in export trade, however little the income is, but in the domestic business, sometimes it is unknown why cargo delay still occurs in the process of transporting before capital is returned."

On the other hand, the opening up of the relevant data, will test the authenticity and standardability of the data issued by the government.

"Now, in some places, the data released by some departments of local governments contradict sometimes so that people can't figure out what data is real." said Mr. Li, "How can we improve the ability of social governance to build a modern government?"

Industrial standard system should be improved and illegal behaviors like data abuse and invasion of privacy must be prohibited according to the law and regulations. In this way, all market participants can fairly share the technology, the systems and innovative vitality big data brings to us.

When big data are widely applied, how will personal privacy be protected, since search engines know what I want to search, shopping websites know what I want to buy and restaurants know what I prefer? When all of such things gradually become real, is it still possible that personal information will not be abused and personal privacy will be violated?

"Security" is a third key word Mr. Li puts forward in the executive meeting on August 19. He said, big data is under continuous innovation and development in industries like the Internet. "Therefore, the government should offer not only 'support' to create a healthy environment for the development of big data industry, but also 'guidance' and 'standard' to ensure information security."

9.

Recently, an explosion in the number of students sitting for the International English Language Testing System (IELTS) required for entry into overseas universities has forced IELTS organizers to increase the frequency of the exam. Last year, around 10,000 people in Shanghai took the exam between May and July. This year that figure has risen to around 17,000, an increase of about 70% over the same period last year. Increasing pressure from competition for jobs is the main reason that so many university graduates choose to continue their studies abroad.

10.

At Princeton University in the U. S., a boy fell deeply in love with a girl; however, from the beginning, he didn't know how he should express his love to her, because he was afraid that he would be rejected.

Finally, one day, he came up with a good idea as to how to approach her. Summoning up his courage, he walked straight up to the girl who was on campus reading a book. "Hello, I wrote something about you in this note." he said to her, "If it's true, would you please give me a photograph of yourself?"

It occurred to the girl that this was another boy who was looking for a pretext to woo her.

11.

China is one of the world's most prolific book producers. However, Chinese people read books at a relatively low rate. While the supply of books has exploded in China in recent decades, Chinese people's interest in books does not keep up with it. According to a survey, Chinese people read 4.39 books per capita a year, a figure that is far lower than that of some developed countries. For example, the Americans read 7 books a year on average, and the French 8.4. Statistics show that only 1.3% of the Chinese people think they read a lot while 53.1% admit that they read too little.

12.

Drunk Driving

An investigation by the World Health Organization indicated that in 2008, about 50%—60% of traffic accidents are related to drunk driving, which has been listed as the main cause of vehicular homicide. In China, drunken driving kills tens of thousands of people in traffic accidents every year and is responsible for the deaths in more than 50% road accidents. For its shocking dangers, it has become the first "killer" that induces traffic accidents.

13.

On October 4, Republican presidential candidate Trump said in a television interview that the Middle East would be more stable if Libya's former leader Moammar Gadhafi, and Iraqi's former president Saddam Hussein still remained in power. He added that he supports Russian air strikes on the strongholds of the extremist group "Islamic State" in Syria.

In an interview with NBC Trump, who is currently leading the other republican presidential primary candidates with a 32% approval rating, talked about the Middle East, Syria and the gun control issue in the U.S.A.

Trump spoke bluntly saying that Iraq and Libya sank into chaos after Qaddafi and Saddam were overthrown and that the Middle East would be more stable if both were still alive and in power. He also indicated that the same things that have happened in Iraq and Libya will take place in Syria.

14.

The Four Great Inventions

The "four great inventions of ancient China" usually refers to papermaking, the compass, gunpowder and movable-type printing. This was first put forward by the British sinologist Joseph Needham and inherited later by many historians of China. It is generally recognized that the four inventions gave a huge push to the political, economic and cultural development in ancient China and that these inventions have also had a great effect on the history of world civilization after its introduction in various ways to the west.

15.

Printing is one of the four great inventions of ancient China. Block printing was invented during the Sui Dynasty and then was improved by Bi Sheng during the Song Dynasty. Both woodblock and movable type, two stages of Chinese printing development, were a precious gift to humanity. With regard to convenience and flexibility, they represented a significant breakthrough and allowed printers to economize on time and effort. Chinese printing facilitated the wide dissemination of knowledge and promoted cultural exchange. Although culture had previously been spread mainly through handwritten materials, writing by hand was time consuming and it was easy to make mistakes. This impeded cultural development.

16.

During the Spring Festival in 1989, my husband and I, newly married, went to his hometown in Qianguzhou Village, Luxi Township, Yongxin County, Jiangxi Province for the first time. That was also the first time in my life that I, in a real sense, spent the Spring Festival in the countryside. As I was the first woman from Beijing ever to visit that village, the people there looked at me inquisitively while sizing me up. At the same time I regarded them with curiosity.

Since then, I have gone back to that village many times—though I don't know exactly how many—mostly to spend the holidays. Considering that I grew up in and live in Beijing, I really don't have a concept of home at all. Because of this, my husband always refers to me as "a person without a hometown".

17.
Bi Sheng (the years of his birth and his death unknown) was a commoner who lived in Yingshan county, Hubei Province, during the Northern Song Dynasty. He originally worked as an engraver in a bookstore. During the Qingli Period (1041—1048), Bi Sheng, based on his experience, invented ceramic moveable-type printing. Unfortunately, however, he passed away before this technology had become widespread. The printing device with carved Chinese characters was kept by his family. His stories are recorded in volume 18 of his book *Sketchbook of Dream Brook or Dream Stream Essay* (*Meng Xi Bi Tan*). Movable-type printing makes use of multi-purpose engraved characters which can be used repeatedly to produce high efficiency printing in large quantity, thus saving time, effort and materials. This represented a qualitative leap, compared with wood block printing and has had an enormous, far-reaching impact on later printing as well as on the progress of world civilization.

18.
It seems more and more Americans want schools to teach foreign languages to children younger than five years old. The most popular way to teach these young children another language is the teaching method called "Immersion". Children in Immersion classes hear only the new language in the classroom. These children play games, sing songs and talk to one another in the new language. Some experts say Immersion classes are the most effective way for young children to learn a language. However, there may be problems when children in the United States begin to learn another language at such an early age. Not many (Few) primary schools continue the effort as the children get older.

19.
Today, most kids in China's kindergartens are the only child of their family. They are clever, studious, and full of imagination and energy. However, they are usually egocentric, undisciplined and more vulnerable. Generally speaking, children aged from 4 to 6 who have just entered kindergarten are egocentric, while children aged from 9 to 10 demonstrate the quality of self-control and not being afraid of setbacks. Therefore, our education program attaches great importance to collectivism, mutual help and love. Children are encouraged to look after themselves and are taught the benefits of sharing with others.

20.
I did not realize that college entrance examinations were a big deal until I was filling out the application form for my university of choice.

That night, my father, wearing a pair of glasses, took the guide book to filling out the application form and sat on the sofa, reading it for a long time in silence. The house was so quiet that the sound of TV advertisements could be heard coming from the next-door neighbor's house. It had been a long time since my father and I had sat face to face like this. It was also the first time I had watched my father, who was in his 40s, reading with presbyopic glasses for an extended period of time.

He had just learned, not long ago, that he was suffering from presbyopia as well as that I was now old enough to take the college entrance examinations.

Wearing presbyopic glasses, my father, though still physically strong, showed a hint of old age. Absorbed in his reading and drawing upon all his life experience and wisdom in order to plan the future for his son, he turned the pages of the guidebook as if he were making a life and death decision.

21.

Bangladeshi police said that on the third of October a Japanese citizen was shot by several masked men in northern Bangladesh. This was the second foreigner killed in that south Asian country in less than a week.

The "Islamic State" claimed that it had carried out the two attacks; it then threatened more killings in retaliation for air strikes on the extremist group. Many embassies and consulates are worried about security in Bangladesh and have thus issued safety warnings to their citizens. Bangladesh's interior minister said, "Three men wearing masks, riding motorcycles, used pistols to murder their victims."

This was the second incident of a foreigner being killed in Bangladesh in less than a week. On September 28, a 50-year-old Italian aid worker was shot in the back by a male motorcyclist while working out near the embassy district in Dhaka. He died after all rescue measures proved ineffectual.

22.

The plan for the first DPRK-US talks since Trump took office has been canceled, owing to the U.S. State Department's refusal to issue a visa to the North Korean special envoy, Cui Shanxi.

According to the *Wall Street Journal*, Cui Shanxi was originally scheduled to hold talks with American officials in New York from March 1 to 2. This was to have been the first planned contact between North Korean and U.S. officials since Trump assumed the office of U.S. president and also the first time that a senior North Korean envoy was to have visited the United States since 2011.

Due to Cui Shanxi's being denied a visa to visit America, the planned meeting has already been canceled. It is still unclear what caused the rejection of the visa. However, outside sources speculate that North Korea's recent missile tests and Kim Jong-nam's murder in Malaysia may have played a role in the visa decision.

23.

Wu Yunduo, born in 1917 in Wuhan, Hubei Province, once worked, in his early years as a miner in the Anyuan Coal Mine. In 1938, he joined the New Fourth Army and was sent to army headquarters to work in a weapon repair unit. In 1939, he joined the Chinese communist party.

In 1941, after the Wan'nan Incident, Wu Yunduo was transferred along with military units to an anti-Japanese base south of the Huaihe River, where he was appointed deputy minister of the New Fourth Army Second Division War Industry Department and director of a bullet factory. Wu Yunduo and eight technicians went, unarmed and defenseless, to Xiaozhuzhuang, Ping'an Township, the Jingou District, Gaoyou County, where they established a factory base in two borrowed straw houses. There, they manufactured all the implements and machine tools necessary for the production of bullets, and soon built this base into a factory, where around 600,000 bullets could be produced annually. Soon afterwards, Wu designed and tested the first mortar projectile.

One day at dusk in 1942, a command came from the New Fourth Army Second Division War Industry Department that a batch of mortar shells that were defective had to be repaired. Wu Yunduo did the de-rusting (removed the rust), reloaded the ammo, and installed the projectile tails and fuses himself...

24.

During his visit to the United States, Xi Jinping gave a speech in which he spoke for nearly two minutes about fighting corruption, which, as he said, involves a vigorous investigation of corruption cases, without a power struggle. This statement regarding corruption and power struggles by Xi Jinping, the supreme Chinese leader, is a very direct public response to the suspicions of people from all walks of life.

In Seattle, the first stop of his visit, Xi Jinping delivered this notable speech in which "fighting corruption" was one of the key phrases. That he spent nearly two minutes talking about this subject in this speech was, when compared with his practice in speeches delivered on previous official visits, extremely rare. While discussing the anti-corruption campaign, his tone remained firm and determined. Xi Jinping then moved on to another topic: *the House of Cards*. When he paused for a moment, his audience broke into applause; he was now looking down from the stage, smiling and laughing.

25.

On the afternoon of October 4, tornadoes, spawned by typhoon Rainbow, struck Shunde in Foshan, Panyu in Guangzhou, and Haifeng County in Shanwei, Guangdong Province. By 10 o'clock this morning, according to local government reporters, this natural disaster had claimed 6 lives—3 in Panyu and 3 in Shunde. In addition, 215 people were injured—134 in Panyu and 81 (6 seriously) in Shunde.

In addition, tornadoes also caused power outages in large areas of Foshan and Guangzhou. The Haizhu and Panyu districts experienced serious water and power outages in large parts of their sub-district communities as well as failing traffic lights and traffic jams.

26.

Last night, a netizen in Xiamen posted a mobile video to reporters with *The Paper* and claimed that the old woman seen in the video had been waiting for several hours at the ferry terminal on Lujiang Road. The image (camera shot) of an agitated old woman with her head buried in her hands weeping and choking with sobs, was very moving.

The old woman, Xing Yuhua, was 76 years old and had come from Beijing. This year, her family had decided to take a trip to Gulangyu Island. At first she was reluctant because she was afraid that it would be too crowded there. On second thought, however, she concluded that "it's all right to take an occasional look at the outside world", and agreed to go. She never expected that this journey would turn into a "nightmare".

Not until 5 p.m. on October 3, when her family rushed excitedly from the airport to the ferry terminal on Lujiang Road did she learn that this place was now accessible to citizens of Xiamen only. An employee at the booking office (customer service window) informed her that all tickets were sold out.

27.

Life is a stage where you choose some things and give up others. Huang Xuhua, revered as "the father of China's nuclear submarines", gave up far more than we can imagine.

Mr. Huang left home to attend school in 1938 and returned home to Guangdong Province on a business trip in 1957. During those 19 years of separation, his mother had no complaints, other than to urge again and again, "When you were a kid, battles were going on everywhere and it was impossible for you to get home. Now that society is stable and transportation convenient, I hope you can come back often to have a look at your old mother."

Mr. Huang readily agreed. Contrary to expectations, however, they did not see each other again for 30 years. "I had no choice but to weaken the family connection now that I was engaged in a job like this. The family were always asking me what I was doing, but how could I respond?" Accordingly, he became a remote "mailbox number" for his mother.

28.

I often think that the meaning of life lies in how we perceive it.

Some people say that life is a dream, a very short one, while others think that life is just a soap bubble. As a matter of fact, these are all pessimistic attitudes toward life. I would say that even if life is really a dream, I would prefer to have an exciting, robust dream, to having a pessimistic one.

Life is simply a stage play. Since it requires great effort to reach that stage, once there, you should give a proper performance like a true entertainer, not a small-time actor, because what we do and say can have a lasting influence.

In the first year of the Republic of China, an Englishman came to our school and gave a talk whose content was really ridiculous. Nevertheless, his squeaky pronunciation of the letter "O" in Chinese pinyin, which was different from that of ordinary people, affected my pronunciation of that letter. Unfortunately, many of my students have been negatively influenced by my pronunciation of "O"...

29.

When we are in love with someone special, our deepest emotional need is to feel loved. Accordingly, many people like to do two things: one is to prove that he loves "me" and the other is to prove he doesn't love "me".

Because they are generally insecure, most people incline to the latter. "He has never said that he loves me, so he certainly doesn't love me that much." Or "She's so independent that she surely doesn't need my company. Is it because I'm simply not that important?"

You need a lot of evidence to prove that he loves you, but only one piece of evidence is enough to confirm that he doesn't. That is why many, after breaking up, often complain as follows: "I have given you so much, but have never felt how much you love me."

But the truth is: sometimes it is not that he doesn't love you, but that he doesn't know how to express it, or that you have not heard his words of love…

30.

On March 22, 2018, Zhang Miman received the 2018 "the World's Outstanding Female Scientist Award" granted by UNESCO. On stage at the ceremony, she appeared in a long Chinese dress and delivered an unscripted speech in fluent English, moving at times freely between French, Chinese, Russian and Swedish. Her graceful manner and humor impressed Chinese netizens so much so that she was affectionately called "an online star scientist", "the rose of Chinese scientific research" and "the real goddess of China".

As a senior member of the Chinese Academy of Sciences, a foreign member of the Swedish Royal Academy of Sciences, and a recipient of the "Romer-Simpson Lifetime Achievement Award", the highest international award in the field of vertebrate paleontology, honor and reputation are nothing new to Mrs. Zhang, the world-renowned paleontologist. Nevertheless, when compared with winning prizes or being a "web celebrity", doing scientific research is still the most important thing for her right now.

31.

In 1986, I served as the President of Shanghai Theater Academy, where there was an old teacher who had studied in the department of Theater as an exchange student at Yale University in the United States before returning to China—allegedly in the same boat as Mr. Qian Xuesen (who later developed into a great Chinese scientist). Though seemingly well qualified, he still had not been promoted to associate professor at the time I took office as president.

This slight appeared to be too much for him; others also thought that he had been wronged from the start. I personally checked his professional profile, only to find that he had neither delivered any lectures nor written any books during the past few decades, nor had he directed any rehearsals of plays, having only left behind some messy bound notes in English. I turned the book over and saw that the English notes consisted of just a few hand-copied snippets, none revealing any original viewpoints whatever…

32.

A U. S. news media survey showed that waiters & waitresses who listen attentively, while nodding or softly repeating a customer's order, have a greater than 70 percent chance of getting a tip than those who concentrate exclusively on memorizing the names of the dishes.

A British media survey came to a similar conclusion. In British restaurants, it is a tradition that peppermints be given to customers after a meal. Compared with waiters or waitresses who give no mints to customers, those who give one receive 3% higher tips, while those who give two get 14% higher tips; If one mint is given first and then another after a short while, the tip will be 25% higher than that given to waiters and waitresses who do not provide mints.

These two media surveys are quite interesting. Actually, the principle is very simple. If you show respect for others, others will naturally show respect for you. In other words, the more you "interact" with your customers, the more rapport you will have and the more tips you will receive.

This is just a matter of a tip. If it is life, then the feedback will be more.

33.

Sharks are such powerful ocean-dwelling creatures that almost no other marine animals are capable of harming them. The fierceness of sharks lies not only in the fact that they stand at the top of the food chain, feeding on nearly all other ocean animals, but also in the fact that they instinctively play with their prey before eating it. For example, when animals such as seals, sea lions and albatrosses are, unfortunately, caught by a shark, the shark will not immediately eat them; rather, it will toss them about in the water and play with them, until, having suffered great torment, they finally expire.

Although they are incredibly powerful, sharks have a deadly natural enemy, the hagfish, which, though too weak and small to play the role of a shark's opponent in terms of strength—the tooth of a shark is dozens of times heavier than a hagfish—has its own "tender" (gentle) trump card to play.

34.

The 1960s was a time of great economic difficulty for China. At that time, my younger sister and I were in junior high and high school respectively, far away from our parents' home. On Sundays, resident students like us got only two meals, which were not enough for us.

My hunger became so unbearable during the long winter that I poured out my woes in a letter to my mother. Several days later, I was quite surprised to receive a small package from my mother and, upon opening it, found two bags of stir-fried wheat powder as well as a letter inside.

I hastily unfolded the letter, which read, "My dear son, right now our country is having economic difficulties, which all of us must bear with. If you/we get through this period, everything will be all right; you must persevere. You and your sister are to share these two bags of stir-fried wheat powder, the product of your father's labor insurance. Mother."...

35.

On August 4, 1875, after drinking morning tea at a merchant friend's house, Hans Christian Andersen (a Danish author, fairy tale writer, and poet) felt unwell and went to lie down. Shortly thereafter he passed away, at the ripe old age of 70.

Not long before his passing, he was in such poor health that one musician said to him, "I would like to write you a funeral march." Andersen replied, "I have written fairy tales for a lifetime. Since most of the people who will attend my funeral will be children, would you please write me a march, the beat of which is best suited to small children's tiny steps."

Upon learning this detail, I was shocked. If one can accomplish one thing throughout one's life, it must be because it is found in every corner of one's spiritual world, even in the details of a funeral. If one really makes it at one thing in one's lifetime, it must be like this: Even at one's funeral, people will not forget it.

36.

After my graduation from an undergraduate program in 2007, I came to Chicago and began my overseas life. Because of the muddle-headed college life I had lived, I vowed to plan and take action in advance, before going to study at a graduate school abroad. Mustering all my strength, I made up my mind to find a summer internship.

Internships require a good resume, so my top priority was to accumulate experience. At the time, I heard that there was a professor in the Finance Department who was working on a research project. In my desperation, I saw an opportunity. I thereupon went and stood in the doorway of his classroom. When his class was over, I rushed up to him and introduced myself, adding that I would love to help him with his research. Probably impressed by my sincerity, he agreed, to my surprise, to accept me as an intern and assistant...

37.

Rats are highly adaptable, so they never need protection from us humans. Whenever their natural instincts have led them into conflict with human interests, human beings have caught and killed them on a large scale. Pandas, on the other hand, because of their highly ornamental and research value, have long been listed as a national treasure and are under the meticulous care of humans.

In commercial culture, those organizations or individuals at the forefront who have the lowest social status and care only about profit and loss, are often compared to rats, in terms of sense of smell, alertness and power to act. Pandas in this culture, however, are of value only because of their rarity.

If you know only how to make money, to which all other relevant knowledge of yours is related, you're learning to be a rat. If you're working on cutting-edge but temporarily unmarketable technology, or studying a profound but unpopular, awkward art, you're learning to be a panda.

38.

Many big-horned antelopes live in the grasslands of northern Namibia in Africa. These animals are medium-sized, have short but solid hooves, and are good at running and jumping. Aside from reaching speeds of up to 95 kilometers per hour, they have such great endurance that they often leave predators behind, giving them no choice but to quit, frustrated and empty-handed.

It is usually thought that big-horned antelopes run as hard as possible in times of danger, but researchers led by British scientist Alan Wilson found, after a long period of observation, that this was not the case.

Alan Wilson and his co-workers fitted some big-horned antelopes and a few cheetahs that frequently make sneak attacks on them with a global positioning system (GPS) and accelerometer necklace. After making thousands of observations of the hunting process, researchers were able to obtain information as to the antelopes' acceleration, trajectory, and speed at every stage. It was discovered that when they are escaping, big-horned antelopes seldom run at their top speed, often maintaining a speed at about 80% of the maximum. Why is that?

39.

The gravitational collapse, which will take place at 1:24:17 p.m., will be observed from the largest observation room of China's Astronomical Observatory, where images from space telescopes in synchronous orbit will be received and projected onto a giant screen, the size of a basketball court.

At present, the screen is still blank and, as yet, few people have arrived. Those who have arrived, however, are authorities in theoretical physics, astrophysics and cosmology. They are seated quietly, waiting for the exciting moment whose meaning they—and only very few others in the world—can truly understand. However, the director of the observatory is pacing restlessly back and forth, because the display screen has unfortunately broken down and the engineer in charge of the repair work has yet to come...

40.

It was nearly half a year before I graduated from my university that I made an important decision: I would spend one year doing charity work and then I would go to work.

There were two reasons for my decision. One was that I had been involved in public-welfare activities in the university, which helped a lot to shape my sound mind and integrated personality, so that I was willing to do more charity work than before; the second was that the target group of our service, the elderly, marginalized by society, were dying and about to disappear into history. As you know, we are actually racing against time in this work.

Compared with my struggle to make this decision, persuading my family to agree was even more difficult, because they simply couldn't understand why I would do charity work instead of going to work and making money after they had worked so laboriously in support of my studies for more than a decade...

41.

I did not realize that I was a legendary "interesting soul" until I met him.

I used to think seriously about what to have for dinner over lunch. When on the subway, I would scrutinize everyone while overhearing them chatting. He, however, eats Chinese sandwiches/food in the same restaurant every day, because he thinks it's a sheer waste of time to browse online food-ordering softwares/order food online. Moreover, no matter how crowded the subway is, he reads a book, because for him, reading becomes more challenging when it is done under difficult circumstances, he says.

After I met him, I began to realize how lazy I was, for not only was I not career-minded enough, I wasn't even making enough of an effort to have fun. In order to be free to ask me out for dinner, he would work late the night before to get all his work done while I, in order to dine with him, would delay writing my already delayed manuscript time and time again...

42.

During the Han and Tang Dynasties, traditional Chinese culture was introduced into Japan. After Jianzhen, a Buddhist monk at the time of the Tang Dynasty, made several trips to Japan, Chinese Buddhist culture and sculpture spread to that country. Afterwards, a large number of Japanese envoys came to China to study Chinese culture, which accounts for the fact that Japanese architecture and the Japanese writing system were subsequently to show a profound Chinese influence. During the Ming and Qing Dynasties, traditional Chinese culture spread to some European countries. The four great inventions of ancient China played an important role in promoting the formation and development of western capitalist society after their introduction to the west. However, traditional Chinese culture had the greatest impact on France, which became the center of "Chinese culture fever" in Europe at that time. We are all amazed at how highly French 18th century enlightenment thinkers esteemed/regarded Chinese culture...

43.

You probably know people who are very smart, spiritually rich and fond of learning. They have many hobbies, dabble in all subjects, and seem to know everything. They are interesting people whom you like to chat with and from whom you can always learn something that you did not know before.

Such people, however, do not achieve anything significant (in life). Although they are self-confident in their youth, they experience a sense of loss when they grow older and feel that they have wasted their talent. When this happens, they may be said to have fallen under the "Da Vinci Curse".

The Da Vinci Curse, a book written by Leonardo Lospennato, was published several years ago.

Leonardo da Vinci was a painter and an architect as well as an expert in human anatomy. Being an all-arounder (a "Renaissance man"), he also achieved a lot scientifically, and produced many technological inventions. The "Da Vinci Curse" means that a versatile man, who is as interested in everything, as was Da Vinci, unfortunately accomplishes nothing in the end.

44.

Recently, I heard from a private education expert that economics is the solution to today's problems, science and technology to tomorrow's, and education to those of the future. As a science fiction writer, I was struck by the fact that science fiction is similar to education in solving future problems.

On occasion, education in Asia, esp. East Asia, is criticized for focusing too much on test-taking ability and placing excessive emphasis on mechanical memorization. Recently there have been changes as schools in Chinese cities are beginning to focus on cultivating students' curiosity and imagination. One manifestation of this is that science fiction has been introduced into schools and even appears in textbooks. However, the uneven distribution of courses focusing on imagination in Chinese education may be a reflection of change of main conflicts of interest in Chinese society...

45.

The Yellow River, a great river in northern China, is about 5,464 kilometers long with a drainage area of about 752,443 square kilometers. It is the fifth longest river in the world and the second longest river in China.

Its middle and upper reaches flow through mainly mountainous regions, while the lower reaches flow mainly through plains and hills. Due to the fact that its middle reaches run through the Loess Plateau, the river is filled with plenty of silt. Consequently, the Yellow River is also known as the world's "sandiest river". Throughout the history of China, however, the constantly changing course of the river has had a great influence on human civilization.

Accordingly, as the main source of Chinese civilization, it is called "The Mother River" by the Chinese people. Every year, 1.6 billion tons of silt is produced, 1.2 billion tons of which flows into the sea. The remaining 400 million tons, is deposited in the river's lower reaches annually, forming alluvial plains conducive to growing crops.

附录4　部分翻译术语

相对来说,以下划线的词/短语为常见的翻译术语。

1. Translation（翻译）is a rendering from one language into another, i.e. the faithful representation in one language of what is written or said in another language.

2. Yan Fu's "three-character guide", namely, the principle of "faithfulness（信）, expressiveness（达）and elegance（雅）", is now still mentioned time and again, though it was first proposed in 1898.

3. Acceptability（可接受性）refers to the adherence of the TT（target text, 目标文本, 即译文）to the norm and conventions of text production, prevailing in the TL（target language,

目标语言,即译文所属语言)。

4. Adequacy(充分性) is the result of the translator's initial decision to subject him/herself to the norms, prevailing in the source culture.

5. In a general sense, the notion of accuracy(准确性) is often referred to in discussing the correctness of a given translation. In this general sense, then, an "accurate" translation (of a word, an utterance or an entire text) is equivalent to a "good" or "right" translation, with no further specifications.

6. Coherence(连贯性) refers to the ways in which an utterance is seen to establish meaningful relations between its parts from a conceptual (i.e. semantic or logical) point of view.

7. Cohesion(衔接性) refers to the ways in which an utterance establishes meaningful relations between its elements by using grammatical and lexical devices.

8. Equivalence(对等) can be seen as a relationship of "sameness" or "similarity".

9. Fluency(流畅度) refers to the idea that a translated text should read like an original and not be recognizable as a translation.

10. Literal translation(直译) is a translation strategy or technique involving a choice of TL equivalents that stay close to the form of the original while ensuring grammaticality in the TL.

11. Free translation(意译), sometimes taken to mean sense-for-sense translation, is an alternative approach generally used to convey the meaning and spirit of the original without trying to copy its sentence patterns or figures of speech(修辞格). This approach is most frequently adopted when it is really impossible for the translator to translate the original meaning literally.

12. Translatability(可译性) can be seen as the capacity of meaning to be transferred from one language to another without undergoing fundamental change.

13. Translation strategy(翻译策略) is used by scholars to refer either to a general mode of text transfer or to the transfer operation performed on a particular structure, item or idea found in the source text.

14. Diction(措辞) means the choice and use of words in literature made in the process of translation.

15. Substitution(替代法) is used to replace the words of the original expression with Chinese synonyms or idioms according to different situations.

16. Explanation(解释法), namely the interpretative method, is commonly used when no corresponding expressions exist in the course of translation activities.

17. Combination(合成法/合译法) is used to join or mix two or more things to form a single unit.

18. Splitting/Division(拆译法) is meant to divide, or to make sth. divide, into two or more parts.

19. Conversion(转换法), the act or process of changing sth. from one form, use or

system to another, especially means the change of parts of speech in translation owing to the syntactical differences between English and Chinese.

20. Amplification/Addition（增译法）means supplying necessary words in the course of translation in order to fully reproduce information in the target language on the basis of accurate comprehension of the original.

21. Omission（省译法）is often adopted when superfluous information in the original text should not be included in the target text for the sake of conformity to the target language.

22. Restructuring（结构重组法）is usually adopted when other methods like division, amplification, omission do not work on the translation of attributive elements, some adverbials or negative sentences according to time or spatial sequence and logic sequence.

23. Context（上下文）is a broad notion that can be used to refer to various aspects of the situation in which an act of translation takes place. According to the perspective adopted in observing a text, the context may refer either to the immediate situation or to the culture in which a text is produced or received.

24. More rationally speaking, the process of translation consists of four phases: comprehension（理解）, transfer（转换）, expression（表达）and proofreading（校对）.

25. Misunderstanding（误解）occurs when the translator does not have a full understanding of the other party（另一方, in form of a text, a person, an organization or even a country）so that confusion even disasters may be resulted in.

参 考 文 献

[1] SOFER M. Translator Self-Training Chinese—A Practical Course in Technical Translation [M]. Rockville:Schreiber Publishing,2002.

[2] PALUMBO G. Key Terms in Translation Studies [M]. London:Continuum International Publishing Group,2009.

[3] 北京外国语大学英语系《汉英词典》组. 汉英词典[M]. 北京:外语教学与研究出版社,2006.

[4] 陈德彰. 热词新语翻译谭[M]. 北京:中国出版集团 中国对外翻译出版公司,2011.

[5] 范祥涛. 研究生科技语篇英汉翻译教程[M]. 苏州:苏州大学出版社,2011.

[6] 方梦之,毛忠明. 英汉-汉英应用翻译综合教程[M]. 上海:上海外语教育出版社,2008.

[7] 傅勇林,唐跃勤. 科技翻译[M]. 北京:外语教学与研究出版社,2012.

[8] 雷晓峰,李静. 科技语篇翻译教程[M]. 西安:西北工业大学出版社,2020.

[9] 刘德军,陈艳君. 旅游资料语篇特点与英译策略[J]. 安徽工业大学学报(社会科学版),2008(3):91-93.

[10] 马祖毅. 中国翻译简史:"五四"以前部分[M]. 增订版. 北京:中国对外翻译出版公司,1998.

[11] 冯庆华,穆雷. 英汉翻译基础教程[M]. 北京:高等教育出版社,2008.

[12] 彭萍. 实用英汉对比与翻译:英汉双向[M]. 北京:中央编译出版社,2012.

[13] 钱歌川. 翻译的基本知识[M]. 修订版. 北京:北京联合出版公司,2015.

[14] 汪福祥. 汉译英难点解析500例[M]. 北京:外文出版社,1998.

[15] 王宪生. 汉英句法翻译技巧[M]. 北京:中国人民大学出版社,2013.

[16] 魏国平. 浅析英汉翻译中词义表达的文化内涵差异与矛盾[J]. 北京第二外国语学院学报,2004(6):36-39.

[17] 武峰. 12天突破英汉翻译:笔译篇[M]. 北京:北京大学出版社,2011.

[18] 武峰. 英汉翻译教程新说[M]. 北京:北京大学出版社,2013.

[19] 谢天振. 当代国外翻译理论导读[M]. 天津:南开大学出版社,2008.

[20] 许建平. 英汉互译实践与技巧[M]. 4版. 北京:清华大学出版社,2012.

[21] 闫文培. 实用科技英语翻译要义[M]. 北京:科学出版社,2008.

[22] 张培基. 英汉翻译教程[M]. 上海:上海外语教育出版社,2009.

[23] 张震久,孙建民. 英汉互译简明教程[M]. 北京:外语教学与研究出版社,2009.

[24] 居祖纯. 汉英语篇翻译[M]. 北京:清华大学出版社,1998.

[25] 外研社《英语学习》编辑部. 英语学习[M]. 北京:外语教学与研究出版社,2002.